TORURE
IN THE EIGHTIES

an amnesty international report

First published 1984 by Amnesty International Publications
1 Easton Street, London WC1X 8DJ, United Kingdom

Copyright © 1984 Amnesty International Publications

ISBN 0-939994-06-2
AI Index: ACT 04/01/84
Original Language: English

Printed in the United States of America.

Amnesty International gratefully acknowledges the
assistance of Sherman Carroll, a former member
of the International Secretariat, in the writing of
chapters one through six of this report.

TORTURE
IN THE EIGHTIES

an amnesty international report

Contents

Introduction

At the detention centre on the Cyprus coast it was well past midnight when a military vehicle stopped abruptly outside. It had driven across the island from Nicosia through the night. Two men went straight inside. One was the colonial Governor, the other his military commander.

> "We walked . . . straight into the room where the
> interrogation was taking place," wrote the governor years
> afterwards. "We could see no sign of ill-treatment. Nor
> could we see any indications of force having been used on
> the villagers who had been interrogated earlier. But our
> visit that night was known throughout the island by the
> next morning. Our night visit did more than all the circulars
> to prevent the use of torture in the Cyprus emergency."

It was a demonstration of political will. The scene was Cyprus during the closing months of the Greek Cypriot insurgency in the late 1950s. The security situation was perilous. Soldiers and civilians had been killed. Intelligence information from captured insurgents was considered essential if their campaign of violence was not to disrupt movement toward a political settlement of the long-standing Cyprus dispute involving Greece, Turkey and the United Kingdom.

Allegations of torture had been brought to the Governor that night. He was not especially surprised. Previously, in 1956, Greece had brought a complaint against the United Kingdom before the European Commission on Human Rights of the Council of Europe concerning whipping and collective punishments in Cyprus. There had also been allegations of brutality during interrogation. Fact-finding by the commission continued, including an on-site visit to the island. The then-Governor, Sir Hugh Caradon, has since described the "salutary influence" of knowing that he and other British officials in Cyprus were subject to an international inquiry by an inter-governmental body with powers to investigate individual complaints about abuses of human rights. On hearing these new allegations concerning torture in a village on the opposite side of Cyprus from his headquarters in Nicosia, he and the armed forces commander set out for their ride through the night.

Clearly, in the 1980s, finding the political will to investigate and prevent torture is in most cases far more complex than the prerogative of a single late colonial commander. Indeed, the reports of torture and ill-treatment from 98 countries set out in this book demonstrate the presence of a conscious decision to torture by some governments and the lack of any will to stop it by many others. While governments universally and collectively condemn torture, more than a third of the world's governments have used or tolerated torture or ill-treatment of prisoners in the 1980s.

Abolishing torture will require a long-term commitment. The launching of a major Campaign for the Abolition of Torture in 1972 by Amnesty International and the publication of its first *Report on Torture* in 1973 marked the beginning of a concerted push to end the use of torture as a tool of state policy. In the decade since, some achievements have been made. More than a million people signed a petition to the United Nations (UN) calling for an anti-torture resolution, a step that helped stimulate the Declaration on the Protection of All Persons from Torture and Other Cruel, Inhuman or Degrading Treatment or Punishment, the Declaration against Torture, in 1975. The UN, other inter-governmental organizations (IGOs) and several non-governmental organizations (NGOs) have worked along parallel lines to develop international standards against torture and machinery to combat its continuing use. Independently, a growing number of domestic human rights groups are working courageously in their own countries to document and publicize torture used by their governments. The news media carry many more items about torture and other human rights abuses than they did a decade ago, not necessarily because there are more such abuses in the 1980s than earlier, but because more independent organizations are investigating these abuses and because editors and journalists are more concerned to conduct their own research into torture allegations and to report on their findings.

Today, due to these national and international efforts, detainees and their families, lawyers and associates are more aware than ever before that international support is available. One such means of direct assistance is the Urgent Action network established by Amnesty International in 1974 to allow a speedy response by cables and express letters from individual participants around the world on behalf of a person known by name who is at risk of being tortured. In 1983 some 30,000 people from 47 countries participate in this network. Between mid-1974 and 1979 Amnesty International interceded on behalf of 1,143 individuals in danger of torture (excluding mass arrests) in 32 countries; between January 1980 and mid-1983, Amnesty International made similar urgent appeals on behalf of 2,687 individuals in 45 countries. This type of action, to be effective, depends on receiving reliable information quickly from those close to a detainee, for torture usually occurs in the first days or weeks in detention. Information leads to exposure, a key to stopping an individual's suffering and to pressing a government to abandon the practice. The increased flow of such information in the last few years indicates not only that torture remains a major international problem in the 1980s, but more positively, that those who live in fear of torture know more and more how to reach abroad quickly for help.

But more — much more — remains to be done. Before the UN is a draft Convention Against Torture and Other Cruel, Inhuman or Degrading Treatment or Punishment. Such a convention could be a truly effective weapon against torture. Amnesty International believes the following points are essential. First, governments should not be allowed the loophole of "lawful sanctions" that might exclude from prohibition some types of punishment that they might legislate (see Chapter 2, page 14). Second, the convention should provide for universal jurisdiction in respect of alleged torturers, who should be subjected to due process of law in any country where they happen to be, regardless of the nationality of the victims or the alleged offender or the country of the alleged torture. There should be no safe haven for torturers. Third, key articles of the convention should apply equally to torture *and* to other cruel, inhuman or degrading treatment or punishment. For example, redress and compensation should be available to victims of all these categories of ill-treatment, and all statements obtained by any such ill-treatment should be excluded from evidence in any trial. Fourth, there must be effective implementation mechanisms (such as a body to receive and investigate torture allegations and the international on-site inspection of detention centres), so as to encourage compliance with the convention. This machinery should not be merely optional.

Revulsion at the extermination camps of the Second World War led to a convention outlawing genocide for all time as a crime against humanity. Today's torture chambers demand a similar international response—a convention to enforce the prohibition of torture and of cruel, inhuman and degrading treatment or punishment, and perhaps more important, a renewed and forceful commitment by individuals, journalists, professional organizations, trade unions, human rights groups and, above all, by governments to expose and denounce torture whenever and wherever it occurs. In 1984 Amnesty International and other NGOs are intensifying the continuing Campaign for the Abolition of Torture. Ordinary citizens by the tens of thousands will be writing to governments to press them to stop torture and to adopt measures to prevent it. A program of specific domestic measures to abolish torture is included in this report. It is addressed to governments individually and collectively as well as to the entire international community.

Torture *can* be stopped. The international legal framework for its abolition exists, as do the investigative methods to verify and expose it. What is lacking is the political will of governments to stop torturing people. It is as simple and as difficult as that. Amnesty International hopes that this new report about torture as well as its continuing campaign against torture will contribute to creating this political will so that our generation can banish torture from the earth.

Torture as an institution

Torture does not occur simply because individual torturers are sadistic, even if testimonies verify that they often are. Torture is usually part of the state-controlled machinery to suppress dissent. Concentrated in the torturer's electrode or syringe is the power and responsibility of the state. However perverse the actions of individual torturers, torture itself has a rationale: isolation, humiliation, psychological pressure and physical pain are means to obtain information, to break down the prisoner and to intimidate those close to him or her. The torturer may be after something specific, like a signature on a confession, a renunciation of beliefs, or the denunciation of relatives, colleagues and friends, who in turn may be seized, tortured and, if possible, broken.

Torture is most often used as an integral part of a government's security strategy. If threatened by guerrillas, a government may condone torture as a means of extracting vital logistical information from captured insurgents. If the government broadens its definition of security, the number of people who appear to threaten it will become larger. The implication of others in banned activities or the intimidation of targeted social sectors like students, trade unionists or lawyers may become the rationale for torture in the new circumstances. Emergency legislation may facilitate torture by giving extensive powers of detention to the security forces. This process may be accelerated if the military take over governmental, police and judicial functions.

The Uruguayan Government's fight against the *Movimiento de Liberación Nacional* (MLN), Movement of National Liberation, or

Tupamaros, an urban guerrilla movement, is an example. Torture began as a police method of interrogation some time in the 1960s. After the army entered the conflict in 1971, torture continued to be used mainly for the interrogation of suspected guerrillas, though on a much larger scale. The Law of State Security and Internal Order came into effect in 1972, granting broad powers to the security forces, and a year later the military took effective control of government behind a civilian façade. The result of these changes is that the emergency legislation introduced in 1972 has been the formal basis for the detention of hundreds of people suspected of non-violent political or trade union activities. Many have been tortured, long after the guerrillas were defeated, by one of several security units of the armed forces and convicted by military courts to long-term sentences. The illegal methods first applied to suspected *Tupamaros* became, by 1975, routine treatment for virtually any peaceful opponent of the Uruguayan Government who fell into the hands of military units.

A specific reason for torture is often to intimidate the victim and other potential dissidents from further political activity. Students detained for demonstrating or leafleting in the Republic of Korea have been tortured and beaten routinely at police stations, then released without charge.

The intimidation of rural populations by means of torture and killings has been part of government strategies to bring the population or land areas under government control. Guatemalan counter-insurgency operations in the early 1980s, for example, included the terrorization of targeted rural populations in an effort to ensure that they did not provide support for guerrillas. Tortured, dying villagers were displayed to relatives and neighbours, who were prevented from helping them. Newspapers in urban areas during this period were allowed to publish photographs of mutilated bodies, ostensibly as an aid to families seeking their missing relatives, but also as a warning to all citizens not to oppose the government.

In specific instances the torturers may want to keep their practices hidden from the local populace. According to a secret Indonesian army manual used in East Timor and obtained by Amnesty International in July 1983, "if the use of force [for interrogation] is required, there should not be a member of the local population present . . . to witness it so that the antipathy of the people is not aroused".

Armed conflict in Afghanistan has led to the involvement of the military and the state security police in torture to obtain intelligence information about the guerrillas, to intimidate the population from supporting them, and to discourage strikes and demonstrations in the towns.

If detainees are charged and eventually tried, a confession may be the primary evidence against them. The increased number of assaults during interrogation during and after 1976 in Northern Ireland was partly a result of a governmental security strategy to obtain confessions that could be used in court (see Chapter 5). In Spain torture and ill-treatment are still used in some police stations to obtain confessions from suspects charged under the anti-terrorist law.

Torture and ill-treatment are also used as punishments, sometimes additional to prison sentences. In Pakistan since 1977 and Mozambique since 1983, prisoners have been flogged, sometimes in public, while serving sentences for political or criminal offences. Caning, flogging and, in a few countries, amputation are inflicted as judicially prescribed punishments.

Prisoners often face further ill-treatment after interrogation, sentencing or confinement. Prisoners on hunger-strike against harsh prison conditions or against their own torture have been severely beaten in the Republic of Korea. One is known to have died in 1982 following such a protest; others have needed hospital treatment. At least 15 military prisoners in Morocco are reported to have died in custody during the period under review, in part as a result of diseases caused by appalling conditions and of a complete lack of medical care. In the USSR in the 1980s, medical personnel, in collaboration with the secret police, continued the practice of administering powerful pain-causing and disorienting drugs to prisoners of conscience who are forcibly confined to psychiatric hospitals for political rather than authentic medical reasons.

Isolated incidents of torture do occur without governmental approval. However, governments are not blameless if they fail to investigate such alleged abuses of authority. Their failure to investigate the offence and discipline the offender may well be taken as a signal by the security agent or agency involved that similar abuses are officially tolerated.

The moral argument

Apologists for torture generally concentrate on the classical argument of expediency: the authorities are obliged to defeat terrorists or insurgents who have put innocent lives at risk and who endanger both civil society and the state itself. The truth is that the classical apology for torture does not fit the facts. It purports to justify undesirable but "necessary" suffering inflicted on an individual only for the purpose of protecting the greater good of the greater number. This apology ignores the fact that the majority of torture victims, even in countries beset by widespread civil conflict, have no security information about violent opposition groups to give away. They are tortured either to force confessions from them or as an acute message not to oppose the government.

The arguments for the abolition of torture do not rest on utilitarian judgments. Security officers who torture may well argue its efficacy to their superiors, especially if it has produced a few successes in a given conflict. But they are not the best judges. It is natural that those who apply illegal methods should argue that so much information could not have been obtained so quickly in any other way. As they become more reliant on torture they are less likely to use other methods of interrogation, and their ability to assess the effectiveness of torture diminishes. Whether the suspects under interrogation possess the sought-for information or not, once made hostile by assaults they may give false information either to mislead their interrogators or because they are eager to stop the pain. Under great mental stress, they may suffer hallucinations that distort the truth, even to themselves.

Even if torture could be shown to be efficient in some cases, it could simply never be permissible. From the point of view of the individual, torture, for whatever purpose, is a calculated assault on human dignity and for that reason alone is to be condemned absolutely. Nothing denies our common humanity more than the purposeful infliction of unjustified and unjustifiable pain and humiliation on a helpless captive. From the point of view of society, the argument of torturing "just once" does not hold. Once justified and allowed for the narrower purpose of combating political violence, torture will almost inevitably be used for a wider range of purposes against an increasing proportion of the population. Those who torture once will go on using it, encouraged by its "efficiency" in obtaining the confession or information they seek, whatever the quality of those statements. They will argue within the security apparatus for the extension of torture to other detention centres; they may form elite groups of interrogators to refine its practice; they may develop methods that hide its more obvious effects; they will find further reasons and needs for it if particular segments of society become restive. What was to be done "just once" will become an institutionalized practice and will erode the moral and legal principles that stand against a form of violence that could affect all of society.

As for the state, if it purports to uphold justice, torture should be banned: torture subverts a basic tenet of just punishment, a prescribed penalty for a proven offence. If a government subscribes to the rule of law, torture should be forbidden: most national constitutions as well as international law in war and peace explicitly prohibit it. If the authorities claim to rule on the basis of any moral or legal authority whatever, torture should be outlawed: it rends the fabric of society, tearing at any threads of trust or sympathy between the citizens and their rulers.

Governments have formally recognized the force of these arguments. No state legalizes torture in its constitution or penal code (although an increasing number of penal codes do allow for such judicial punishments as flogging and amputation). The Geneva Conventions, ratified by more than 150 states, confirm torture to be a crime in both international and non-international armed conflicts. Several UN declarations and treaties as well as human rights instruments of regional IGOs prohibit torture. The UN is currently drafting a convention that could make torture a crime under international law. The law does not and must not accommodate torture.

The methods, victims and agents

The truth is, of course, that well into the 1980s torture remains an evil. The methods vary: for example, the long-used *falanga* (beating on the soles of the feet, also called *falaka*); the use of quicklime inside a hood made from the inner tube of a tyre, as reported by Guatemalan torture victims; the Syrians' "black slave", an electrical apparatus that inserts a heated metal skewer into the bound victim's anus; the *cachots noirs* in Rwanda, black cells totally devoid of light in which prisoners have been held for as long as a year or more. Some methods—pain-causing drugs administered forcibly to prisoners of conscience in Soviet psychiatric hospitals, the forcible use of techniques of sensory deprivation, and the electrodes that have become an almost universal tool of the torturer's trade—make the verification of torture and ill-treatment especially difficult.

In many countries the victims of torture include virtually all social classes, age groups, trades and professions. Criminal suspects as well as political detainees are subject to torture in many countries although the information available to Amnesty International deals mostly with political cases. In El Salvador children have reportedly been tortured, and in Iran under the government at the time of writing children held with their mothers in the women's block of

Evin Jail have been forced to witness the torture of their mothers. Women often face special degradation at the hands of their male torturers. Relatives of wanted people in Syria, including adolescents, have reportedly been held as hostages and tortured to force suspects to give themselves up. Foreign nationals seeking asylum in the Congo have allegedly been tortured to force them to confess to espionage. Victims in Ethiopia have allegedly included members of several ethnic and religious minorities suspected either of supporting armed groups fighting for territorial independence or of obstructing the revolution.

Sources of evidence about torture include an increasing number of first-hand accounts from victims, witnesses and people who have seen torture victims shortly after torture. (A short discussion of medical and other evidence of torture prefaces the country entries in Chapter 7, pages 90-94.) During the 1970s a number of governments changed that had practised torture: in 1974, Portugal and Greece; in 1979, Iran, Nicaragua, Equatorial Guinea, Uganda, the Democratic Kampuchea Government, *Khmer Rouge*, and the Rhodesian administration headed by Prime Minister Ian Smith. Besides confirming that torture had indeed occurred in each of these countries on a large scale, these changes of government and the subsequent discoveries and trials provided new and detailed evidence about the inner workings of torture agencies. Unfortunately the governments that succeeded to power have not always prevented the recurrence of torture, as has happened in the 1980s in Iran, Uganda and Zimbabwe.

The agencies involved in torture give an indication of the degree of governmental responsibility for it. Frequently several military and police intelligence units as well as police forces and perhaps prison employees in the main population centres are implicated, thus demonstrating the widespread institutionalization of the practice.

Where trials of security agents accused of torture have been pursued vigorously, additional evidence of torture methods and the training of torturers has come to light. An analysis of this rare type of evidence was published by Amnesty International following several of the trials of accused torturers in Greece in the mid-1970s.[1]

---

1 See *Torture in Greece: The First Torturers' Trial, 1975* (London, Amnesty International Publications, 1977). A documentary film entitled *Your Neighbour's Son*, made by an independent team of Danish film-makers and Greek actors is based on similar material. The film is available in English, Danish, Greek and other languages, from the Danish Section of Amnesty International, Frederiksborggade 1, 1360 Copenhagen K, Denmark.

Testimonies from security agents who have participated in or witnessed torture and who have defected and gone into exile are also available, in particular from Argentina, Guatemala and Uruguay.

The psychological conditioning of the individual torturer can be described on the basis of this evidence. The Greek experience (1967-74) is known in greatest detail. After basic training young conscript soldiers from known anti-communist families were selected for special training for the military police. Further screening produced the chosen few to be trained as torturers. This "distinction" carried special privileges — prestige, the use of a car, non-commissioned officer rank, extra pay and time off, and a posting in the metropolis rather than the provinces or the frontier. Most were from country or working class families, so these privileges and the guaranteed public service job after leaving active duty were strong incentives to accept a post in the elite corps. They were not initially aware of the duties of this corps. A large part of their training consisted of beating and being beaten by fellow conscripts. The officers who trained them ordered them to eat the straps to their berets, to kneel and swear allegiance to portraits of commanding officers, to perform demeaning acts like pretending to make love to a woman in front of other soldiers. After ideological indoctrination and psychological conditioning, they were assigned first to guard prisoners, then to arrest suspects, and finally to torture them. Hesitation to torture led to ridicule, more beatings, threats of transfer and loss of privileges, and threats to the economic livelihood of the conscript's family.

The general picture that emerges of torture agencies from these trials and testimonies is of an elite group, often specially trained to torture, who have an elevated view of their role in protecting state security against "subversives". State propaganda reinforces this view, as does any real violence perpetrated against the state or their colleagues by opposition groups. If they are aware that their acts are criminal, they also know that their superiors will protect them in the unlikely event that the state attempts to prosecute them. Under pressure to get results (logistical information, confessions, names of the suspect's associates), they know that their future career depends on getting those results regardless of the method.

"Preconditions" for torture

The accumulated evidence also gives a clear picture of the "preconditions" for torture. Emergency or other special legislation that allows wide powers of arrest and detention may facilitate torture. Suspects can be held on the vaguest of suspicions; crimes against the state are given broad, elastic definitions.

Torture most often occurs during a detainee's first days in custody. These vulnerable hours are usually spent incommunicado, when the security forces maintain total control over the fate of the detainee, denying access to relatives, lawyer or independent doctor. Some detainees are held in secret, their whereabouts known only to their captors. The authorities may deny that certain detainees are held, making it easier to torture or kill them or to make them "disappear".[2] Incommunicado detention, secret detention and "disappearance" increase the latitude of security agents over the lives and well-being of people in custody.

The suspension of *habeas corpus* and other legal remedies, trials of political detainees in military courts, the lack of any independent means to examine and record a prisoner's medical condition—such conditions allow the security forces to conceal evidence of torture from lawyers, civilian magistrates, independent doctors and others who would be capable of taking action against their illegal activities.

Further incentives are trial procedures that do not exclude from evidence statements extracted under torture or during long periods of incommunicado detention, a government's refusal to investigate allegations of torture, its peremptory denial that torture occurs in the face of mounting evidence such as deaths in custody, its obstruction of independent domestic or international investigations, the censorship of published information about torture, and the immunity from criminal and civil prosecution given to alleged torturers.

Torture today takes place in the face of an increasing international consensus against torture. The UN and several regional IGOs have definitively prohibited torture in international law. They have created bodies that deal with allegations of torture and other gross violations of human rights. Numerous NGOs, among them Amnesty International, have collected, analysed and published information about torture as part of a worldwide effort to help individual victims and groups of victims and to press governments to abolish torture. International codes of conduct have been adopted to dissuade medical professionals and law enforcement officials from participating in torture and other forms of cruel, inhuman or degrading

---

2 Amnesty International considers that a "disappearance" has occurred whenever there are reasonable grounds to believe that a person has been taken into custody by the authorities or with their connivance and the authorities deny that the victim is in custody.

treatment or punishment.[3] A particularly significant development in recent years is the increased number of domestic non-governmental groups that work to protect human rights and to fight torture in their own countries. All of these developments reflect a mounting body of legal, ethical and religious thought and actions that condemn torture as alien to any concept of human dignity. Chapter 4 of this report looks at the development and use of international law by IGOs, international NGOs and domestic human rights groups to combat torture and to create the political will, country by country, to abolish it.

A few governments have taken positive steps against torture in their own countries. Some alleged torturers have been brought to justice, although often only as an exceptional measure. In other countries, combined domestic and international pressure have helped create the political will for the government to control its security agents more closely. Chapter 5 of this report looks at two such situations in the 1970s, Northern Ireland and Brazil.

Since it is governments that are responsible for torture, only governments can in the end effectively prevent it. Chapter 6 offers a set of legal and administrative safeguards and remedies that any government can introduce if it seriously wishes to abolish (or prevent) torture and ill-treatment.

Torture is not only committed by governments: it has been used by opposition forces and by groups such as "death squads" acting with or without government acquiescence. As a matter of principle Amnesty International condemns all acts of torture inflicted on prisoners, regardless of the motives or identities of the perpetrators. Where torture is inflicted by non-governmental entities, Amnesty International considers that it is within the jurisdiction of governments to determine criminal responsibility and to bring those responsible to justice—such authority being exercised by states in conformity with their commitments in international law. This report addresses the steps needed to ensure that states themselves do not become the perpetrators of torture.

---

3 The word "torture" is used in accordance with the definition accepted by the UN (see pages 13-17 below). For convenience, the term "ill-treatment" is used in the country entries synonymously with the more legally correct phrase "cruel, inhuman or degrading treatment or punishment", practices that are likewise prohibited by international law. Unless otherwise indicated, the references to torture made here are meant to cover these forms of ill-treatment as well.

Definitions

To combat torture, and ultimately to abolish it, are the objectives of this report and of Amnesty International's long-term work against torture. Much has already been done by the international community. In the field of international law, the UN took a major step in 1975 by defining torture, a step that allows rulings by domestic courts or IGO human rights bodies to be based on a common understanding of the concepts involved. Article 1 of the Declaration against Torture, adopted unanimously by the UN on 9 December 1975, elaborates the following definition:

> "1. For the purpose of this Declaration, torture means any act by which severe pain or suffering, whether physical or mental, is intentionally inflicted by or at the instigation of a public official on a person for such purposes as obtaining from him or a third person information or confession, punishing him for an act he has committed, or intimidating him or other persons. It does not include pain or suffering arising only from, inherent in or incidental to, lawful sanctions to the extent consistent with the Standard Minimum Rules for the Treatment of Prisoners.[1]

> "2. Torture constitutes an aggravated and deliberate form of cruel, inhuman or degrading treatment or punishment."

This definition bears examination since it is the most authoritative international text now adopted. The main definitional elements contained in the term "torture" are the severity of physical or mental pain or suffering caused to the victim, the deliberateness of

---

1 The Standard Minimum Rules for the Treatment of Prisoners were adopted by the First UN Congress on the Prevention of Crime and the Treatment of Offenders, held at Geneva in 1955, and were subsequently approved in 1957 by the Economic and Social Council of the UN. They purport "to set out what is generally accepted as being good principle and practice in the treatment of prisoners and the management of institutions".

the act, the fact that the act has a purpose, and the direct or indirect involvement of state officials in the act. For the first time the concept of causing severe *mental* suffering was explicitly accepted as part of the international prohibition of state torture. It therefore follows that modern psychological methods of extreme coercion of detainees are prohibited. The purposes mentioned are broad, covering not only the extracting of information and confessions but also acts inflicted to punish or to intimidate the victim or others. However, the exclusion of "lawful sanctions" from the prohibition opens a potentially serious loophole for governments that is only partially closed by reference to the Standard Minimum Rules. (Unfortunately the draft Convention against Torture currently before the UN reiterates this loophole without the qualifying restriction.)

The definition does not attempt to clarify precisely what is meant by "cruel, inhuman or degrading treatment or punishment" although torture is said to be a form of such ill-treatment that is "aggravated and deliberate". Judicial attempts to interpret these concepts or to distinguish clearly among them in case law have proved difficult. What is clear, however, is that the scope of these terms was meant by the drafters to be broad. The relevant UN debates indicate that government representatives accepted that the phrase "cruel, inhuman or degrading treatment or punishment" was not clearly definable and that the scope of its application was meant to be extensive. The UN confirmed this intention in 1979 by adopting a commentary to Article 5 of the Code of Conduct for Law Enforcement Officials, which states: "The term 'cruel, inhuman or degrading treatment or punishment' has not been defined by the General Assembly but should be interpreted so as to extend the widest possible protection against abuses, whether physical or mental."

The difficulty of applying these terms in case law can be seen from the Northern Ireland Case that was before the Council of Europe from late 1971 until 1978. In 1976 the European Commission of Human Rights found, unanimously, that the United Kingdom's combined use in Northern Ireland in 1971 of five techniques in support of interrogation (hooding, wall-standing, subjection to continuous noise, deprivation of sleep and deprivation of food and drink) constituted "torture". In 1978 the European Court of Human Rights, by a large majority (13 to four), disagreed with the ruling of the Commission. In the Court's view the five techniques did not amount to torture although by an even larger majority (16 to one) it found that these practices did constitute inhuman and degrading treatment.

Amnesty International has criticized the restrictive standard set by the Court in this ruling. While accepting that the five interrogation techniques had been used systematically and that their object was to extract confessions and information and to implicate others, the Court held that the five techniques "did not occasion suffering of the particular intensity and cruelty implied by the word torture as so understood". This is a surprising statement given that the Commission had found convincing evidence of weight loss, mental disorientation and acute psychiatric symptoms during interrogation in some of the 14 suspects subjected to these techniques.

Whereas the Commission based its conclusion on its own findings of fact, the Court did not re-examine the evidence directly or call witnesses, although it was empowered to do so. The only hint of its reasoning lies in the unexplained statement that the severity of suffering caused was not sufficiently intense to warrant labeling the methods used with "the special stigma" of torture. This is a regrettable conclusion, as noted by several dissenting judges whose separate opinions indicate that the Court's majority was inclined to regard only physical methods and physical pain as constituting torture, whereas the internationally accepted definition of torture also covers mental suffering and psychological methods.

Were the definition not to do so, some forms of sophisticated techniques of sensory deprivation that have been scientifically developed and used since the 1930s, especially in industrially developed countries, would avoid the stigma of properly being called torture.

Two points emerge from the contradictory rulings in the Northern Ireland Case. First, the treatment in law of torture, whether by definition or in jurisprudence, must keep pace with modern technology, which is capable of inducing severe psychological suffering without resort to any overt physical brutality. Second, it is not necessary to delineate precisely the border between torture and other forms of ill-treatment in order to condemn a particular act. The prohibition in international law of cruel, inhuman or degrading treatment or punishment is as unequivocal as that of torture.

It *is* necessary, of course, to indicate what constitutes or might constitute cruel, inhuman or degrading treatment or punishment. It is clear that there is a lower borderline and that not all forms of treatment or ill-treatment rise above it. It is also clear that these are somewhat elastic terms that have evolved through jurisprudence and the development of international human rights standards and will continue to do so in the world's common understanding of what constitutes a gross abuse of a human being's inherent dignity.

Amnesty International's developing practice in this area is reflected in the abuses that are covered by this report. For some acts there is clear guidance provided by international standards. Article 7 of the International Covenant on Civil and Political Rights prohibits medical or scientific experimentation without the free consent of the subject, thereby ruling out experimental techniques of behaviour modification forcibly used on prisoners. The Human Rights Committee, the body that monitors compliance with the Covenant by States Parties, ruled in July 1982 that corporal punishment falls within the Covenant's prohibition of torture and cruel, inhuman or degrading treatment or punishment. Thus flogging and punitive amputations can be said to violate international standards. The UN Standard Minimum Rules for the Treatment of Prisoners prohibit corporal punishment and confinement in a dark cell as punishments for disciplinary offences by prisoners. The Standard Minimum Rules forbid punishment by "close confinement" and reduction of diet unless the prisoner has been certified as medically fit to withstand the punishment. By implication any punishment of a prisoner that damages his or her physical or mental health is thus prohibited.

Some practices that are not in themselves prohibited by international standards may nevertheless cause concern in particular circumstances. Solitary confinement or other isolation in itself is not generally regarded as a cruel or inhuman treatment or punishment. However, Amnesty International raised the issue of prolonged isolation from other prisoners with officials of the Federal Republic of Germany in 1979 in the belief that it had caused mental and physical harm to prisoners' health and constituted a "cruel, inhuman or degrading treatment or punishment". Considerations of the age, sex and state of health of the prisoner must be weighed as well as the duration of a particular treatment or punishment, its known or likely physical or mental effects on the prisoner, and the deliberateness of the act as evidenced by such things as discrimination shown toward particular prisoners. Reduction of diet, denial of adequate medical care whether deliberately or by negligence, forcible feeding, compulsory labour and numerous other undesirable forms of treatment or punishment may be rendered cruel, inhuman or degrading by the circumstances in which they are imposed.

Amnesty International's practice is to intercede in all cases where there is a risk of torture. With regard to other cruel, inhuman or degrading treatment or punishment of prisoners, Amnesty International seeks to set standards and encourages a government to conform to those standards. This general approach does not preclude taking up individual cases as a means of illustrating general problems in the treatment of prisoners.

In the case of prisoners of conscience, for whom Amnesty International always seeks immediate and unconditional release, the organization may take action on any aspect of their treatment and conditions.[2]

---

2 "Prisoners of conscience" are men and women detained anywhere for their beliefs, colour, sex, ethnic origin, language or religion, provided they have not used or advocated violence.

The process of torture

In many of the countries covered by this report the torture of political prisoners can be said to have become routine. But routine for whom? For the organs of state that require torture to help suppress political opposition. For the security agents who go routinely to their job, like any other worker, except that their job is torture. For the victim, however, torture can never be "routine". It is a calculated assault on one's mind, one's body and human dignity. In these pages torture victims tell their own stories. While it is impossible to verify every one of these allegations, Amnesty International believes that each one is representative of torture as practised in the 1980s in the countries mentioned.

No experience of torture is typical, but there are discernible patterns in the thousands of personal testimonies, affidavits and statements that have reached Amnesty International in the 1980s. For the individual victim torture can mean being seized at night, violently, while family and neighbours are terrorized into helplessness; being blindfolded and beaten in the police van or the unmarked car; the vague reasons, if any, given for the detention; the threats of execution, of rape, of family members being killed in "accidents"; the preliminary questions at the police station or army barracks about present health, medicines, past illnesses, so as not to go too far in the procedures that follow; the sometimes senseless questions ("Why were you born in Tunceli?") for which there are no answers—and throughout, the anticipation and the fact of brute force, without limit, without end, the knowledge of being beyond the help of family or lawyer, of being totally at the mercy of those whose job it is to have no mercy.

Torture usually means isolation: abduction, secret detention, incommunicado detention beyond the reach of family, friends and legal assistance. Blindfolding during days of interrogation and torture serves to increase the sense of being alone and defenceless. Iranian political prisoners released in 1982 tell how it is used at Evin Jail, the Revolutionary Court headquarters in Tehran:

"The worst thing in Evin is being held blindfold for days
on end waiting for someone to tell you why you are there.
Some people are left blindfold for days, weeks or
months. One man has spent 27 months like this. None of
the prisoners appear to know what he is being held for.
After 27 months, he sits, largely in total silence nodding his
head from one side to the other. Sometimes he just sits
knocking his head on the wall. Obviously, they keep people
blindfold to add to the fear. But when they suddenly
whip off the folds to question you, you are almost blind,
the light is painful and you feel dizzy. You can't
concentrate on any single thought."

Essential to torture is the sense that the interrogator controls
everything, even life itself. The pistol cocked at the temple, the
meticulous procedure of mock execution by firing-squad, burial alive
in a deserted area: each is a means of demonstrating to the victim
that the team of torturers has absolute power. "This is nothing but
the introductory exercise", a South Korean security agent told a
prisoner in 1979 after beating and stamping on him and burning his
back with cigarettes. "You can test the limit of your spiritual and
physical patience when you are taken to the basement, where there
are all kinds of torture instruments from ancient times to the
modern age."

"We are six teams trained in Turkey and given full responsibility,"
a torturer told Suleyman Kirteke, a former trade union official
detained in Turkey in 1981. "You will be killed whether you talk or
not. For the cause of death we will say either suicide or a gun battle.
You have no way out." Whether this torturer's claim that he was a
member of a team trained to torture is true or not, the purpose is
to convince the victim that he or she is powerless in the hands of
those with the techniques, the equipment and the determination to
destroy any vestige of resistance.

Torture means degradation: insults, sexual threats or assaults,
forcible eating of one's excrement, humiliation of one's family.
Another torture victim from Turkey witnessed a married couple
being tortured together in 1981:

"In the presence of four or five torturers they were
undressed and made totally naked. Their blindfolds were
removed. A torturer would play with the genital organs of
the wife, squeezing her breasts and caressing her hair while
the husband watched. The reverse would be applied to the
husband. While his wife watched they would give electric
shocks to his penis, hang him by his feet. They would

threaten to rape his wife unless he would admit the accusations made against him. This was one of the tortures that the husband could not bear. And because of that he would admit a lot of crimes that he did not commit.''

Torture often means breaking down under extreme pressure and severe pain, whether the confession signed or information given is true or false. ''Eventually, I was forced to answer in the way they wanted me to since the pain became intolerable,'' said Fernando Benjamín Reveco Soto, who was tortured in 1982 by the *Central Nacional de Informaciones* (CNI), the Chilean secret police.

''When it was finally over I was examined by a doctor. . . . The next day . . . the interrogation continued, accompanied by hard blows to my face and body. They applied intense electric current to my hands. . . . For 21 days I was held in the CNI's hidden premises. . . . On each of the first 14 days which followed my arrest I was subjected to both physical and psychological torture. . . . I was seen by the doctor after nearly all the torture sessions. . . . I was given a document to sign which stated that I had been well treated. It also contained statements which I had made under pressure, and included others which I had never made at all. When I refused to sign I was threatened with further torture. Under such circumstances, I had to sign.''

Other Chilean former prisoners mention this ''doctor'' as well. Besides being medically examined on arrival at this CNI centre in Santiago, six people reported to Amnesty International delegates who visited Chile in 1982 that they had been given non-therapeutic medicine to make them lose their self-control and cooperate with their interrogators. The reported medical knowledge of the person(s) who examined these detainees indicates that he was either a doctor or had had a thorough medical training. It is not uncommon in many countries that a doctor is present to supervise interrogation under torture or available to ensure that the victims can survive to be tortured further and that they do not ''escape'' through unconsciousness or death.

''All I can remember is seeing myself dead,'' Guatemalan doctor José Hurtado told a friend after he was released into the care of the International Committee of the Red Cross following 40 days in custody in June and July 1982. Responding to international appeals on Dr Hurtado's behalf, the government, which had initially refused to acknowledge his detention, showed film of the prisoner inside the National Police Hospital where he was said to be undergoing treatment for a stomach ailment. He was seen in a severely weakened condition, clutching a hot water bottle.

* * * *

Torture victims tell of different reasons why they were tortured. Frequently the purpose is to obtain a confession, often to a deed the person did not commit. In the Republic of Korea, six staff members and an associate of an institute that runs an educational program for labourers, farm workers and women were arrested in March 1979 and later charged with forming a "pro-communist group" because they had, among other alleged acts, listened to North Korean radio broadcasts and possessed Marxist-Leninist books. One of the defendants told the court: "They hit me with a bat; after placing a stick behind my knees, and making me get down on my knees, they stepped on my thighs. They said, 'Even a well-trained spy from North Korea will confess when we do this.' When the stick was broken, they brought another to continue."

Hüseyin Yildirim, a lawyer now living in exile in Sweden, was tortured in Turkey, apparently to intimidate him from acting as defence counsel to members of the Kurdish Workers' Party (PKK) on trial in Diyarbakir. On 11 October 1981 Hüseyin Yildirim was taken from the prison he was visiting in order to help a father find his son, to the Political Branch of Police Headquarters, where he was held for three days in solitary confinement. On the fourth day he was questioned, in particular about the PKK and one of his clients. On the fifth day he was taken to Istihkam Army Engineers' Unit, where his hair was shaved and his eyes blindfolded. He was then taken somewhere else. Just before entering this place he was hit several times, then taken into a room and told to speak. He replied that he was a lawyer, in response to which he was hit in the face and stomach and fastened to a wooden cross naked. He was given electric shocks on his ears, tongue and penis. He was questioned about the PKK, asked why he acted as lawyer for members of the PKK and asked to promise not to do so in future. He fainted and when he regained consciousness found himself lying in water. Five or six men (he does not know whether they were police officers or not) beat the soles of his feet *(falaka)*. He fainted several times and does not know how long the *falaka* continued. He was once again asked to promise not to act for PKK clients in future, but refused to do so. He was taken to another room and beaten with batons, he thinks by soldiers.

In the Soviet Union psychiatrists administer drugs as a form of punishment to prisoners of conscience detained in psychiatric hospitals. The drugs may serve to compel the prisoner to renounce his or her religious or political beliefs, or they may be given as "treatment" for a prisoner's continuing "delusions". In the summer of 1980, for example, Vladimir Tsurikov, a 35-year-old worker from Krasnoyarsk, was interned for the third time in the USSR in connection with his peaceful attempts to emigrate. He describes the effect of drugs forcibly given to him:

> "The triftazin [stelazine] made me writhe, and my legs began to twist about in a ridiculous way. I lost the ability to walk, while simultaneously feeling very restive and also feeling sharp pains in my buttocks at any movement—a result of the sulfazin [a one per cent solution of elemental sulphur in oil]. Fainting fits began, recurring very often: I fell and hit my head on the floor and on the brick walls. The pain prevented me sleeping or eating. The sulfazin made my temperature rise, and it then stayed around 40 degrees centigrade. Sometimes I experienced slight shivering and my tongue hung out. . . . This nightmare lasted a week, until I was invited to chat with some medical students. I couldn't walk, so I was carried. In the auditorium it turned out that I couldn't move my tongue. I was taken back and they began to give me anti-parkinsonian drugs, which made me feel a bit better. I was still suffering from the sulfazin, and I had got much thinner, but at the next meeting with the students I was able to talk with them."

Like at least nine other known dissenters who were forcibly confined to psychiatric hospitals shortly before foreign visitors arrived in Moscow to attend the Olympic Games in July 1980, Vladimir Tsurikov was released very shortly after the Games ended.

Some prisoners are beaten in prison when there is no clear reason for it. A released Zairian prisoner sentenced to 10 years' imprisonment on the charge of "insult to the President" (he was accused of saying that President Mobutu had had another prisoner beaten and tortured), told Amnesty International in 1981 that he was regularly beaten after sentencing in 1978, while he continued to be held incommunicado for six months. During this period he was beaten approximately every other day. Following a meal, he would be told to lie down on the concrete floor of his bare cell, and he would be set upon by four or five (sometimes eight) guards.

* * * *

Different security agencies develop their own methods and procedures for interrogating prisoners under torture. The Venezuelan-born film director Nelson Arrieti described his interrogation in El Salvador after being abducted by security forces in January 1981 from a hotel lobby in the capital, San Salvador:

"There were three different levels, you might say, three types of interrogation and three types of interrogator. The first was the most brutal, with a great deal of beating. There was a lot of violence. They threatened to kill me, and shouted at me to tell them everything I knew about the revolution and the guerrilla movement. This is the typical brutal policy which produces a basic fear in the prisoner and which is intended to demoralize him.

"The second type is on a higher level. This is carried out by a policeman whose language is less crude, who asks general questions, without beatings, using a more refined language.

"The third type is the trained policeman who does not administer beatings or make threats, but who tries to explain the problem and who converses with a certain degree of ideological understanding. He is the type of man who tries to be friendly and make promises. He allows the prisoner to relax emotionally. His intellectual resources and investigative methods are better. I recall that it was these policemen who offered me a light sentence and offered to help me if I signed a telex for the international press, declaring that the Junta had played a beneficial role and that agrarian reform had been a success and that the revolutionary movement had failed. They make you fear for your life. 'Your life is in our hands' . . . that is the situation in a nutshell. 'If you say nothing, it makes no difference, you are still condemned because we know everything.'"

Some interrogators develop a particular expertise. "Sometimes someone would take over who apparently was a specialist at slapping," reported a political prisoner in the Philippines in 1979. "He asked only one question and this repeatedly, together with a sharp and hard slap to the face or ears." In March 1980 Amnesty International interviewed and medically examined 14 Iraqi exiles who alleged that they had been tortured in Iraq. In many cases the interrogators were said to have pretended to adopt a "kind" and "understanding" approach at some stage; for instance, they would engage in discussions about politics and pretend to support the victim's views, or they would promise them such things as good jobs, entrance to college, passports and "women" if they confessed or signed a declaration that they would remain politically unaffiliated.

One man described how he was "befriended" by a "kind man", ostensibly a fellow detainee, who would frequently ask for him to be brought to his cell, show concern and understanding about his predicament and offer to help him. The detainee could not be certain but believed him to be a security "plant" whose job was to break him down; he found this kind of psychological pressure difficult to resist.

Torture has its own sardonic slang: Chilean former detainees described several of the terms used: *el quirófano*, the operating theatre, in which the detainee is made to lie on a table for long periods with the upper half of the body unsupported, making it a great strain to keep the whole body horizontal; *la parrilla*, the grill, a metal bed to which the victim is strapped while being given electric shocks; *la bañera*, the bath, holding the victim's head under water almost to the point of drowning; *pau de arara*, parrot's perch, suspension head down from a horizontal pole placed under the knees, with the wrists bound to the ankles; and *el teléfono*, blows with the palms of the hands on both ears simultaneously. A released prisoner held by Zaire's internal security service in 1982 reported that prisoners were made to drink their own urine, *le petit déjeuner*, and then beaten systematically on the shoulders, *le déjeuner*.

* * * *

The immediate and long-term effects of such intense physical and psychological abuse are oppressive. On a mission to Chile in 1982 Amnesty International delegates medically examined Adriana Vargas Vásquez, a 31-year-old factory worker who had been tortured in March 1980. She described the early effects of the torture. She completely lost all sense of time after one day's torture. After electrical shocks and suspension from the *pau de arara* she had especially painful breasts, wrists and ankles. She had swelling and discolouration in places where she had received blows, and there were small black scabs where electrodes had been applied. She lost about 6 kg while in detention for four days. She had almost no appetite initially after her release and suffered for about 20 days from nausea but did not vomit. She developed a urinary tract infection. Her genitals became inflamed two months, and again four months, after her release. Among other symptoms, she experienced abdominal pain and headaches when she menstruated, persistent headaches in the back of the head and around the temples, impaired memory, difficulty in concentrating, dizziness, insomnia, nightmares, depression to the point of feeling suicidal, proneness to weeping, and anxiety attacks triggered especially by loud noises.

Clearly, there is a great need for medical treatment both immediately after torture and over a longer period, including psychiatric treatment in many cases. Suicide is a not uncommon result of torture, either in prison to avoid further pain or after release due to the oppressive suffering that persists. Following the extreme ill-treatment of suspects held in connection with the May 1980 violent disturbances in Kwangju, Republic of Korea, four prisoners reportedly formed a suicide pact rather than be tortured, and one of them succeeded in committing suicide. Kanagaratnam Gunapalasingham, a Sri Lankan cigar manufacturer, committed suicide in September 1981, having been detained, tortured and released in May. Amnesty International possesses his affidavit submitted before a justice of the peace on 2 August 1981. The medical expert who examined him on his third admission to hospital for treatment of physical and mental after-effects of torture told Amnesty International that Kanagaratnam Gunapalasingham was refusing food and drink and was unable to talk, expressing himself only by way of gestures. He had difficulties in passing urine. The doctor said that he had found signs of haematoma (clotted blood) in both the big toe folds and on both heels consistent with the allegations made by Kanagaratnam Gunapalasingham in his affidavit that needles had been driven into both his toes and heels. The doctor told Amnesty International the patient had hysterical attacks, continuously referring to the army assaults. The medical expert concluded that he was profoundly psychiatrically disturbed possibly as a consequence of torture.

Torture victims often need social, medical and psychological help after release. Systematic examinations of torture victims conducted by Amnesty International's Danish Medical Group, established in 1974, show that practically all victims suffer from multiple mental and physical sequelae (after-effects) to torture.[1] In a few countries groups of doctors, psychologists and social workers have formed in response to the urgent needs of the victims who come to them for help. These groups sometimes work in the countries where torture occurs, but more often such help is available only for those victims living in exile.

As one means of treating these victims (and their families, who often have psychosomatic symptoms), several independent doctors and other health workers created a rehabilitation centre for torture victims at the University Hospital of Copenhagen. The centre draws on the experience of medical specialists who have examined and treated victims from several countries. One of the 20 torture victims treated at the centre since it was established in 1982 was a 35-year-old man who had been tortured six years previously by,

---

1 See, for example, the Amnesty International Danish Medical Group's first publication, *Evidence of Torture*, (Amnesty International Publications, London, 1977).

among several methods, *falanga*. Years later he suffered from pain in his feet and back. He could not walk more than a few hundred metres without great pain in his legs. Following careful physical examination, he was treated with ultrasound techniques and physiotherapy. Two months later he was able to walk, run and play football without pain. In addition, psychological help relieved some of his sleep disturbances, anxiety attacks and other persistent mental symptoms.

A great many torture victims, of course, cannot obtain medical help. Some fear to seek it even after release. An ex-detainee held in late 1981 at an army camp in northern Sri Lanka reported being tortured by an army major who put his two thumbs into the victim's eyes, pushing them in until blood came out. "My eyesight is bad at the moment. After dark I cannot see very well. I do not dare to go to an eye specialist. I am afraid that they might tell officials that I told them how I got my injuries."

Many others remain in prison, their situation uncertain and vulnerable. International support for them remains vital. After an Amnesty International mission to Morocco in 1981, where delegates visited Kenitra Central Prison, Amnesty International received this message from a prisoner currently held there who had previously been tortured and had campaigned together with other prisoners of conscience for improved conditions:

> "It is incontestable that our situation has improved in prison, but our situation is very precarious, since it is based on no judicial text (the government does not recognize having political detainees, and we are officially considered common criminals). In other words, the 'privileges' we have obtained thanks to the struggles we have waged in prison and the support given to us at the international level by many organizations, above all Amnesty International, all these 'privileges' are constantly threatened."

Action against torture

The prohibition of torture in international law is absolute: "No one shall be subjected to torture or cruel, inhuman or degrading treatment or punishment", states Article 7 of the International Covenant on Civil and Political Rights. The covenant reflects the growing body of international law that unequivocally condemns torture. This prohibition cannot be derogated from: no government may use terrorism, foreign aggression, threats to national security or any other argument of public emergency to justify torture. Nor is the prohibition made relative by cultural or religious differences among or within societies, or by victims' differences in tolerance to pain. On the contrary, the prohibition of torture and all other forms of cruel, inhuman or degrading treatment or punishment is universal, covering all prisoners, countries and situations.

This individual right gains its moral force from the concept, as stated in the Universal Declaration of Human Rights (1948), "of the inherent dignity and of the equal and inalienable rights of all members of the human family". Historically this declaration of human dignity was the response of the newly formed UN to the "barbarous acts which . . . outraged the conscience of mankind" prior to and during the Second World War.

The legally binding force of the prohibition of torture derives from two sources of international law: treaties and "international custom, as evidence of a general practice accepted as law".[1] The Geneva Conventions, the International Covenant on Civil and Political Rights and the regional human rights conventions, all of which prohibit torture, are legally binding on the states that ratify them. International customary law can be inferred from such things as multilateral declarations of common policy among states, the number of domestic constitutions that uphold a given norm, and the acceptance by domestic and international courts of internationally agreed standards. The absolute prohibition of torture may

---

1 Article 38(1) of the Statute of the International Court of Justice at The Hague.

be considered to reflect international customary law, and it is therefore legally binding on all states, even on those that are not parties to any human rights treaty and those that did not exist when the prohibition of torture was formulated in international instruments.

Among the treaties that prohibit torture is the International Covenant on Civil and Political Rights, which was adopted in 1966 and entered into force in 1976 after being ratified or acceded to by 35 member states. The significance of this treaty lies not only in the breadth of the specific human rights norms elaborated in it, but also in the fact that it is legally binding on ratifying states.

Clear evidence that torture is now prohibited in international customary law as well can be found in the numerous multilateral resolutions and declarations indicating a commonly declared policy among states to prohibit torture. The Universal Declaration of Human Rights forbids torture absolutely. In 1975 the UN adopted the Declaration on the Protection of All Persons from Torture and Other Cruel, Inhuman or Degrading Treatment or Punishment. The adoption by acclamation of the Declaration against Torture came at a time when 144 states were members of the UN, as compared with 56 at the time of the adoption of the universal declaration, thus adding further weight to the claim for the universal applicability of the prohibition of torture.

Pursuant to the Declaration against Torture, the UN drafted and adopted the Code of Conduct for Law Enforcement Officials and the Principles of Medical Ethics, in 1979 and 1982 respectively, which govern the conduct towards detainees by members of the two professions most directly responsible for prisoners' care.

Further evidence that the prohibition of torture is firmly established in the rules of international law is provided by the number of domestic legal systems that expressly incorporate it. A 1978 survey of 136 constitutions and other legal instruments cites legal provisions by 112 nations that either explicitly forbid torture or can reasonably be interpreted as doing so.[2] Such domestic judicial rulings as in the Filártiga case mentioned below on page 33, which held that torture is a violation of international law, are additional evidence that the prohibition of torture now constitutes a part of international customary law.

The accompanying list of international instruments adopted during the last three and a half decades leaves little doubt that "the law of nations" unequivocally and unconditionally condemns

---

2 Steven Ackerman, "Torture and Other Forms of Cruel and Unusual Punishment in International Law", *Vanderbilt Journal of Transnational Law*, Vol. 11, Autumn 1978, pp. 667-68 and Appendix 1, pp. 691-702.

International instruments that prohibit torture

Global

Universal Declaration of Human Rights (1948), Article 5: "No one shall be subjected to torture or to cruel, inhuman or degrading treatment or punishment."

Geneva Conventions (1949): Common Article 3 of the four Geneva Conventions forbids "cruel treatment and torture of persons taking no active part in the hostilities". Common Article 3 also proscribes "outrages upon personal dignity, in particular, humiliating and degrading treatment". Under Article 99 of the Third Geneva Convention, "no moral or physical coercion may be exerted on a prisoner of war in order to induce him to admit himself guilty of the act of which he is accused".

International Covenant on Civil and Political Rights (1966), Article 7: "No one shall be subjected to torture or to cruel, inhuman or degrading treatment or punishment. In particular, no one shall be subjected without his free consent to medical or scientific experimentation."

UN Declaration on the Protection of All Persons from Torture and Other Cruel, Inhuman or Degrading Treatment or Punishment (1975), Article 3: "No State may permit or tolerate torture or other cruel, inhuman or degrading treatment or punishment. Exceptional circumstances such as a state of war or a threat of war, internal political instability or any other public emergency may not be invoked as a justification of torture or other cruel, inhuman or degrading treatment or punishment."

Regional

European Convention for the Protection of Human Rights and Fundamental Freedoms (1950), Article 3: "No one shall be subjected to torture or to inhuman or degrading treatment or punishment."

American Convention on Human Rights (1969), Article 5 (2): "No one shall be subjected to torture or to cruel, inhuman or degrading punishment or treatment. All persons deprived of their liberty shall be treated with respect for the inherent dignity of the human person."

African Charter on Human and Peoples' Rights (adopted 1981, not yet in force), Article 5: "All forms of exploitation and degradation of man, particularly . . . torture, cruel, inhuman or degrading punishment and treatment shall be prohibited."

Special rules and codes of conduct

UN Standard Minimum Rules for the Treatment of Prisoners (1957), Article 31: "Corporal punishment, punishment by placing in a dark cell, and all cruel, inhuman or degrading punishments shall be completely prohibited as punishments for disciplinary offences."

UN Code of Conduct for Law Enforcement Officials (1979), Article 5: "No law enforcement official may inflict, instigate or tolerate any act of torture or other cruel, inhuman or degrading treatment or punishment, nor may any law enforcement official invoke superior orders or exceptional circumstances . . . as a justification of torture or other cruel, inhuman or degrading treatment or punishment." In this code of conduct, the term "law enforcement officials" is said to include all officers of the law who exercise police powers, especially the powers of arrest or detention.

UN Principles of Medical Ethics (1982), Principle 2: "It is a gross contravention of medical ethics, as well as an offence under applicable international instruments, for health personnel, particularly physicians, to engage, actively or passively in acts which constitute participation in, complicity in, incitement to or attempts to commit torture or other cruel, inhuman or degrading treatment or punishment."

torture and all other forms of cruel, inhuman or degrading treatment or punishment.

Yet these international (and national) commandments are violated by dozens of governments. Therein lies the importance of international human rights law. It sets an indisputably universal legal standard to which torture victims may appeal for protection and redress against their own government and which individuals and domestic groups fighting for human rights as well as international human rights bodies, both inter-governmental and non-governmental, can use to hold an offending government accountable.

The remainder of this chapter looks at several of the legal remedies available and at some of the actions that have been taken in recent years against torture by victims, their families and by domestic groups courageously combating torture committed by their own governments, and at the actions of several IGOs and international NGOs.

Action by victims and their families

To whom does one turn for help when a relative, friend or associate is in danger of being tortured? What actions do families take domestically and internationally to try to stop the torture or seek redress? Speed is especially important in the first few days of detention and interrogation. Because relatives are often not informed where a detainee is held during this initial period of interrogation, they may have to pursue their inquiries personally at police stations and military barracks—often receiving little or misleading information about the detainee's whereabouts, legal status and physical condition.

Where emergency legislation or broad powers of arrest and detention exist, the security apparatus may be empowered to hold a detainee for long—sometimes indefinite—periods in incommunicado detention. Families try any well-placed friend or contact in the bureaucracy, judiciary, military or other official body who might intervene.

Often, however, the only legal procedure available is to apply to the courts to test the legality of a detention, for example, by an application for a writ of *habeas corpus*, *amparo*, or the equivalent. In theory, *habeas corpus* is a mechanism that provides for judicial restraint on the security forces. In practice, it depends for its effectiveness on the independence, integrity and courage of the judiciary and on the susceptibility of the security forces to control by the judiciary. In some countries *habeas corpus* is rendered inoperative in political cases or during states of emergency because the law is so drafted as to make a wide range of detentions legal, making it easy to satisfy the test of legality provided by *habeas corpus*. Elsewhere, judges may not respond to petitions for *habeas corpus*, or if they do, the security forces may simply ignore them.

Other court procedures may be available, even if only after torture has occurred. In Chile, for example, more than 200 people as of mid-1982 had filed complaints alleging torture with domestic courts. Most of them were submitted after 1980. Paraguayan law allows a private party to bring a criminal action, with the permission of the court, against perpetrators of a crime. In a case of international significance, the parents of Joelito Filártiga, a 17-year-old youth who died under torture in 1976, brought a criminal action against his alleged torturers, including Américo Peña-Irala, the Inspector General of Police of Asunción. In February 1983 a Paraguayan Court of Appeal upheld a ruling of the lower court acquitting the accused of the murder of Joelito Filártiga.

In March 1979, however, the police inspector was temporarily resident in New York when he was arrested for overstaying his visa. Joelito Filártiga's father, Dr Joel Filártiga, and his sister Dolly were in the United States (US) at the time. Under a little-used provision of US law, the Alien Tort Statute (Title 28 of the *United States Code*, Section 1350), Dr Filártiga and Dolly Filártiga filed a civil action for damages against their compatriot in a US court. The US Alien Tort Statute provides that: "The [US Federal] district courts shall have original jurisdiction of any civil action by an alien for a tort [private or civil wrong] only, committed in violation of the law of nations or a treaty of the United States."

Although the initial ruling in federal district court found that the US courts did not have jurisdiction to hear the case, in June 1980 the US Federal Court of Appeals for the Second Circuit ruled that torture, when officially condoned, is a violation of international law. In the Court of Appeal's view, the international treaties and declarations that prohibit torture are an expression of the evolving "law of nations", and as a consequence a US federal district court would have jurisdiction under the Alien Tort Statute to hear the Filártiga civil suit against Américo Peña-Irala.

In the meantime, the former inspector had been allowed by the trial court to return to Paraguay. The trial court in May 1983 entered a judgment of $375,000 against Américo Peña-Irala. It is doubtful, however, whether the family will be able to collect any part of this sum because the former inspector is no longer in the US. Nevertheless, the courage and persistence of this Paraguayan family led to a land-

34

mark decision in a foreign court that opens a new domestic remedy in international human rights law. That is an important precedent in a world where the enforcement of human rights law remains principally at the national level. The decision further added a bilateral governmental dimension to the concept of human rights enforcement. In the words of the US Court of Appeal's judgment, "the torturer has become, like the pirate and slave trader before him . . . an enemy of all mankind".

Action by national groups

An encouraging feature of the world human rights map is the growing number of local and national organizations that are courageously prepared to confront their own governments with their records on human rights abuses, including the onerous charge of torture. Examples are non-governmental human rights groups, bar associations, trade unions, churches, minority rights groups and political parties.

They usually concentrate on actions through the courts, such as applications for writs of *habeas corpus*, and on the collection of primary data about individual cases of torture and other human rights abuses which they may be able to submit to international organizations. By collating data over a period of time, some groups are able to discern patterns of human rights violations of particular social sectors and may therefore be able to challenge the government's position that any human rights abuses that occur are merely the excesses of individual officials. An important humanitarian aspect of their work is direct assistance to torture victims after release.

Besides actions in court and humanitarian work, some such groups may be able to publicize specific human rights abuses nationally and internationally or bring attention to human rights violations by various techniques such as vigils or hunger-strikes, often undertaken in conjunction with similar actions by prisoners and torture victims themselves. The specific aim of each of the types of action described below is to press the government to bring its practice into line with international law.

A brief review of a few of these groups—by no means a comprehensive survey—will give an idea of what they have done against torture as part of a larger effort to re-establish respect for human rights in their countries.

In many African countries the existence of organized domestic opposition to torture is severely limited by the absence of effective legal remedies. Against this background, it is all the more notable when some domestic groups speak out against torture or other human rights violations. Church leaders have taken on this role in Uganda both under President Idi Amin and under President Milton Obote's government, in Zimbabwe before and after independence, in Namibia, South Africa, Lesotho and elsewhere.

For several years Ugandan religious leaders of the Anglican, Orthodox, Roman Catholic and Muslim faiths have protested directly and publicly to the Uganda Government about violations of fundamental human rights in their country by security officers, including violence towards civilians at road-blocks and the stripping and searching of women at gun-point. Religious leaders and worshippers have themselves been subjected to violence. After an attack on an army base by guerrillas from the vicinity of the Rubaga Cathedral in Kampala in February 1982, soldiers of the Uganda Army disrupted an Ash Wednesday children's mass at the cathedral. Cardinal Emmanuel Nsubuga, Archbishop of Kampala, protested to the government that priests and worshippers had been threatened by soldiers and that Article 5 of the universal declaration "was openly violated when, according to evidence from two medical superintendents of Nsambya and Rubaga hospitals, patients who had been victims of [the] shooting were dragged out of our hospitals without the authority of the medical staff." The government formally apologized for the Rubaga incidents.

In South Africa, the Detainees' Parents Support Committee (DPSC), composed of members of each of the country's racial groups, was formed in 1981 to highlight the plight of political detainees and to seek improvements in their conditions and treatment in security police custody. The DPSC pressed for detainees to receive visits from relatives and in early 1982 compiled some 70 statements by former detainees alleging torture or ill-treatment. The DPSC also recommended to the authorities the introduction of the right of access to detainees by lawyers, relatives and doctors; an enforceable code of interrogation practices and the establishment of independent, effective machinery for supervising the treatment of detainees. However, such measures had not been implemented by mid-1983.

At a general meeting of all Moroccan bar associations, the associations issued a persuasive document in June 1982 calling for an end to the violations of judicial independence in Morocco and for the right to a proper legal defence. The bar associations publicly called on the government to honour the safeguards that exist in domestic law for detainees but that are systematically ignored in political cases during the period of incommunicado detention in police custody *(garde à vue)*. In outlining the legal safeguards that would help secure respect for detainees' rights in Morocco, the statement of the bar associations referred to Islamic tradition, the Moroccan constitution, the Universal Declaration of Human Rights and the International Covenant on Civil and Political Rights.

In Syria, some 217 Damascus lawyers began in June 1978 to press publicly and via the Syrian bar association for a change in government policy towards political freedom. By early 1980 the bar association was joined by national and local associations of doctors, pharmacists, dentists, teachers and engineers in making public demands for the observance of civil and political rights. Among the demands of the General Congress of Syrian Engineers in February 1980, for example, was a call to punish "anyone who tortures citizens physically or morally or treats them in a degrading manner". Following a national one-day strike in support of their demands, hundreds of lawyers, doctors and engineers were arrested, many of whom have remained in detention without trial since April 1980.

In the USSR, the forcible confinement to psychiatric hospitals of political and religious non-conformists, without medical justification, is sometimes aggravated by subjecting these prisoners of conscience to serious physical ill-treatment: forcible injections or over-doses of disorienting and pain-causing drugs, insulin-shock therapy, immobilization in straitjackets or wet canvas, and often severe beatings. One unofficial group created by Soviet citizens to monitor these violations of human rights was the Working Commission to Investigate the Use of Psychiatry for Political Purposes, formed in Moscow in 1977. During the next four years it documented more than 70 cases and investigated a further 260 cases of the political abuse of psychiatry.

Working with the group were two practising psychiatrists, Dr Alexander Voloshanovich and Dr Anthony Koryagin, who examined 55 prisoners of conscience released from mental hospitals or people in danger of being detained and sent to psychiatric hospitals. They concluded that there was no medical justification for the forcible confinement or treatment of these people.

In February 1980 Dr Voloshanovich emigrated from the USSR in the face of official harassment. Within a year, all six remaining members of the working commission, including Dr Koryagin, were arrested and are now serving terms of up to 12 years' imprisonment and internal exile on charges of "circulating anti-Soviet slander" and "anti-Soviet agitation and propaganda".

In May 1983 the Human Rights Society of Pakistan named nine political detainees whom it alleged had died as a result of torture while in custody since the military coup in 1977 that brought President

Mohammed Zia-ul-Haq to power. The society's report, based on an eight-month investigation, mentions long-term incommunicado detention and lengthy interrogation sessions as preconditions for torture.

In Sri Lanka the Civil Rights Movement (CRM) was founded in 1971 during a state of emergency when some 16,000 political prisoners were being held. It subsequently firmly established itself as "a group which examines laws, proposed laws and the workings of government in the light of basic principles of human rights . . . common to a wide spectrum of political groups and parties". In 1978 it made a successful attempt to prevent the reintroduction of the "cat o'nine tails" (a multi-thonged whip for flogging sentenced prisoners); it objected to the perpetuation in 1979 (the UN's Year of the Child) of laws to allow the whipping of juvenile offenders; and in 1980 publicized its query to the Inspector General of Police about news reports that the Sri Lanka Police were considering the use of the "shok baton" (a battery-operated truncheon that could be used for torture). In 1983 the CRM reiterated its long-standing and public demands for an end to police assaults and for the introduction of independent machinery to investigate complaints against the police. In June 1983 it criticized proposed emergency legislation aimed at allowing the police in the north, an area of civil unrest where there have been many allegations of torture, to dispose of dead bodies without post-mortem inquiries. The CRM pointed out that such powers could create again "the excesses of 1971, when similar powers resulted in deaths under torture, indiscriminate killings and executions without trial by the security forces".

In Indonesia the independent Legal Aid Institute has publicized cases of torture and police brutality. In 1982 they were joined by the Indonesian Lawyers' Association in publicly supporting the attempts of Drs Haji A.M. Fatwa, a Muslim teacher and former government official from Jakarta, to obtain a judicial hearing for compensation against three military officers who allegedly beat him in October 1980, leaving him in need of hospital care. Despite the government's statement that the three officers who had ill-treated Haji Fatwa had been disciplined, his claim for compensation has not been able to proceed owing to the harassment of his lawyers, who have been forced to withdraw from the case.

In late 1981, 28 defendants in the Republic of Korea were accused of organizing or participating in two separate groups—one for students, one for workers—supposedly with the purpose of fomenting anti-state activities. The main evidence against the accused were their confessions, which they renounced in court on the grounds that they were obtained under torture during incommunicado detention that lasted between 20 and 40 days. The families of all of the prisoners issued a public appeal to the authorities in early January 1982, shortly before the end of the trial, asking for an end to torture, a return to the rule of law and the release of the detainees on the grounds that the prosecution charges were based on illegally obtained confessions. Following severe harassment, several were warned not to refer to torture again.

The same month, Protestant church leaders supported the families' appeal. All 13 clergy from seven different church groups who signed the petition were warned by the authorities that its publication would lead to investigation of themselves. All copies of a Christian newspaper in which they did publish the petition were confiscated. At the end of February the Justice and Peace Commission of the Korea Catholic Church publicly condemned the torture of the 28 defendants and called generally for an end to "the utilization of torture as a device for political revenge".

Torture in some countries of Latin America is often associated with "disappearance" or murder following detention. A number of human rights groups have been formed to combat human rights violations, including torture, in such countries as Argentina, Bolivia, Chile, Colombia, El Salvador, Guatemala, Haiti, Honduras and Mexico. The cost in terms of personal safety to themselves and their closest relatives has sometimes been considerable. For example, the Jesuit priest Fr. Luis Espinal was a member of the Bolivian Permanent Assembly for Human Rights, a group that monitors and publicizes human rights abuses in Bolivia and gives legal advice to prisoners and their relatives. In March 1980, during the brief civilian government of President Lidia Gueiler, Fr. Espinal was bound, gagged and shot dead, allegedly by paramilitary agents who were harassing civilian sectors and the government with military support. The Medical College of La Paz confirmed after examination of his corpse that he had been tortured prior to his murder. In February 1983 the civilian government of President Hernan Siles Zuazo announced the prosecution of paramilitary agents implicated in the murder of Fr. Espinal and other Bolivians during the early 1980s.

In Chile there are several human rights groups assisting torture victims, among them the *Vicaría de la Solidaridad*, Vicariate of Solidarity, which works under the sponsorship of the Archbishop of Santiago. The *Vicaría* and its predecessor, the ecumenical *Comité para la Paz*, Committee for Peace, have submitted thousands of petitions for *amparo* to Chilean courts since the 1973 coup, in an effort to protect detainees from "disappearance" or torture. April 1983 witnessed the public announcement in Chile of the newly formed *Comisión Nacional contra la Tortura*, National Commission against Torture, a group of 23 prestigious civic and church leaders whose principal task, according to its President, is "to create the space for witness . . . [being] as objective as possible". At its inaugural news conference in Santiago the national commission presented evidence about the alleged torture of 12 of a group of 34 people who were detained for alleged political activities in March and banished *(relegado)* without trial to Pisagua in the north of the country.

Action by inter-governmental organizations

Several of the IGOs that work for the protection of human rights have developed bodies and procedures to deal with allegations of torture and other cruel, inhuman or degrading treatment or punishment. At the outset it is important to note that the limitations on the effectiveness of these inter-governmental mechanisms are considerable. They have generally been more successful in elaborating international norms against torture than in implementing them. None of these IGOs can force governments to stop torture; they cannot enforce their recommendations. Consequently the principal sanction of IGOs is to bring international pressure to bear on governments by investigation and, in some cases, by public exposure.

The following section indicates some of the actions taken against torture by IGO human rights bodies in recent years. Because these bodies have an increasingly significant role to play in exposing the use of torture, it is important that their procedures be workable, effective and accessible. In Amnesty International's experience, structures and procedures that incorporate the following principles tend to increase the effectiveness of IGO human rights bodies:

a. The members of the human rights body should be independent of governmental pressure.

b. It should be able to undertake responsible fact-finding. It should not take a government's response at face-value. It should have sufficient staff to pursue its own investigations.

c. It should be able to act quickly to prevent torture in individual cases, and its procedures for the review of cases and situations should be swift and efficient.

d. It should be capable of acting on its own initiative where it has reasonable cause to believe that torture has occurred.

e.   It should be empowered to receive complaints from people who allege torture, from individuals acting on their behalf, from member states of the IGO and from NGOs.

f.   Significant parts of its proceedings, at a minimum its conclusions and recommendations, should be made public. Public reports of the body's decisions and recommendations should be broadly disseminated and publicized.

g.   A government's non-response to allegations or its inadequate compliance with the human rights body's findings should cause the body to infer acceptance of the facts as alleged. Non-compliance should be persistently pursued and publicly reported.

In setting forth these principles, Amnesty International does not suggest that all IGO human rights bodies should be uniform. A diversity of IGO procedures may strengthen the overall efforts to eradicate torture, each body bringing its own weight and capacities for action to bear.

The Human Rights Committee

The Human Rights Committee was established in 1976 pursuant to the terms of the International Covenant on Civil and Political Rights. Its 18 members are elected for four-year terms by the States Parties to the covenant; they meet thrice yearly. They are elected as independent human rights experts serving in their personal capacities and are empowered to consider the compliance of all States Parties with the covenant, by considering reports from States Parties about their performance under the covenant. Under Article 40(4) of the covenant, the committee may also make "such general comments as it may consider appropriate". These general comments constitute an authoritative interpretation of the covenant.

In a key interpretation of its own procedures concerning individual complaints, the committee decided to receive complaints from individuals other than the victim of a human rights violation—normally a close relative or an appointed lawyer—as the victim is often in prison, dead or otherwise prevented from filing a complaint. In August 1979, in its first decision on an individual complaint, the committee found that the alleged torture of Professor José Luís Massera in Uruguay and the detention of his wife and son-in-law in conditions seriously detrimental to his health were breaches of Article 7 of the covenant. Two of the three prisoners who were the subject of this complaint are now released. Although the committee called for his release in 1979, as of mid-1983 Professor Massera, now aged 68, remains in prison, having suffered permanent physical injury to one leg as a result of torture in 1975. After four years in detention, Professor Massera, a renowned mathematician, was sentenced in 1979 to 20 years' imprisonment on a charge of "subversive association".

The Uruguayan Government has failed to comply with the specific views of the Human Rights Committee regarding the 28 individual cases on which decisions had been reached by the end of March 1983. Nine of these decisions refer to breaches of Article 7 of the covenant. In no case of a current or released prisoner has the government fulfilled recommendations to provide "effective remedies, including compensation". It is incumbent upon other governments, particularly those that are States Parties to the covenant, to press the Uruguayan Government to fulfil its obligations by responding positively to the findings of the Human Rights Committee, as the flouting of the human rights machinery can only endanger its future observance.

United Nations machinery

Primary among the special UN agencies that deal with torture is the UN Commission on Human Rights, established in 1946. Although it initiated the drafting of the Universal Declaration of Human Rights in 1948, it did not consider itself empowered to investigate complaints of torture or other human rights violations until some two decades later. Its 43 members officially represent their governments.

One procedure of the UN commission allows it to consider significant human rights abuses in different countries. Resolution 1235, adopted by the Economic and Social Council (ECOSOC) in 1967, instructed the UN commission "to examine information relevant to gross violations of human rights and fundamental freedoms, as exemplified by the policy of *apartheid*" in southern Africa. Since 1967 this procedure has been broadened and has allowed the UN commission to examine torture allegations in public session from several countries. Under the "1235 procedure" working groups composed of members of the UN commission acting in their personal capacities have examined human rights situations in southern Africa, Israeli-occupied territories and Chile. In February 1975, for example, the UN commission created an *Ad Hoc* Working Group (since superseded by a Special Rapporteur) on the Situation of Human Rights in Chile. This body reported twice yearly, once to the UN commission and again to the UN General Assembly. After three years of discussions with the Chilean Government, the working group was allowed to visit Chile in July 1978. They took testimony from torture victims and government security agents, examined security police and medical records on former prisoners and visited detention centres where torture had allegedly occurred. Their investigations revealed numerous inconsistencies in the government's version of events in several cases of torture, including the identification of a secret detention centre said by the authorities to be a "recreational centre" for security police.

The "1235 procedure" has also been a useful means of obtaining public discussion among government representatives about specific cases of systematic torture and other gross human rights violations. Special rapporteurs, representatives or delegates of the UN Secretary General have been authorized to investigate human rights violations in several countries, including Bolivia, El Salvador, Democratic Kampuchea, Guatemala, Iran and Poland. Torture was specifically mentioned in respect of Iran.

Another procedure has been developed under Resolution 1503 adopted by ECOSOC in 1970. It authorizes the UN commission to consider communications that reveal a "consistent pattern of gross and reliably attested violations of human rights".

The UN commission has reviewed allegations of torture and other human rights abuses in a significant number of countries under the 1235 and 1503 procedures. These procedures offer a form of sanction, for no government wishes to stand accused of torture before other governments, even in closed session.

The UN has developed two further mechanisms to assist individual torture victims directly. The Secretary-General can in certain cases exercise his "good offices" to protect individuals from human rights abuses by contacting governments to express urgent concern or to ask for information about detainees at risk of being tortured. In 1981 the General Assembly created the United Nations Voluntary Fund for Victims of Torture (for which contributions are invited from governments and other sources) to assist torture victims financially through relief, rehabilitation and legal aid.

Organization of American States

The two bodies empowered by the Organization of American States (OAS) to monitor member states' implementation of norms against torture and other human rights abuses are the Inter-American Commission of Human Rights (IACHR) and the Inter-American Court of Human Rights. The IACHR has some of the most flexible procedures for dealing with human rights abuses of any of the IGO human rights bodies. Created in 1959 at a meeting of OAS foreign ministers, it was reconstituted by the American Convention of Human Rights (1969), which came into force in 1978. The IACHR came into existence before the adoption of the American Convention and retains its original jurisdiction over all OAS member states, not just those that have ratified the convention.

Its seven members are elected in their personal capacities by all member states. It acts on allegations of torture received not only from an alleged torture victim but "any person or group of persons", or "any NGO entity [non-governmental organization] legally recognized in one or more member states". It sends emergency telegrams and makes other urgent approaches to governments concerning individuals at risk of torture; it reviews information about individual cases and country situations; it can act on its own initiative; it can seek authority "to conduct on-site observations in the territory of a state, with the consent, or at the invitation, of the government in question". Even without the government's consent the IACHR can issue a report on its investigations. On-site visits can add to the balance and credibility of the findings. Since the late 1970s the IACHR has issued subsequent reports on such visits to investigate torture and other violations of human rights in Colombia, Haiti, Panama, Nicaragua under President Somoza, El Salvador and Argentina.

Following its visit to Argentina in September 1979, the IACHR concluded that "unlawful physical force and psychological and mental torture were practised in special interrogation centres commonly known as *chupaderos* ["roughing-up centres"] and, in some cases, were carried out over several months of interrogation sessions". The report on this visit, submitted to the governments in December 1979 and published in April 1980, lists 18 types of physical and mental torture alleged by complainants. The section of the report dealing with torture concludes:

> "Methods of this nature, evidencing similar characteristics, the generalized use of them throughout the country, the large number of cases that have been denounced, and the organized transfer of detained persons from one place to another, inevitably lead to the conclusion that these practices were not unknown to persons occupying the highest positions in the government and the Armed Forces.
> "Whatever the measures initiated by the Government to prevent torture, they have been deplorably ineffectual."

Council of Europe

The European Commission of Human Rights and the European Court of Human Rights are empowered by member states of the Council of Europe to receive complaints of breaches of the European

Convention for the Protection of Human Rights and Fundamental Freedoms. Under the convention member states can bring applications to the European commission and, where the states in question have accepted the court's jurisdiction, can seek a review or confirmation of the commission's findings before the European court. The majority of member states have further accepted that individual citizens of their countries can petition the European commission once all domestic legal remedies are exhausted.

The commission and the court have ruled on a wide variety of individual petitions concerning alleged breaches of Article 3 of the European convention, the article that categorically prohibits torture and inhuman or degrading treatment or punishment. Complaints from individuals have alleged various forms of ill-treatment, from flogging and solitary confinement to abuses related to asylum, racial discrimination and treatment received in mental hospitals. There have also been a few inter-state cases involving allegations of systematic torture or ill-treatment. Since the mid-1950s the European commission, and in some instances the court, have reviewed cases filed by states concerning the use of corporal punishment and collective punishments by the British in Cyprus, torture and other human rights violations in Greece, British interrogation techniques and other human rights violations in Northern Ireland, and the serious misconduct of Turkish troops in Cyprus. Currently under review by the European commission are two further applications lodged against Turkey, one by Cyprus and the other by Denmark, France, the Netherlands, Norway and Sweden.

Whereas the Greek Case and the complaints against Turkey have mainly concerned the establishing of whether particular acts occurred, the Northern Ireland Case was more an issue of whether the acts, which were not generally in dispute, were sufficiently severe and deliberate to constitute a breach of Article 3 (see page 50).

The strength of the Council of Europe's human rights machinery lies in its ability to adjudicate complaints based on international human rights law and on the careful evaluation of evidence in judicial proceedings. This feature should not be undervalued in a world where human rights abuses are too frequently subject to the sway of international politics rather than to careful adjudication. Its main limitation is that member states have not empowered the European commission to investigate allegations of torture or other human rights abuses on its own initiative. Even though all but four member states (Cyprus, Greece, Malta and Turkey) have recognized the right of individual petition, this procedure does not lend itself to the investigation of the systematic use of torture. Since only member states can initiate this type of complaint, action against even so gross a human rights violation as the widespread use of torture is dependent on member governments' willingness to "prosecute" another West European government on a very damning charge. If that degree of political will is lacking, as it often is, torture victims may not find remedy in the human rights machinery provided by the European convention.

Organization of African Unity

African heads of state attending the Organization of African Unity (OAU) Summit in Nairobi in July 1981 adopted the African Charter on Human and Peoples' Rights, Article 5 of which prohibits torture and cruel, inhuman and degrading punishment or treatment. This treaty will come into force when a majority of the member states have ratified it; as of May 1983 only seven of the 51 member states had done so; a further 11 had signed but not ratified it. Once it comes into force, the charter will authorize the creation of the African Commission on Human and People's Rights, which will be permitted to consider complaints of torture and other violations of the charter brought against States Parties to it. At present, the OAU possesses no effective regional mechanism which can deal with cases of torture committed by governments of OAU member states.

The possibility that an African regional human rights mechanism may be established should not obscure the fact that other international human rights instruments, in particular the International Covenant on Civil and Political Rights and the Optional Protocol to this Covenant, are open to ratification by African governments. Few have signed or ratified them.

* * * *

The IGO human rights bodies that monitor torture and other violations of international human rights law face a daunting task in attempting to persuade governments to comply with their recommendations. First, the essential determination of facts may not prove easy, for with such a serious charge as torture they must establish the facts with considerable certainty. Accused governments will usually deny the allegations, arguing that the treatment in question does not warrant the stigma of being called torture, or claiming that whatever may have occurred was due to unruly police officers rather than to an officially condoned administrative practice. The lack of enforcement machinery and the political pressures on all IGO human rights bodies mean that their effectiveness in stopping torture largely depends on the willingness of governments to act on their recommendations.

Because of these inherent weaknesses, it is all the more important that governments that inflict torture be pressed by other governments directly, via all available *bilateral* channels, to stop torture and to comply with the findings of IGO human rights bodies. There are a multiplicity of bilateral contacts—diplomatic, aid, trade—that could be used. As an indication of their concern about human rights, governments could instruct their embassy officials abroad to collect information about torture. They could send observers to trials of defendants in other countries who allege torture, and they could publicly condemn the use of torture in named countries. Governments that supply military, security or police training and equipment to other governments should ensure that these transfers of equipment and training do not facilitate torture. Governments should refrain from sending anyone to another country where they can reasonably be expected to be tortured. All appropriate measures should be made to persuade a government to comply with the recommendations of IGO human rights bodies. Unless governments use appropriate pressure to persuade governments to comply with recommendations of IGO human rights bodies, the international human rights procedures risk being discredited.

Action by international non-governmental organizations

International NGOs, among them Amnesty International, have become increasingly active against torture in recent years. Some NGOs investigate and publicize individual allegations or widespread patterns of torture. NGOs often intercede directly with governments to try to protect people likely to be tortured. Research studies into the legal framework of states that practise torture' and on-site missions to investigate reports of torture are among the different methods of NGOs. The education of their own constituents and of the general public about torture is often part of their concern, as is their moral, legal and sometimes financial support for torture victims and their relatives.

The International Committee of the Red Cross (ICRC) plays a unique role in ameliorating the conditions in which people are held in custody. It is the only institution that regularly visits prisoners held by their opponents, whether in their own or a foreign land. It has done so for more than a hundred years. In 1981, the ICRC visited 489 places of detention, and between 1971 and 1981 its delegates carried out approximately 15,000 visits in some 80 countries. The ICRC is concerned with the conditions of (not the reasons for) a prisoner's detention. Its delegates attempt to establish the facts about these conditions, including allegations of torture and of cruel, inhuman or degrading treatment or punishment. Having established the facts with reasonable certainty, its delegates may react in different ways according to the gravity of the case, for example by bringing incidents of torture to the attention of government ministers or the head of state. The ICRC does not make its delegates' findings public since this would endanger its future visits to prisoners. Unfortunately, even in many countries where the ICRC has access to some prisoners, the governments deny its delegates access to detainees under interrogation, who are the prisoners most in danger of torture. The ICRC has consequently set itself the "permanent objective . . . in all countries accepting its presence, to endeavour to have access to detainees from the time of their arrest".

The International Commission of Jurists (ICJ) focuses on national and international legal matters related to the development and observance of human rights norms. Through its quarterly *Review*, country reports and occasional studies, it provides facts about and analyses of torture and other human rights issues. The ICJ publicizes cases of lawyers and judges who speak out against torture committed by their governments, and who are themselves victimized. A significant part of the ICJ's work against torture is the drafting and promotion of international instruments. Its draft Principles for a Code of Ethics for Lawyers, Relevant to Torture and Other Cruel, Inhuman or Degrading Treatment or Punishment is addressed especially to defence and prosecuting lawyers, lawyers in government service, judges and other judicial authorities.

The ICJ was involved in the preparation of the initial draft optional protocol to the future convention against torture that was before the UN Commission on Human Rights in 1983. A special international committee of independent experts empowered by States Parties to the convention and to its optional protocol is envisaged by the draft optional protocol routinely to inspect all places where people in custody are to be found. The ICJ also submitted to the Council of Europe a draft instrument for the European region that contains similar ideas.

International medical NGOs have addressed questions of medical help for torture victims (see page 47), better methods of verifying torture scientifically (see page 92) and ethical aspects of the involvement of medical personnel in torture and ill-treatment. The World Medical Association's Declaration of Tokyo (1975) forbids doctors to "countenance, condone or participate in the practice of torture or other forms of cruel, inhuman or degrading procedures, whatever the offence of which the victim of such procedures is suspected, accused or guilty, and whatever the victim's beliefs or motives, and in all situations, including armed conflict and civil strife''. The objections to ill-treatment made by police surgeons in Northern Ireland (see page 58), the disciplining of a forensic doctor in Brazil who falsified the death certificate of a man who died under torture (see page 72), and the alleged involvement of medical personnel in torture in Chile and their presence at floggings in Pakistan show the need for an international medical ethical standard regarding doctors' complicity in torture and ill-treatment.

The resolution adopted in 1975 by the International Council of Nurses on the Role of the Nurse in the Care of Detainees and Prisoners provides similarly explicit guidelines for nurses. In 1977 at its Sixth Congress, the World Psychiatric Association (WPA), in response to allegations of the abuse of psychiatry for political purposes, especially in the USSR, adopted the Declaration of Hawaii. It calls on psychiatrists "not [to] participate in compulsory psychiatric treatment in the absence of psychiatric illness" and to "refuse to cooperate" in "actions contrary to scientific or ethical principles".

The above examples are but a few of those that could be cited to show that while their mandates and methods may differ, many international NGOs share the common aim of abolishing torture and cruel, inhuman or degrading treatment or punishment of prisoners.

Pressure for improvements

The previous Chapter showed that there are serious domestic efforts underway to stop torture in the 1980s. This Chapter examines two countries where such pressure had some positive impact during the 1970s. In both situations there is sufficient public information available to identify the governmental decisions and policies that allowed or encouraged increases in torture or ill-treatment and to assess steps taken to contain or reverse that brutality.

The province of Northern Ireland in the United Kingdom poses the classic dilemma of how far a society that regards itself as a liberal democracy is prepared to allow illegal methods in its resistance to "terrorism". The case study concentrates on the 1976-79 period of ill-treatment (not on the "in-depth" interrogation techniques used in 1971) and provides an opportunity to examine the effect of emergency legislation on the role of the judiciary, police conduct and the process of interrogation generally. It is also possible to identify the main pressures for reform and their consequences by looking at the role of the news media, the Council of Europe, police surgeons working inside official channels, Amnesty International itself and finally a government-appointed independent committee of inquiry (the Bennett Committee) whose report led to new preventive measures now in force and to a sharp reduction in the number of complaints of assault during interrogation by 1980.

Brazil is chosen for several reasons. It is a developing country, albeit one of the more economically developed among Third World countries. Although torture occurred there following a coup in 1964 and especially after the "coup within the coup" in 1968, improvements have been possible after years of persistent pressure, and despite resistance to the improvements from officers within the ruling military authorities. Torture occurred in Brazil under a legal system that after 1968 was based on presidential decree. Torture in Brazil aroused major international concern and protests in the early 1970s from many quarters, including the Vatican. Most important, the domestic pressure for liberalization from many sources helped create a climate in which torture for political purposes in urban areas decreased. Besides describing specific actions against torture by prisoners themselves, their families, support groups, students, professionals, their associations and others, this section reviews in some detail the highly significant role of the Brazilian Church as a "voice of the voiceless".

Northern Ireland

In January 1976 the European Commission of Human Rights in Strasbourg concluded that the authorities in Northern Ireland and the British Government were responsible for practices in 1971 amounting to torture and inhuman treatment of detainees under interrogation by the police, in breach of Article 3 of the European Convention on Human Rights.[1] In the meantime, the British Government gave the British Parliament in 1972 and the European Court of Human Rights in 1977 unqualified undertakings that the most objectionable techniques of interrogation would not be used again. Yet despite this declared concern (which led the European Court to state in 1978 that is was hardly plausible that practices in breach of Article 3 would continue or recommence), complaints of assault during interrogation in early 1976 in Northern Ireland were increasing.

A pattern recurs

Between 1976 and 1978, one in 11 detainees arrested under emergency legislation in Northern Ireland filed official complaints of assault by the Royal Ulster Constabulary (RUC).[2] Prior to May 1977 almost all such complaints came from members of the Roman Catholic community, detained as "Republican" suspects. Starting in May and June, with the advent and collapse of a Protestant-led strike,

1 European Commission of Human Rights, *Report of the Commission on Application No. 5310/71, Ireland against the United Kingdom of Great Britain and Northern Ireland*, adopted 26 January 1976, pp. 402 and 468. The European Court of Human Rights, in their judgment on this case in January 1978, modified the Commission's findings, omitting the word "torture" but confirming that there had been an "administrative practice" of inhuman and degrading treatment in breach of Article 3. For a discussion of the significance of this judgment in international law, see Chapter 2 to this report, page 15.

2 This ratio is calculated on the basis of data given in the *Report of the Committee of Inquiry into Police Interrogation Procedures in Northern Ireland* (hereafter

"Unionist" detainees also began to file complaints.

The 443 complaints of assault during interrogation filed in 1977 represented a 101 per cent increase over 1976, although fewer suspects were detained. An Amnesty International mission to Northern Ireland in late 1977 investigated 78 cases, both "Republican" and "Unionist". It found that ill-treatment by the RUC had taken place. The alleged methods included such physical and psychological abuses as beatings, bending of limbs, prolonged standing, burning with cigarettes, threats of death and threats to the suspect's family.[3]

It is important to ask why the preventive measures taken and assurances given by the British Government, following the exposure by Irish and British journalists (and by Amnesty International) of the torture of 14 detainees and the ill-treatment of hundreds more in 1971, did not prevent the assault of suspects from becoming a frequent and tolerated practice in Northern Ireland from late 1975 or early 1976 until early 1979 and to examine what steps were taken to reduce the number of complaints so significantly by 1980.

The law and interrogation

Northern Ireland security needs in 1972, in the British Government's view, dictated a review of arrest and trial procedures. The officially appointed Diplock Commission recommended changes that became law in the Northern Ireland (Emergency Provisions) Act 1973, which altered the rules of evidence for the admissibility of confessions. In English and Northern Ireland common law a judge can allow in evidence only a voluntary statement made by the accused, "in the sense that [it has] not been obtained from him by fear of prejudice or hope of advantage, exercised or held out by a person in authority, or by oppression".[4] The Diplock Commission concluded that this common law test was "hampering the course of justice in the case of terrorist crimes",[5] and the 1973 act altered the

---

called Bennett Report), (HMSO London, Cmnd. 7497, March 1979), paragraph 44 and Appendix 2. The ratio given in paragraph 313 of the Bennett Report (one in eight detainees held under emergency legislation filing complaints of assault during interrogation between 1975 and 1978) appears to be erroneous in that this calculation is based on the number of complaints by *all* detainees in Northern Ireland, not just by those held under emergency legislation.

3 Amnesty International, *Northern Ireland: Report of an Amnesty International Mission* (London, 1978), p. 4 (hereafter called Amnesty International Report on Northern Ireland).

4 *Judges' Rules and Administrative Directions to the Police*, Home Office circular No. 31/1964, principle (e). The Judges' Rules are in the form of advice to police officers on what will and will not be allowed as evidence in a trial.

5 *Report of the Commission to consider legal procedures to deal with terrorist activ-*

test of voluntariness. Whereas the common law test renders inadmissible confessions obtained by "oppression", section 6 of the 1973 Act had the effect of disallowing confessions only if the accused "was subjected to torture or to inhuman or degrading treatment".[6] Since the 1973 act applied only to Northern Ireland, the police in the province became exempt from restraints applying elsewhere in the country. Although the Diplock recommendations and the new act did not specifically make physical violence or psychological coercion lawful, they did imply that a confession previously disallowed by judges due to police misconduct in obtaining it might henceforth be admitted in evidence. Furthermore, Lord Diplock recommended that the law prohibit the threat of physical violence, but this prohibition was not included in the 1973 act. The omission could only encourage the view that a degree of coercion would be tolerated.

Until late 1975 this change in law did not significantly alter police interrogation practices. Prior to this time the security strategy of the government was based either on executive internment without trial or on quasi-judicial internment regulated by commissioners. Neither system required a high level of proof to ensure a suspect's continued detention. Indeed, the purpose of these systems was to put *suspected* terrorists or their sympathizers out of action even when there was not sufficient evidence to convict them in a court of law. As internment was phased out gradually during 1975, however, evidence became essential to the conviction of terrorist suspects in the trials that Lord Diplock had recommended to replace internment. In Northern Ireland forensic evidence is difficult to obtain in hostile areas. Witnesses are subject to fear and intimidation. Intelligence information, whether from informers or detainees, until recently has rarely been used in court. Under these circumstances, the RUC came to rely almost exclusively on confessions as evidence against the accused. For example, during the first half of 1978, 75-80 per cent of all convictions for politically motivated offences were based solely or mainly on confessions.[7]

Between 1972 and 1975 there were allegations of ill-treatment

---

ities in Northern Ireland (hereafter called Diplock Report), (HMSO London, Cmnd. 5185, December 1972), paragraph 87.

6 The phrase quoted from section 6 was taken verbatim from Article 3 of the *European Convention for the Protection of Human Rights and Fundamental Freedoms*. Section 6 of the 1973 Act became section 8 in the consolidated version of this act in 1978.

7 Bennett Report, paragraph 30. The figures were prepared by the Director of Public Prosecutions for Northern Ireland and were thought by the Bennett Committee to be accurate for 1976 and 1977 as well.

during interrogation, but the numbers were few and no pattern emerged. The need to get confessions for convictions in court, however, brought changes in 1976. The RUC took over from the army in all but the most hostile neighbourhoods. New RUC crime-squads were formed to specialize in interrogation. Centralized police interrogation centres were opened or planned at Castlereagh police station in Belfast and Gough Barracks in County Armagh. In July, the new Chief Constable, Kenneth Newman, issued an internal directive that made an important distinction between the "interview" of a suspect, which would lead to a specific criminal charge and to which common law protection of the Judges' Rules on admissibility of evidence would apply, and the "interrogation" of suspects, which was for general questioning and gathering intelligence. By implication, because this more general questioning need not lead to a charge for a specific offence, the Judges' Rules need not apply. Since available evidence indicates that approximately two-thirds of those arrested in Northern Ireland under emergency legislation at that time were released without charge,[8] this relaxation (or implied suspension) of the Judges' Rules and of the protection they afford suspects had special significance for "interrogations". During 1976 complaints of assault during interrogation increased by approximately 85 per cent over 1975, whereas arrests increased by only 49 per cent.

The government's view of interrogation

Successive British governments throughout the 1970s had a common policy on interrogation: to protect police discretion to question a suspect in private for extensive periods without the intrusion of the courts, lawyers or any other independent person. One consequence of this policy was the failure to safeguard suspects' rights and physical integrity. Besides relaxing the rules governing the admissibility of confessions in court, the government gave the police new powers in 1973 to hold persons suspected of politically motivated crimes incommunicado for up to three days (increased to seven days under the Prevention of Terrorism (Temporary Provisions) Act, 1974).

A prominent factor in the rapid decline in police standards was the prolonged failure of government ministers and senior RUC officers to intervene with interrogators, directly and forcefully, to show that assault and illegal coercion would not be tolerated. On the contrary, the increased number and seriousness of complaints in 1976 and 1977 came when the government was pressing the police

---

8 Bennett Report, appendix 1, gives precise statistics for September 1977 until August 1978: only 35 per cent of those detained were charged.

for confessions to use in court. Since the 1971 Compton Committee (which actually justified the use of the interrogation techniques subsequently identified as torture by the European Commission of Human Rights), no government-initiated inquiry has specifically investigated allegations of ill-treatment in Northern Ireland. All such inquiries have dealt with legal or police procedure, not with individual allegations of brutality. No British Government took any decisive action before 1979 to halt the abuses that had begun to increase three years earlier, and to this day (to Amnesty International's knowledge) no government minister having responsibility in this area has accepted that ill-treatment took place in the late 1970s.

The extension of police discretion

Nor did the RUC command intervene despite the increasing evidence of misconduct by plain-clothes detectives in the middle and lower ranks. In April 1977, a senior police surgeon wrote to one of the government authorities, complaining that although police surgeons forwarded reports on a prisoner's injuries to the appropriate police station, "no senior officer has ever seen fit to ring up to see me or my colleagues about the injuries noted".[9] Several police interrogators were found at fault in civil proceedings, and the Police Authority chose to settle other claims out of court. In some instances these complaints were of serious assault and the damages paid were substantial. Yet no police officer ever admitted ill-treating a suspect, and no internal disciplinary proceedings were brought against any police officer.

The RUC took the position that allegations against its officers were part of an orchestrated campaign to sully the reputation of the force throughout the community, thereby damaging its aim of gaining acceptance for its law-enforcement role, especially by the Roman Catholic community, and thus reducing its effectiveness against paramilitary groups. In the official RUC view the injuries sustained by prisoners were either self-inflicted or resulted from attacks made by the detainee on police officers, who then had to restrain the suspect. Chief Constable Newman asserted in June 1977 that the increasing number of allegations of police brutality were a sign, not of police mis-

9 Letter of 14 April 1977 from Dr Robert Irwin, Secretary of the Forensic Medical Officers Association in Northern Ireland, to Dr Terence Baird, Chief Medical Officer at the Department of Health and Social Security, Belfast. Quoted in Peter Taylor, *Beating the Terrorists?* (London, Penguin Books, 1980), p. 180. This and other details concerning pressure for improvements from within the system are available due to the research, after the events, by the well-known British journalist Peter Taylor, who conducted personal interviews with the police surgeons and authorities involved.

conduct, but of growing police success in combating terrorism. He also pointed out, correctly, that suspects had strong motives to file false complaints of assault against their interrogators. They might need to justify their confessions to their own paramilitary groups, and their only defence in court was often to claim that their confessions had been extracted under torture, or inhuman and degrading treatment. If the confession could be ruled inadmissible on that statutory ground, under section 6 of the 1973 act, the accused would probably go free since it was usually the only evidence available.

The legislation earlier in the decade had increased police powers without providing for corresponding safeguards to protect the rights of suspects. The RUC sought (and were allowed) to increase police discretion over the interrogation process, violating the common law principle of access to a lawyer and undermining the machinery for the investigation of complaints against the police. None of the 78 people whose cases of alleged ill-treatment were examined by the Amnesty International mission in 1977 had been allowed to see a lawyer while in police custody. The majority of them had specifically requested to see a lawyer soon after arrest. The Judges' Rules state that "every person at any stage of an investigation should be able to communicate and to consult privately with a solicitor (lawyer) . . . provided that in such a case no unreasonable delay or hindrance is caused to the process of investigation . . .", but this latter proviso was invariably interpreted by RUC officers so as to deny access to a lawyer. Detainees spent as many as seven days in incommunicado detention. It appears that the discretion assumed by RUC investigating officers to exclude lawyers was not the practice at this time elsewhere in the United Kingdom.[10]

Concerning complaints machinery, the RUC frequently pointed out, correctly, that it was more elaborate in Northern Ireland than anywhere else in the United Kingdom. However, the oversight role of the independent Police Authority does not cover complaints of criminal assault, which are referred to the Director of Public Prosecutions (DPP). Furthermore, the DPP does not have an independent investigative staff, and all complaints against the police are investigated by the RUC itself. Chief Constable Newman often argued that the DPP's decision not to prosecute a police officer was an indication that the allegations were false. In fact, the DPP himself reminded the Chief Constable in November 1977 that the failure to bring a prosecution against a police officer did not indicate that the complaint itself was untrue. In a review of 300 complaints from the first nine months of 1977, wrote the DPP, he had found some evidence of assault in about half of them, some of which were

10 Bennett Report, paragraph 271.

medically documented. But he had found a level of evidence high enough to make conviction possible, and therefore to warrant prosecution, in only one case.

The government-appointed Bennett Committee found that from 1972 until the end of 1978 only 19 police officers were criminally prosecuted for ill-treating terrorist suspects out of the hundreds of complaints that had been filed. Of these 19, only two were convicted, and both these convictions were set aside on appeal. In five of the cases resulting in acquittals, civil proceedings in respect of the same incidents resulted in the police paying damages to the complainants.[11]

The main reason for this low number of prosecutions was that in order to bring prosecution, the DPP must be satisfied—beyond reasonable doubt—that the assault was committed by an identifiable police officer and can be proved in court. Nevertheless, Chief Constable Newman continued to maintain that the general lack of prosecutions cleared the RUC of allegations of misconduct. In other words, no crime had been committed because the officers responsible could not be convicted.

The judiciary

In ordinary circumstances one would expect judges in the United Kingdom to provide a measure of protection to suspects by their rulings on arrest and interrogation procedures. Given their independence as well as the degree of discretion allowed judges in English and Northern Ireland common law, it is fair to ask why cruel, inhuman and degrading treatment took place in spite of the role and authority of the Northern Ireland judiciary.

The primary role of the judiciary in the UK, according to the Judges' Rules, is to "control the conduct of trials and the admission of evidence . . .; they do not control or in any way initiate or supervise police activities or conduct." Nevertheless, the courts' decisions do influence police practices indirectly by indicating, after the fact, what kind of conduct by the police makes evidence inadmissible in court. In Northern Ireland interrogating officers attend trials of terrorist suspects regularly in order to give evidence, and they do take note of the attitude of the courts. The Bennett Report cites the evidence of an officer who testified in a civil proceeding that because the courts had accepted confessions made after "interviewing hours

---

11 Bennett Report, paragraphs 157 and 338. While standards of proof in civil cases may be lower than in criminal cases, a substantial number of successful civil suits should at least stimulate a serious investigation by the authorities of the allegations of ill-treatment.

on end with no sleep'', he continued to interrogate prisoners in this way.[12]

One means of protecting detainees' rights during interrogation left unused by the courts is to disallow confessions obtained during incommunicado detention. Principle (c) of the Judges' Rules, cited earlier, protects the right of access to a lawyer. Although it can be argued that section 6 of the 1973 Act negated this principle in Northern Ireland, Mr Justice Bennett, citing police practice and court precedents elsewhere in the United Kingdom in 1977, implied that discretion was still available to Northern Ireland judges to exclude confessions obtained after the police had denied a prisoner's request to see a lawyer. In no case in Northern Ireland involving people charged under emergency legislation did judges exercise this discretion.[13] In effect, judges did not help to ensure the detainee's right of access to a lawyer, which they could have done by disallowing evidence obtained during incommunicado detention, some of which was allegedly the result of ill-treatment.

More extreme assaults, especially if medically documented, presented judges with little difficulty in disallowing the confession of the accused. But in less clear-cut cases the Northern Ireland judiciary seemed uncertain of their authority to intervene positively. Several Northern Ireland judges attempted to interpret the degree of judicial discretion over disallowing from evidence confessions obtained by coercion that in their view was short of torture and of inhuman or degrading treatment (the language of section 6 of the 1973 act). After reviewing some of these judgments, the Bennett Committee found that "the uncertainty, despite the standards upheld and applied by the courts, about what is permissible and what is not . . . may tempt police officers to see how far they can go and what they can get away with."[14] The police interrogators appear to have interpreted the judges' too frequent silence as assent.

Pressure from the police surgeons

The most striking single action taken by any official in Northern Ireland to prevent ill-treatment was Chief Constable Newman's order on 21 April 1978 to install "spy-holes" in the doors of interview rooms at the Gough Barracks interrogation centre so that senior officers could monitor interrogations. The suggestion came from the Senior Medical Officer (SMO) at Gough, Dr Denis Elliott, who

---

12 Bennett Report, paragraph 178.

13 Bennett Report, paragraphs 271-276. Elsewhere in the United Kingdom denial of access to a lawyer is common, but only for the first 24 hours in detention.

14 Bennett Report, paragraph 84.

had held a long-awaited meeting with the Chief Constable the previous night to discuss prisoners' injuries that doctors were continuing to see. During the next five months there were no complaints of assault filed by prisoners interrogated at Gough for terrorist offences.

Also in attendance at the meeting in April were Dr Charles Alexander, SMO at Castlereagh police station in Belfast, and Dr Robert Irwin, Secretary of the Forensic Medical Officers Association, who had himself seen many injured detainees from Castlereagh. Since late 1976 doctors employed by the independent Police Authority or by the government's Department of Health and Social Security (DHSS) as police surgeons had documented injuries that they were convinced could not be dismissed as self-inflicted. In March 1977 Dr Irwin's association informed the Police Authority of its concern about the increasing number of injuries to prisoners. Both individual doctors and groups of doctors kept pressing their employers and the RUC command to respond to their demands. They cited the decision of the European Commission of Human Rights about the 1971 events, which was still under consideration by the European Court, as cause for doctors to play an active role in protecting prisoners from abuse and the police from false allegations.

The doctors kept their appeals within the system's administrative channels, shunning publicity. In the wake of a national television program about Castlereagh, however, having failed for months to get a personal interview with the Chief Constable, their association's executive committee stated publicly in October 1977 that they had sought a meeting with him to discuss injuries to detainees. In November, doctors at Castlereagh and Gough informed their employer that they would resign unless action were taken to stop the assaults. When taking up his post as SMO at Gough on 1 November, Dr Elliott stipulated that if there were serious police misconduct towards detainees, he would request a transfer to his previous post. The cumulative pressure of the national television program, the visit of the Amnesty International mission to the province in late November and early December 1977 and the doctors' steadfastness appears to have had an impact. Complaints of assault during interrogation dropped from the autumn 1977 average of 40 a month to eight in December. The association's representatives noted this improvement in their discussions with the Amnesty International mission in December as an explanation of why the mission had examined released prisoners with recent but not fresh injuries.

In March 1978 the Police Authority informed the government that the doctors had noted a renewed pattern of injuries, that resignations might soon follow, and that the doctors wished their assessment of the recent decrease in injuries given in December to Amnesty International to be withdrawn. The next month Dr Irwin's association wrote formally to the Police Authority on this last point; four doctors at Gough, where Dr Elliott was SMO, wrote to the Police Authority in order to protest against the continuing injuries in custody, and Dr Elliott himself formally requested a transfer. Their pressure seems to have conveyed a sense of urgency to the government and the RUC command. The Amnesty International mission had collected considerable medical evidence, and a report would soon appear. Resignations at this time by police surgeons would have been an acute embarrassment to the government. Chief Constable Newman met Drs Alexander, Elliott and Irwin on the evening of 20 April and took decisive action the next morning. Besides the new "spy-holes" to be installed, the meeting discussed a suggestion to install closed-circuit television in interrogation rooms so that senior officers could monitor interrogators' conduct. The Chief Constable objected that this would be costly, to which Dr Irwin replied that it would be cheaper than having to return to the European Court.

Amnesty International published its report in June 1978. The immediate result was the government's appointment of the Bennett Committee of Inquiry into police procedures which ultimately led to the introduction of administrative safeguards to protect detainees and to a drop in the number of complaints of ill-treatment.

In August a new job description was agreed for police surgeons which formally extended their duties. SMOs would henceforth have access to any prisoner at all reasonable times, not just when the police called them in, and they would occasionally tour the police station, making use of the new "spy-holes". ·

During the remainder of 1978, while the Bennett Committee received evidence, complaints of assault declined but did not cease. Their report was published in March 1979 and their major recommendations were accepted by the government in June. But the Bennett Report did not lay the doctors' fears to rest. A few days before its publication Dr Irwin broke the doctors' long public silence and gave a nationally televised interview. He described some of the 150 injured prisoners he had personally examined—injuries he believed were not self-inflicted—during the past three years, some as recently as the month before. One week after publication of the Bennett Report, Dr Elliott resigned in protest at the "undisciplined" treatment of prisoners at Gough and at the failure of either the government or the RUC to acknowledge that ill-treatment had occurred during the past three years. Drs Elliott and Irwin, whose actions had done so much to bring about an official inquiry, now underlined the importance of its recommendations.

The significance of an independent inquiry

The Bennett Committee addressed the balance between the efficiency of police interrogation and the protection of suspects' rights. Its terms of reference prevented an investigation of individual complaints. Nevertheless, it examined considerable medical evidence that revealed "cases in which injuries, whatever their precise cause, were not self-inflicted and were sustained in police custody". Nor did the government permit a general review of the emergency legislation or a specific one of section 6 of the 1973 act. Such a review might have led to recommendations for statutory protection of prisoners. Given these restrictions, the committee recommended self-regulation by the police: for example, closed-circuit television monitoring of interrogations by senior officers; more detailed record-keeping on detainees; and the offer of a medical examination once every 24 hours. Even the recommendation for access to a lawyer after each 48 hours in custody, without exception, was to be incorporated in a revised RUC code of conduct, rather than in legislation. The report thus offers an impressive set of preventive administrative measures that, if fully implemented, would significantly reduce the likelihood of torture or ill-treatment of suspects.

Once implemented, these measures did reduce the number of allegations of assault and ill-treatment in Northern Ireland. The average number of complaints filed in the first three months of 1979 was 20 a month. This was somewhat down on the 1978 monthly average of 22, but in April 1979, the first full month after the Bennett Report appeared, the number of complaints dropped sharply to 8.[15] More significantly, the administrative measures introduced seem to have prevented the recurrence of the previous pattern of ill-treatment.

At present a very high percentage of convictions in non-jury trials in Northern Ireland are based solely or mainly on confessions. However, Amnesty International's approaches to the British Government about current police and judicial procedures used in Northern Ireland have not concerned allegations of ill-treatment. They have concerned the use of continuous, oppressive interro-

---

15 Statistics on complaints of assault during interrogation were made available by the RUC to Peter Taylor. Those given here are drawn from his book *Beating the Terrorists?* The monthly average for 1978 would be higher except for the low figures for June and July which were eight and nine. respectively. It may be significant that the Amnesty International report on Northern Ireland was leaked in May and was published officially in June.

gation, which has resulted in a steadily high rate of confessions for which no objective corroborating evidence is presented in court. Under these conditions it is doubtful whether the 48-hour rule concerning absolute right of access to a lawyer provides adequate protection for detainees under interrogation.

* * * *

There are several generalizations to be drawn from this examination of ill-treatment in Northern Ireland in the late 1970s:

1. The attitude towards the treatment of detainees shown at the top of the command structure within a security agency and by ministers responsible for their conduct affects officers' attitudes and actions right down the line.

2. Emergency legislation (or the interpretation of existing law by the courts) that extends the powers of the security forces specifically at the expense of detainees' legal guarantees may be perceived by the security forces as a signal that the law, the government and the courts will tolerate official violence towards and coercion of detainees.

3. When emergency legislation extends the powers of the executive, the judiciary must increase its vigilance on behalf of suspects and defendants if their rights are to be protected.

4. Post-facto investigations, prosecutions, civil suits and internal disciplinary proceedings may not be sufficient by themselves to stop abuses. The responsible authorities must take direct preventive actions, particularly those measures that will guarantee detainees access to individuals independent of the security forces, for example, the detainees' lawyer, doctor and relatives. This is all the more true in a legal system that does not provide for contemporaneous judicial supervision of interrogation.

5. Organized pressure from within the security system for respecting the rights of suspects is most likely to be effective when complemented by external pressures, in particular from the news media, which in some societies can play a relatively independent watchdog role in bringing alleged abuses of authority to public attention.

6. The existence and use of inter-governmental human rights machinery, although lengthy and capable of being obstructed by a government, can act as a restraint on human rights abuses if the government fears the findings, the expense, the embarrassment or even the propaganda that may result.

Brazil

"Toward the end of 1970 we sent a group of officers from the First Army to England to learn the English system of interrogation," said a retired Brazilian general.[16] But, according to the general, the "English system" of breaking a suspect psychologically was too slow for the Brazilian security forces.

Speed was considered essential in order to destroy the small urban guerrilla groups that operated in Brazil from 1967: if the guerrillas and their supporters were to be captured, information had to be extracted quickly from each suspected guerrilla before his or her associates knew of the detention, which was in many cases an illegal kidnapping. Hundreds of political prisoners were tortured each year following the military hardliners' "coup within the coup" in December 1968. Even after the short-lived guerrilla groups had been crushed during 1970, torture continued on a large scale and in a highly organized manner until the end of the presidency of General Emílio Médici in early 1974.

Under the presidency of General Ernesto Geisel (1974-1979) there were attempts to assert control over the security forces and to curb their worst abuses, but after five years of free rein, certain security agents and their protectors within the military coalition resisted the liberalizing *abertura* program promoted by General Geisel. Nevertheless, by the end of the decade, allegations of torture for political purposes were rare in urban areas, where the central government's control was more direct and where organized non-violent opposition pressed for reform.

1968-1973: The government's war on "permanent subversion"

In addition to the guerrilla groups, the Brazilian Government faced student and labour unrest in the late 1960s that, in its view, threatened both the economic development and national security of the country. The "doctrine of national security", first defined in Brazilian law in March 1967, provided a rationale for the military's political role and became identified under the presidencies of General Artur da Costa e Silva (1967-1969) and General Médici (1969-1974) with rapid industrialization.

The legal framework for the most intense period of repression was provided by Institutional Act No. 5, signed on 13 December 1968 by President Costa e Silva, the second general to rule Brazil

16 Antonio Carlos Fon, *Tortura, A história da repressão política no Brasil* (São Paulo, *Global Editora*, 1979), p. 72.

after the military coup in 1964. The new act was the military hard-liners' response to the 1968 student unrest and the events that followed. An opposition deputy had spoken in Congress against violence used to suppress student demonstrations; the government convened Congress in special session to remove his immunity from prosecution so that he might be tried for libel of the military; about 100 deputies from the government's own party voted with the opposition and defeated the government. The Federal Supreme Court that same day granted writs of *habeas corpus* for 46 student leaders arrested in October in São Paulo for attempting to convene a convention of their banned national union. The military government's reaction to these parliamentary and judicial rebuffs was to centre all remaining political power in its own hands. The president suspended Congress and several state legislatures, removed three troublesome justices from the Supreme Court (the Chief Justice resigned in protest), deprived hundreds of Brazilians of their political rights, retired 68 prominent university professors, and ordered a crackdown on all dissenters. Among the draconian measures allowed by the act and the one that had the most direct bearing on the practice of torture was the suspension of the right of *habeas corpus* for anyone charged with crimes against national security. None of these executive actions were open to judicial review. A "coup within the coup" had occurred.

By mid-1972 Amnesty International had compiled a list of 1,081 people allegedly tortured since 1968, based on corroborated evidence from victims, accounts by eye-witnesses, clergy, lawyers and journalists, as well as on international press reports (few domestic accounts were published due to direct censorship established in 1968). The report concluded that torture of a systematic nature had been on the increase and had been practised since 1968 "with a steadily increasing expertise in the police stations and interrogation centres in Brazil".[17] The government's only response was to ban the mention in the news media of the organization's statements on Brazil. It undertook no inquiry into the allegations.

One striking feature of repression during this period was the number of security agents and agencies involved in torture. Together with its report, Amnesty International submitted to the government a confidential list of 472 security agents allegedly responsible for torture, belonging to various official and "unofficial" agencies. Besides the political police (*Departamento de Ordem Política e Social*, sometimes known as *Departamento Estatal de Ordem Política e Social*, depending on location) (DOPS/DEOPS), each of

---

17 Amnesty International, *Report on Allegations of Torture in Brazil* (London: Amnesty International Publications, 1972), p. 85.

the armed forces—army, navy and air force—had its own specialized intelligence units, each of which was implicated in torture. In addition, special joint police and military units were created to hunt down the urban guerrillas. The best known was the counter-insurgency agency *Operação Bandeirantes* (OBAN), set up in São Paulo in 1969 and soon replicated in Brasília and Rio de Janeiro. Existing only as unregistered units for several years, they were formally recognized in 1972 as the *Destacamento de Operações e Informações — Centro de Operações de Defesa Interna* (DOI-CODI), Detachment of Operations and Information — Centre of Internal Defence Operations. (DOI is a pun on the Portuguese for "it hurts".) Often there were so many agencies involved in the same town or state that relatives and friends had difficulty in locating a political detainee. The effect was to confuse anyone trying to prevent kidnappings and incommunicado detention, the period when almost all torture took place. It was also convenient to the higher authorities in the chain of command who could plead ignorance of the whereabouts of a detainee.

Deaths in detention were frequent, very often as a result of torture. In January 1974, at the end of General Médici's presidency, Amnesty International submitted a list of 213 deaths of people who had died while in custody since 1964 to the UN Commission on Human Rights. With a repetitiousness straining credulity, the government claimed that many of them had died while trying to escape or had been run down by a motor vehicle.

The methods used in what many Brazilians came to call their "industry of torture", reportedly taught to interrogators in special training courses, were as varied and brutal as those used anywhere in the world: electric shocks from portable generators; partial drowning by covering the mouth and pouring water into a tube inserted into the nostrils; severe beatings with wooden, rubber or aluminium paddles, sometimes perforated and inflicted on the palms of the hands, soles of the feet or the buttocks so as to induce pain and swelling without leaving permanent marks; forced walking on the open rims of tin cans; sexual violation and numerous other methods. One or more of these methods were usually employed in combination with the *pau de arara*, parrot's perch, made notorious by Brazilian torturers. Said by political prisoners to have been formerly used on slaves in Brazil, it consists of suspending a naked prisoner upside-down from a bar placed under the knees, with the wrists tied to the ankles. The pressure of the body's weight on the knee joints and forearms causes intense pain after half an hour; many victims with weak hearts are thought to have died on the "perch".

1974-1976: The sealed coffin

In March 1974 General Geisel became the fourth military president to rule Brazil since the 1964 coup. He had promised during the electoral campaign to introduce liberalizing measures. Pressure was mounting for an end to censorship, torture and the most evident abuses of state power, not only from the church and trade unions, but also among the military regime's initial social base of political support, the urban middle class. The first worldwide oil crisis and sharp rise in Brazil's payment for imported oil in 1973 began to erode the so-called economic miracle, its benefits to the middle class, and thereby their main economic rationale for supporting the government. Middle-class attitudes towards the need for liberalization were further affected by the fact that many of the young people who were tortured, imprisoned or killed were from middle-class families.

Abertura, "opening", was the undefined concept that was widely used to describe a process of government-controlled relaxation of security measures. President Geisel, in the face of opposition from the military hardliners, sought to bring the security agents under greater control. Press censorship was relaxed, and newspapers for the first time since the 1964 coup carried stories about detention and torture. Congressional and state elections scheduled for November 1974 were allowed to go ahead in a climate of freer campaigning by the two legal political parties. The elections gave the opposition *Movimento Democrático Brasileiro* (MDB), Brazilian Democratic Movement, enough gains to pose a potential electoral threat to the military's power and led, ironically, to a reassertion of the *linha dura*, hard line, within the military coalition.[18] Early 1975 witnessed a renewed campaign against members of the political opposition. About 2,000 "communist sympathisers" were detained throughout Brazil, including not only active members of the Moscow-oriented *Partido Comunista Brasileira* (PCB), Brazilian

18 The size of this potential electoral threat in the more industrialized centres can be estimated from the election results in São Paulo, Brazil's largest and most industrialized city. The opposition MDB candidate for the Senate from the city of São Paulo gained 70 per cent of the votes. Only 19 per cent went to the government-backed *Aliança Nacional Renovadora* (ARENA), National Renewel Alliance, party candidate; 11 per cent of the ballots were blank or spoiled. In middle-class residential areas the opposition won by almost 2:1, and in the working-class areas and the shanty towns the margin was 8:1 against the government. In the state of São Paulo, voting for the Chamber of Deputies gave the opposition a 7:4 ratio of votes over the ARENA party. See Commission of Justice and Peace of the Archdiocese of São Paulo, *São Paulo: Growth and Poverty* (São Paulo, 1976), English translation (London: Bowerdean Press in association with the Catholic Institute for International Relations, 1978), pp. 94 and 100.

Communist Party, but also journalists, lawyers, trade unionists and members of the legal MDB party, which had campaigned in the elections for the restoration of *habeas corpus* and an end to torture and kidnappings. The government attributed MDB electoral gains to communist support and dismissed calls for inquiries into human rights abuses as "subversive".

Torture again became widespread. The *Washington Post* (19 October 1975) reported that documents in their possession contained allegations of torture inflicted on at least 600 Brazilians during the first three months of 1975. Reports reaching Amnesty International during this period indicated that almost all new political detainees were subjected to ill-treatment ranging from psychological intimidation to the most brutal forms of torture. During the 12 months ending in April 1976, Amnesty International issued urgent appeals on behalf of about 200 detainees known by name, who it feared would be tortured. It also concluded on the basis of reports received from different cities and states that "systematic torture continues to be practised throughout Brazil".

A turning point against this resurgence of brutality occurred in late 1975 when deaths of detainees who had been tortured in the São Paulo headquarters of the Second Army mobilized popular anger. The Brazilian Justice and Peace Commission of the Roman Catholic Church described the Second Army Headquarters as "a huge torture complex which has at its disposal the most modern and sophisticated equipment, and which requires an increasing number of staff—jailers, drivers, executioners, typists, public relations officers, doctors and others—to run". It was these institutions of torture and the officers who commanded and protected them that remained as a pressure group within the regime opposed to even the modest liberalization favoured by President Geisel.

Between August 1975 and January 1976 four victims of torture died at Second Army Headquarters. Two detained military officers died in August and September, and on 25 October a nationally known journalist, Vladimir Herzog, died in custody only hours after he had voluntarily presented himself for interrogation. A statement issued two days later by the Second Army Command said that he had hanged himself by his belt after confessing to being a member of the Communist Party. Public anger was remarkable. Over 400 Brazilian journalists and the *Ordem dos Advogados do Brasil* (OAB), Brazilian Bar Association, condemned his death and demanded a full inquiry. Pressed for an inquiry, the government appointed its own, which announced in December that its findings corroborated the earlier official version of suicide. Security police returned his body to the family in a sealed coffin—a frequent practice that prevented the disclosure of evidence of torture, and in this case also prevented

Jewish pre-burial rites. Paulo Evaristo, Cardinal Arns, Archbishop of São Paulo celebrated a memorial mass for him in São Paulo cathedral attended by 30,000 people, which became a symbol of protest.

This degree of social protest and disturbance appears to have influenced President Geisel. When a fourth death occurred at Second Army Headquarters in January 1976, that of Manoel Fiel Filho, a metal worker, President Geisel summarily dismissed hard-liner General Eduardo D'Avila Melo from his post as commander of the Second Army. Operations of its intelligence unit were temporarily suspended. President Geisel could hardly have made the point more forcefully that superior officers would henceforth be held responsible for abuses of power by their subordinates.

This public show of conflict within the military over security measures was preceded by another internal confrontation over censorship. Written censorship orders issued by the Ministry of Justice existed from September 1972 until 8 October 1975, just two weeks before Vladimir Herzog's death. Although other forms of prior censorship continued until 1978, the fact that President Geisel did not re-institute the stricter written censorship orders to ban any mention of Vladimir Herzog's death or of the protests that followed was an indication that the hardliners would no longer be allowed total impunity to torture and kill.[19]

1977-1979: Reforms conceded

After early 1976, the incidence of torture declined although there were disturbing exceptions to this pattern. Less widespread torture continued throughout 1977. During 1978 Amnesty International received substantial and serious torture allegations and interceded urgently between July 1977 and June 1978 on behalf of 51 named detainees who it feared would be tortured—still a high number but a significant decline from the 200 urgent appeals issued two years earlier.

The annulment of Institutional Act No. 5 in late 1978 followed by a new Law of National Security, made effective in January 1979, and the subsequent introduction of measures such as medical examinations for detainees, curtailed the use of torture for political purposes in urban areas, although the torture of peasants, especially where there are land disputes, and of *marginais*, vagrants, and petty

---

19 This analysis is based on examinations of the written censorship orders by Brazilian journalists. See Joan Dassin, "Press Censorship—How and Why", special Brazil issue of *Index on Censorship* (London, Vol. 8, No. 4, July-August 1979), p. 16.

criminals continues to occur. (See entry on Brazil on page 148 of this report.)

Still, this limited victory over the use of torture in Brazil is significant. What forces helped restrain its practice? President Geisel himself was thought to oppose the practice from his earliest days in office. Whatever his motivation—whether a personal abhorrence or a political judgment about domestic opposition to it or about the need to control the worst abuses that might damage Brazil's reputation for political stability with its foreign creditors—the fact is that torture for political purposes had virtually disappeared in urban areas by the end of the Geisel presidency. Torture could not be retained as a central element of political repression if the program of liberalization was to proceed, a program that both the government and influential industrialists believed was necessary to economic development as the period of rapid growth was coming to an end.

The need to get control of the security apparatus for purposes of domestic political stability was almost certainly a factor as well. Even when a military commander did intervene to stop torture, as the commander of the First Army reportedly did prior to 1974 in Rio de Janeiro, members of the military intelligence unit transferred detainees whom they intended to torture to other states where the authorities agreed with their methods.[20] Certain police officers at the beginning of President Geisel's term appeared to be virtual freelance specialists in torture and assassination. The social protests in response to the deaths in custody in late 1975 as well as the fact that many victims of repression were from well-placed families created further pressures to bring those undisciplined military and police personnel under at least a degree of central government control even though there was little effort to punish them for their crimes.

There were various pressures put on the government throughout the 1960s and 1970s, both international and domestic, that helped move the government to act against torture in the latter half of the 1970s. At the international level, NGOs were active in documenting and publicizing torture in Brazil. Amnesty International's 1972 report on allegations of torture in Brazil had an impact not only among those outside Brazil concerned about torture there, but also within the country itself. The report circulated in Portuguese in Brazil, and as a result case material soon began to arrive at the organization's London headquarters from areas not previously covered by Amnesty International's research.

Among IGOs, the Inter-American Commission on Human Rights (IACHR) of the Organization of American States was particularly

20 Fon, *op. cit.* p. 72.

active after 1970 in considering complaints that came before it from Brazilian individuals and groups and from NGOs. In the case of a trade union official alleged to have died as a result of torture in May 1970, the IACHR stated in a virtually unprecedented resolution that "the acts reported in the record of this case constitute *prima facie*, in its opinion, a very serious case of the violation of the right to life".[21] A second petition received by the IACHR in 1970 came from a very large number of claimants whose allegations of torture were said to be representative of many other unidentified victims. The IACHR decided to consider this very complex submission as a "general case", which meant, among other things, that the case could be examined even though domestic legal remedies had not been exhausted. After considering this complex case over two years, including the government's submissions, the IACHR decided that although "absolutely conclusive proof" had not been obtained, "the evidence collected in this case leads to the persuasive presumption that in Brazil serious cases of torture, abuse and maltreatment have occurred to persons of both sexes while they were deprived of their liberty."[22] In 1974, due to lack of cooperation from the government, the IACHR moved its hearings into open session. Despite persistent efforts by the IACHR to obtain specific improvements in domestic remedies, their lengthy proceedings involving Brazilian cases resulted in no admission of state responsibility, no investigation of allegations or prosecution of those accused of torture, no financial compensation paid by the state to victims or their surviving relatives, and no objectively verifiable changes of security procedure to protect detainees.

Persistent accounts of torture and other human rights abuses affected Brazil's bilateral relations with its long-time ally the United States. During the 1968-1973 period of harsh repression in Brazil, President Richard Nixon's administration singled out Brazil as its major diplomatic and economic ally in South America. It also defended the Brazilian Government's record on torture before US Congressional hearings in 1971 and 1973.[23] In the late 1960s and

---

21 IACHR, *Report on the Work Accomplished During its Twenty-Eighth Session (Special), May 1 through 5, 1972* (OEA/Ser. L/V/II.28, Doc. 24, Rev. 1, August 1972), pp. 26-27. For an analysis of the IACHR's work on Brazil, see the case study in Lawrence J. LeBlanc, *The OAS and the Promotion and Protection of Human Rights* (The Hague: Martinus Nijhoff, 1977), pp. 122-138.

22 IACHR, *Report on the Twenty-Eighth Session (Special)*, pp. 21-22.

23 On the 1971 hearings, see Amnesty International's *Report on Allegations of Torture in Brazil*, 1972, pp. 57-73. On the 1973 hearings, see the statement of Stephen Low, Country Director for Brazil, US State Department before the Subcommittee on International Organizations and Movements in *International Pro-*

early 1970s, Brazil was the major recipient of direct investment from the United States in the manufacturing sector in South America.[24] It was also the largest recipient in South America of US arms transfers between 1966 and 1975 under all programs,[25] and of police equipment and training under the US Public Safety Program, 1961-1973.[26] US Congressional hearings in 1971 and 1974 on torture in Brazil, as well as similar hearings concerning other countries, helped to persuade many US legislators that their country had become politically identified with police terrorism in Brazil and elsewhere: their concern led to the abolition of the US Office of Public Safety and the closing in 1975 of its International Police Academy in Washington, and to further legislation in 1976 that directed the US President to conduct US international security assistance programs so as to "avoid identification of the United States through such programs with governments which deny to their people internationally recognized human rights and fundamental freedoms".

The following year, in the early months of President Carter's administration, the US State Department criticized Brazil's record on human rights, singling out torture as a major problem, in a report to the US Congress. Although Brazil was only one of several dozen countries mentioned in the report, the Brazilian Government took pre-emptive action in March 1977, one month before publication of the report, cancelling its 25-year program of military assistance. It rejected the report and refused a previous offer of $50 million in US military aid credits. The US Congress then prohibited military credit sales to Brazil, and the Brazilian Government responded by ending all formal military cooperation between the two countries. Ironically, while the period of the largest US security assistance to Brazil coincided with the development of Brazil's most repressive security agencies, the human rights reporting mechanism in the US that triggered the bilateral dispute came too late to bring pressure

tection of Human Rights: The Work of International Organizations and the Role of US Foreign Policy (Washington, D.C.: US Government Printing Office, 1974), pp. 199-202.

24 Source: US Department of Commerce, cited in *United States Foreign Policy, 1969-70: A Report of the Secretary of State* (Washington, D.C.: US Government Printing Office, Department of State Publication 8575, March 1971), p. 108.

25 Source: US Arms Control and Disarmament Agency, *World Military Expenditures and Arms Transfers, 1966-75*, cited in *Latin America Political Report*, (22 April 1977, Vol. XI, No. 15), p. 115.

26 Sources: US Agency for International Development reports, and hearings held by the US House of Representatives, Committee on Appropriations, 1972, cited in Michael Klare, *Supplying Repression* (Washington, D.C.: Institute of Policy Studies, 1977), Table II, pp. 20-21.

on Brazil even if the government had been open to it. The US Public Safety Program for Brazil had been phased out on schedule in 1972. Furthermore, Brazil's domestic arms industry had developed to the point that the government was not vulnerable to the type of pressure that might have followed from the State Department report: by 1973 only 2.5 per cent of its military budget was affected by the cut in US assistance. Indeed, some observers saw the Brazilian Government's move as coinciding with its wish to reduce the import of US arms in favour of promoting the growing Brazilian arms industry.[27]

The most effective initiatives against torture were taken domestically by Brazilians themselves. In general, their actions were protests against many forms of the abuse of power, of which torture was a prominent feature. Several relatives of torture victims took courageous action, pressing the authorities for an end to incommunicado detention of detainees or for full inquiries into deaths in custody. Several committees were formed in the mid-1970s to work for a general amnesty for political prisoners. They also worked openly for an end to torture and other abuses of prisoners' rights. Political prisoners themselves in different prisons went on hunger-strike against the torture or ill-treatment of themselves or fellow prisoners. Also in 1977, a group of 110 army and air force officers sent a manifesto to President Geisel calling for an "end to censorship and inhuman repression" and for a return to full democracy.

Several social groups that had been targets of the worst repression became or remained vocal against torture. There was a nationwide reappearance of student demonstrations in the second half of 1977 that focused on, among other things, the treatment of prisoners. Two press organizations formally protested about the March 1978 beating of a journalist in Guarulhos, São Paulo, after he had published a report about the torture of political prisoners and the death of a miner while in the custody of the Guarulhos police. Some 400 journalists had vigorously protested about the death of their colleague Vladimir Herzog in 1975. Official censorship of articles about torture and other acts of repression drove several major newspapers to the articulate protest of printing black or blank spaces, recipes for inedible "sweets", and verses in Latin on their censored news pages.

Among various professional groups and individuals who opposed

27 Of course, the impact of a bilateral governmental initiative in the area of human rights is not restricted to the governmental level. The US State Department report was prepared in the context of the Carter Administration's newly formulated policy on human rights, from which Brazilian human rights groups gained a degree of legitimacy.

torture were the lawyers in São Paulo who attempted to reopen the official inquiry into the death of Vladimir Herzog. They filed suit against Dr Harry Shibata in October 1977, accusing him of falsifying a death certificate after he admitted publicly that he had signed the official autopsy report citing suicide as the cause of death without having seen the body. Three years later the São Paulo Regional Medical Council disciplined Dr Shibata, the head of the São Paulo Forensic Medical Institute. The Brazilian Bar Association denounced individual cases of "disappearance", torture and killings by government agents from at least the mid-1970s on and worked persistently for the restoration of the right of *habeas corpus*.

The courts were subject to the general trends of repression throughout the decade. Given the government's obvious interference with the courts—in trials for "crimes of subversion" four of the five judges were military officers, often with no legal training—the determination of some judicial officers is all the more noteworthy. Hélio Bicudo, a prosecutor in São Paulo, brought charges in 1970 against the head of the political police (DEOPS) in São Paulo, Sergio Fleury, who had become nationally known as alleged torturer and founding member of the "death squad" in that city. Several unsuccessful attempts were made to prosecute him. A judge in Guarulhos ordered that he and four others be remanded in custody in 1978 to face charges of the murder of three *marginais* 10 years earlier. Less than 48 hours after the arrest warrant was issued, the judge was removed from the case. Sergio Fleury and his four defendants were later acquitted.[28]

Under pressure from domestic human rights groups, the authorities did allow at least some disciplinary actions against lower police officials to proceed, for example, the suspension, pending an inquiry, of two Brazilian police officers in the southern town of Pôrto Alegre accused of complicity in late 1978 in the abduction of four Uruguayans, including two children, and their forcible return to Uruguay. The two adults were subsequently acknowledged as being held incommunicado by Uruguayan authorities; they were sentenced to five years' imprisonment by a Uruguayan military court in 1981. In December 1981, also in Pôrto Alegre, it was possible for a federal judge to award damages to a prisoner who had been seriously injured in April 1975 by the Pôrto Alegre political police. In a very promising decision, the judge ruled that the Brazilian state was responsible for the security and physical condition of the prisoner, who was in good health before his detention. In June 1983, the

28 Sergio Fleury died later in unexplained circumstances. His death was believed by many Brazilians to have been at the hands of former "colleagues" who feared that his eventual prosecution would implicate them in torture and murder.

Federal Appeal Tribunal in Brasilia upheld a lower court's decision that the state was responsible for the death in 1975 of the journalist Vladimir Herzog.

'The voice of the voiceless'

The church, throughout military rule, has been the only domestic social institution capable of mounting a sustained critique of governmental repression. Brazilian clergy and lay workers have ministered to political prisoners and their families, identified themselves with their suffering, and stood firm when face to face with the state in the country's police stations.

Profound changes occurred in the Roman Catholic Church in Brazil in the 1950s and 1960s. As the world's most populous Roman Catholic country, Brazil experienced an acute shortage of priests. The Vatican issued a call for foreign priests to go as missionaries to Brazil, a call that led to the opening up of the previously insular clergy to European priests influenced by progressive post-war theology. The shortage of clergy also led to the recruitment of young, educated lay workers from middle-class urban families in Brazil, who became radicalized by the poverty and indifference to it that they encountered in their daily work. The progressive wing of the church engaged itself in local struggles for economic and social rights. They supported rural unions, local political "conscientization" programs, and regional economic development projects. Clergy and lay workers soon came into conflict with local authorities; many were arrested in the years before and after the 1964 coup and were subsequently adopted as prisoners of conscience by Amnesty International.

As the repression hardened following the December 1968 "coup within the coup", clergy (mainly Roman Catholic but also a number of Protestant foreign missionaries) became second only to students as the targets of human rights abuses. Dom Helder Câmara, Archbishop of Olinda and Recife, became a symbol of church opposition to torture and repression. In May 1969, his assistant, Father Antonio Henrique, was killed by a right-wing vigilante group. In 1973 a number of lay workers associated with Dom Helder Câmara were arrested, held for short periods, and in some cases tortured. In 1970 Bishop Waldir Calheiros of Volta Redonda protested about the arrest and torture of members of the *Juventude Operária Cathólica* (JOC), Young Christian Workers, and was himself charged as a subversive. Convicted in 1971 of sympathy with guerrilla groups were four Dominican priests, all of whom were tortured during interrogation. One of these torture victims, Fr. Tito de Alençar Lima, took his own life in a period of intense psychological depression following torture. Two further priests were arrested and tortured in 1972.

The late 1960s marked a turning-point in the church's open criticism of the government. The repeated allegations of systematic torture drove many clergy, including an increasing number of the hierarchy, to take stronger stands against many aspects of governmental repression. In 1969 the Archbishop of Ribeiro excommunicated the local chief of police and his assistant—a type of church action since taken elsewhere in South America—because they had used torture to obtain information from political prisoners, including the Mother Superior of a local convent and a number of priests.

Clergy diligently collected information about torture and presented it to the Vatican in December 1969. The Papal Nuncio to Brazil sent Pope Paul VI a similar report. These dossiers led to the Pope's specific denunciation of torture in his Easter Message in March 1970, generally regarded as addressed to Brazil.

Cardinal Arns, Archbishop of São Paulo, took up the cause of 36 prisoners to whom he ministered at the Presidio Tirandentes prison in São Paulo when they went on hunger-strike in 1972 to protest about their inhuman conditions. When the government removed the prisoners to a prison on the borders of the state of São Paulo, where there would be less visibility for their protest and less protection for them, Cardinal Arns issued an international appeal to "save the lives of the 36 prisoners". He was then banned from visiting detainees. The next year he conducted a memorial mass for a young geology student who died in police custody and whose body was refused to his parents for burial—moving the Cardinal to remark in his memorial sermon, "Even Christ after his death was returned to his family and friends; the representative of Roman power was able to do that much justice."

Individual priests increasingly intervened to stop torture, sometimes by going in person to detention centres, and on at least one occasion by insisting on being arrested with parishioners who had been detained, so as to force their release. Among many such offers of clerical protection to prisoners throughout the decade was the action by the Bishop of Curitiba in the state of Paraná, who intervened in March 1978 to save a journalist from further torture and to win the release of 11 people arrested on charges of indoctrinating nursery-school pupils with Marxist ideas.

The hierarchy also became more outspoken collectively as opponents of torture. Four regional bishops' conferences censured the government in 1972 on a number of issues, including its continued reliance on arbitrary arrest and torture. In response to an appeal from 279 intellectuals in early 1973, the 12th Convocation

of the *Conferência Nacional dos Bispos do Brasil* (CNBB), National
Conference of Brazilian Bishops, made an open attack in March on
repression, accusing the government of "unimagined violence,
murdering students who marched peacefully in the streets and
workers who organized strikes for higher wages and the return of
their rights". The CNBB said that jails were inadequate to hold the
"avalanche of citizens of every social class" who had been detained,
making it necessary to turn army barracks into "dungeons" in which
military interrogators operated free from outside observation or
restraint. In effect, the collective hierarchy of the Brazilian church
gave permission within the church to denounce political repression.

During the presidency of General Geisel, the church continued
to seek an end to torture as part of a program of social, economic
and political reforms. In February 1977 the Committee for Human
Rights of the Archdiocese of São Paulo denounced the government's
"arbitrary measures of repression", arguing that "security, as the
good of the nation, is incompatible with a permanent insecurity of
the people". Their report was later endorsed by the CNBB. The
extent of repression against the church was revealed by the CNBB
in 1979: since the 1964 coup, it reported that there had been hundreds
of death threats to and kidnappings of priests as well as hundreds
of raids on churches; eight members of the clergy had been murdered
and 11 banished from the country; of the 122 arrested, 34 had been
tortured. A further 131 lay workers had been arrested.

The local Christian base communities, begun by church workers
on a small scale in 1960, comprised more than 50,000 local groups
involving approximately two million people by 1978. These groups
of 10 to 50 Christians meeting regularly, guided by lay or clerical
"pastoral agents", provided support for human rights activities as
well as pressure for social, economic and political reforms. They
were instrumental in creating the more overtly political *Movimento
Custo de Vida*, Cost of Living Movement, among urban slum-
dwellers, which organized mass rallies and petitions to support its
economic demands. The church at all levels also gave its support to
the growing number of Brazilian amnesty committees that in
1977/1978 became a broadly based campaign for a general amnesty
for political prisoners and exiles as well as the reintroduction of
parliamentary democracy and civil liberties.

In the 1980s the church remains an active opponent of torture
where it continues in Brazil. The Archbishop of Rio de Janeiro
protested in 1981 that common criminal prisoners had been beaten
and tortured in Ilha Grande prison. His protest led to the trial and
conviction in 1982 of the prison governor, his chief of prison
security and two other officials; an appeal is pending. The church

weekly newspaper, *O São Paulo*, stated in February 1980 in an editorial, "The enormous abuses which still exist are perpetrated against common prisoners." The church's Land Pastoral Commission has reported that squatters and small land-holders in rural areas, mainly in the Amazônia region, are systematically tortured, detained and flogged as a means of forcing them to abandon the land they occupy.

* * * *

It is possible to make several generalizations from the pattern of torture and the efforts to suppress it in Brazil in the 1970s:

1. While torture is illegal in most countries, once a state's security agencies are unleashed to commit such gross crimes, it may prove difficult for the government itself to restrain them, much less dismantle or discipline them. They can become pressure groups for their own privileges and can even threaten a government's stability, either directly from within the regime or indirectly by causing popular anger and unrest.

2. The failure of the authorities in different districts to provide a central register of detainees and of their places of detention, especially when coupled with such legal distortions as the abrogation of *habeas corpus*, makes the locating of detainees extremely difficult and can put their safety and lives at risk.

3. Outspoken domestic opposition to torture can help create the political will to stop it. The most obvious successes against the use of torture in Brazil, for example, concerned political detainees in urban areas where broadly based, organized opposition to it was possible, whereas to stop it when the victims are socially or geographically isolated has proved more difficult.

4. The international exposure of torture not only puts a government on the defensive; it can also strengthen domestic opposition to torture. Reports, hearings, declarations and the like, especially when based on detailed information, can provide moral support and a degree of physical protection for those within the country who risk torture to oppose it.

5. International agreements against torture are a form of contract between governments. If one party to the contract fails in its obligations, other states should act. To be effective, such actions, whether bilateral or multilateral, must be taken early enough to affect the emergence or institutionalization of torture and should be part of a consistent pattern of action.

Safeguards and remedies

In response to allegations of torture by victims, families, domestic groups or international organizations, governments usually respond (if they respond at all) by denying the facts or by contending that whatever allegations may be true are isolated incidents and the work of a few excessively zealous security agents. This will not do. Torture occurs as a result of a failure of *governments* to exercise their legal responsibilities to prevent it and to investigate and redress alleged abuses of authority by its agents. The fact that torture or other ill-treatment occurs in dozens of countries while it is prohibited by the laws or constitutions of at least 112 countries shows that a simple legislative prohibition is not sufficient to ban torture. Where the political will exists, however, a government can stop torture. Conversely, if few objectively verifiable preventive and remedial measures have been taken, then it is fair to conclude that a government's opposition to torture is less than serious.

The Human Rights Committee, in an authoritative "General Comment" adopted in July 1982, pointed out that it is not sufficient for the implementation of Article 7 of the International Covenant on Civil and Political Rights, the prohibition of torture and of cruel, inhuman or degrading treatment or punishment, for states to make such practices a crime. Since the practices occur despite existing penal provisions, states should take additional preventive and remedial steps to ensure effective control. At the very least, in the Committee's view, these measures should include the following:

> "Complaints about ill-treatment must be investigated
> effectively by competent authorities. Those found guilty
> must be held responsible, and the alleged victims must
> themselves have effective remedies at their disposal,
> including the right to obtain compensation. Among the
> safeguards which may make control effective are provisions
> against detention *incommunicado*, granting, without
> prejudice to the investigation, persons such as doctors,
> lawyers and family members access to the detainees;

provisions requiring that detainees should be held in places that are publicly recognized and that their names and places of detention should be entered in a central register available to persons concerned, such as relatives; provisions making confessions or other evidence obtained through torture or other treatment contrary to Article 7 inadmissible in court; and measures of training and instruction of law enforcement officials not to apply such treatment.''

Any universally applicable set of domestic measures to stop torture must include those listed by the Human Rights Committee. Based on its own experience, Amnesty International has elaborated in this chapter a more comprehensive body of legal and administrative measures that governments could adopt. These measures derive from evidence provided by personal testimonies of torture, the work of domestic groups and international organizations combating torture and the historical improvements in particular countries that are described in this report. At the end of this report there is, in addition, a 12-point program that sets out in summary form the most critical steps that governments should take to prevent torture (see page 249).

Preventive safeguards

Many of the following safeguards derive from international human rights instruments either already in effect, in draft or under discussion. Others are suggestions made by national or international committees of inquiry appointed either by a single government or by an IGO. Together, they form a convincing set of measures to prevent torture that any government can adopt. As such they would help fulfil the obligation placed on states by Article 4 of the UN Declaration against Torture, which calls on each state to "take effective measures to prevent torture and other cruel, inhuman or degrading treatment or punishment from being practised within its jurisdiction". In general, these safeguards are meant to protect both detainees and security officers, the former from ill-treatment, the latter against pressure to become involved in such practices.

Official directives condemning torture

The head of state, head of government and heads of different security forces should state unequivocally that they will not tolerate, under any circumstances, the ill-treatment of detainees by officials at all levels under their responsibility. Security agents in many countries regard themselves as outside the law and responsible only to their superiors. The force of such clear orders from the top, when disseminated to all security agents, should not be underestimated as a signal that detainees' rights and the law itself must be respected.

Restriction of incommunicado detention

Almost invariably the victims of torture are held incommunicado, both for purposes of interrogation and to allow any marks of torture to disappear. Ensuring prompt and regular access to one's own lawyer, doctor and family and to a court of law would diminish the likelihood of ill-treatment, especially during the first hours and days of detention when, in Amnesty International's experience, ill-treatment is most likely. Prompt appearance before a court of law would provide an opportunity for magistrates and judges to assess the legality and necessity of the detention as well as the treatment of the detainee.

a. Access to the detainee

The following questions provide an indication of a government's willingness to provide safeguards against the abuse of incommunicado detention. Does the government allow the courts the independence to enforce writs of *habeas corpus*, *amparo* or similar remedy whenever a detainee is not brought quickly before a court of law? Does the government require that the detaining authorities allow prompt and regular access to the detainee by his or her lawyer as well as prompt and reasonable access by members of the family? Can an independent physician chosen by the family gain access to the detainee upon reasonable request, even if the detainee has not made such a request?

b. Access to a lawyer

This safeguard deserves special elaboration. Regular communication and consultation with a lawyer are of the utmost importance to ensure, among other legal guarantees, that statements taken in evidence from the detainee are given freely and not as a result of coercion. Such consultations must occur at a minimum before and between interrogation sessions and in a degree of privacy if the lawyer's presence is to serve as a credible restraint on the interrogators' potential abuse of power.

Domestic legislation

The UN Declaration against Torture calls on each state to ensure that torture is an offence under its criminal law (Article 7). The criminal code should treat torture as a crime and establish appropriate penalties for those found guilty of its practice. Incitement to torture or complicity in torture should likewise constitute criminal offences. In recognition of the fact that the crime of torture is forbidden by international law, domestic legislation should stipulate that the crime of torture is not subject to any statute of limitations. It should oblige the government to seek the extradition of its own officials accused of torture if they flee to another country to avoid prosecution, and to prosecute or extradite foreign officials accused of torture elsewhere but now residing within its jurisdiction, providing they do not risk torture or execution. In some legal systems a law could also allow individuals to initiate criminal proceedings against officials accused of torture if public authorities did not do so.

Repeal of provisions of emergency legislation that diminish detainees' rights

Provisions of emergency legislation or executive decrees that weaken safeguards against the abuse of authority—for example, by allowing unchecked periods of incommunicado detention or suspending the right of *habeas corpus* or its equivalent—may facilitate torture. The promulgation and continued enforcement of such legal provisions is often taken as a signal by the security forces that neither the government nor the courts will interfere with their methods. The repeal of such measures would be an objective signal to the contrary.

Regular system of visits to places of detention

Detention centres should be visited regularly and routinely by individuals independent of the detaining authorities. These individuals may be appointed by independent national bodies, or they may be delegates from international bodies such as the International Committee of the Red Cross. They should be able to communicate with detainees without prison staff being present.

Training in human rights norms for all security agents

All personnel involved in law enforcement duties—military, police and prison staff—should receive proper education and training concerning the Nürnberg Principles and the individual responsibility of officials at all levels; the prohibitions against torture given in the Universal Declaration of Human Rights and the International Covenant on Civil and Political Rights; and in the principles contained in the UN Code of Conduct, the UN Standard Minimum Rules for the Treatment of Prisoners and the UN Declaration against Torture. Domestic laws and regulations against torture should of course be included. These texts should be translated as necessary and disseminated to all central and local authorities involved in the process of arrest, interrogation, detention or the administration of justice. An absolute prohibition of torture and ill-treatment as crimes under domestic law should be visibly displayed in every detention centre in the country.

Separation of authority over detention and interrogation

Detainees subjected to torture are often held in custody and interrogated by the same agency. The formal separation of these two security functions would allow some protection for detainees by providing a degree of supervision of their welfare by an agency not engaged in interrogating them.

Notification to detainees of their rights

At the moment of detention or arrest, or promptly thereafter, detainees are entitled to know why they have been detained or arrested, where held and by which agency. They should also receive an explanation, orally and in writing, in a language that they understand, of how to avail themselves of their legal rights, including the right to lodge complaints of ill-treatment.

Role of the judiciary

The degree of a government's commitment to an independent and positive role for the judiciary in preventing torture can be observed in several ways. First, does the law require that arrests (excepting solely people apprehended in the act of committing a crime) and all continued detention occur only on the written order or warrant of a judicial authority? Second, does the law stipulate that the courts should respond to applications for *habeas corpus* or its equivalent within a brief and specified period? Do the courts so respond? Third, what protective measures for detainees are available to the judiciary if a detainee who appears in court seems to have been tortured in custody? For example, can the court release the detainee or at least remove him or her to another detention centre? Fourth, do the courts have power to supervise and call into question the activities of the security services? Do the courts exercise these measures? Fifth, has the government explicitly instructed all prosecuting authorities not to submit in evidence before the court confessions or other evidence which may have been obtained as a result of torture or oppression of the defendant or any other person? Does the law require judges to exclude all such evidence? By consistently excluding such evidence, judges would provide the investigating and prosecuting authorities with an objective disincentive to torture.

Prohibition against the waiving of certain rights

Some governments allow detainees to waive their right to be presented before a judicial authority within a prescribed period of time. While such a waiver may appear superficially to be voluntary, it is often the result of extreme coercion. Likewise, the practice of having detainees sign statements that they have not been ill-treated in custody is in effect a waiver of the right subsequently to file a complaint about ill-treatment. Such a signed statement can have no probative value whatsoever, and its very existence casts doubt on its content. There is no reason to have a detainee sign a statement that he or she was well-treated in custody—unless of course it was not the case. The legal prohibition of any such statement or waiver of essential rights would remove the temptation to obtain them by force.

Medical safeguards

The presence and formal independence of a fully qualified doctor at all detention centres can provide protection from ill-treatment. In practice, the government must recognize the principles that it is a serious breach of medical ethics for health personnel to be involved in torture and that the medical officers on duty are responsible for the health of detainees and must have the clinical independence to perform this duty. One indication of independence would be if medical officers were responsible to an authority other than the security forces or prison administration. Further procedures for the medical examinations of all detainees could include the following:

a. the offer of an examination on arrival at a detention centre, before interrogation begins;

b. the offer of an examination every subsequent 24 hours while under interrogation and immediately prior to transfer or release;

c. these offers to be made personally by the medical officer on duty, who would explain the importance of having complete records of the detainee's condition in detention;

d. detainees to be informed in the written notice of their rights about the importance of these examinations;

e. all examinations to be conducted in private by medical personnel only;

f. any refusal by a detainee to have any of these examinations to be witnessed in writing by the medical officer;

g. daily visits to each detainee by a medical officer, and access by the detainee to the medical officer on duty at any time on reasonable request;

h. detailed record-keeping by medical personnel of such matters as the weight of the detainee, marks on the body, psychological state and complaints related to health or treatment;

i. these records to be treated as confidential, as in any doctor-patient relationship, but capable of being communicated at the detainee's request to his or her lawyer or family;

j. examination by the detainee's own doctor at the request of the detainee or of his or her lawyer or family, not in the presence of prison guards.

Governments should make obligatory post-mortem examinations of all individuals who die in custody or shortly after release, from whatever cause. Such post-mortem examinations would need to be conducted by an independent forensic pathologist, with access granted by law to the examination, evidence and any subsequent hearings to a representative of the family, their lawyer and doctor.

Record-keeping by the detaining authority

There should be no doubt where and in whose care a prisoner is at any given time. An accurate central register of detainees in each district, in the form of a bound book with numbered pages, with a record of their time of arrest and places of initial and subsequent detention would prevent secret detention and the "disappearance" of persons in custody. It would also give families and lawyers the possibility of locating the detainee. Each detention centre should be required to keep a detailed contemporary record, again bound with numbered pages, of the time of arrest, identities of the authorities who performed the arrest, time of appearance before a judicial authority, times and durations of each interrogation session, times when statements were given, and a complete record of who was present at all of the above instances. All officers present at the taking of a written statement could be required to countersign the statement.

Such records could be supplemented by a personal data sheet giving information about the times of medical examinations, who conducted them, times and places of interrogation, identities of interrogators by name or number, a record of meals and of requests or complaints made by detainees or on their behalf. This data sheet would accompany the detainee when transferred, and the officer in charge of the detainee would sign the data sheet.

Legitimate force used against a detainee or violence by the detainee against guards, interrogators or his or her self could be recorded on this data sheet. Evidence of injuries sustained in custody in the absence of any such record would be an indication that these injuries were more likely to be the result of illegal violence used by officials than of any above-mentioned (but unrecorded) causes.

All records would be available to the detainee and his or her legal adviser.

Procedures internal to the interrogating authority

Strict procedures are needed to regulate the process of interrogation itself. A clear chain of command within the agency would indicate who is responsible for supervising interrogation procedures and practices and for disciplining officers who violate these procedures. The procedures could include such matters as the regular and personal supervision of interrogation by senior officers, as well as specified limitations on the duration of interrogation sessions and the number of interrogators. Perhaps no universal guideline can be established, but one government-appointed inquiry recommended in the late 1970s that there should be a limit of no more than two interrogators at a time and no more than six in all; that each session should end at regular meal-times; and that in general no session should begin or continue after midnight. Whatever the particulars of the procedures, detailed records would have to be kept if they were to be effective as preventive measures.

Particular precautions would also have to be taken to avoid the abuse during interrogation of women and juvenile detainees. Procedures should stipulate that a female officer be present during all interrogation of women detainees and that the questioning of juveniles take place in the presence of a parent or guardian. It would be a further commitment to preventing torture if the government published the interrogation procedures currently in force and periodically reviewed both procedures and practices, inviting submissions and recommendations from civil rights groups, defence lawyers, bar associations and other interested parties.

Code for treatment of detainees

The government should adopt and publish a code of conduct for all security agents who exercise powers of detention and arrest that would be in accord with the UN Code of Conduct for Law Enforcement Officials. Besides a categorical prohibition against torture and ill-treatment and against obtaining statements by force or threats of force, the code would need to oblige security agents (a) to oppose the use of torture or ill-treatment, if necessary by refusing to carry out orders to inflict such treatment on detainees, and (b) to report such abuses of authority to their superior officers and, where necessary, to the authorities vested with reviewing or remedial powers. Proven breaches of the code would result in specified disciplinary penalties for the agents involved. Agents who comply with the code should be entitled to protection and support from their superiors and colleagues.

Ratifications and declarations concerning international human rights norms and mechanisms

A further sign of a government's will to prevent torture would be the ratification of the International Covenant on Civil and Political Rights, its Optional Protocol providing for individual complaints and any further conventions against torture; a unilateral declaration of adherence to the UN Declaration against Torture, as requested by the General Assembly; and a declaration by the government that it will cooperate with international inquiries into allegations of torture by appropriate IGOs and NGOs.

Remedial measures

The safeguards outlined in the previous section must form the first line of defence against torture and ill-treatment. However, preventive safeguards and *post-facto* remedies are closely linked. The purpose of several of the safeguards mentioned above is to facilitate the full investigation of complaints, and one reason for implementing complaints machinery and other remedies is to deter future ill-treatment.

Complaints machinery

If elaborated and implemented, complaints procedures provide redress to persons previously tortured and a degree of deterrence against the future ill-treatment of others. Without adequate complaints machinery, justice may not be done and certainly will not be seen to be done. As a result, the security agency is likely to forfeit credibility in the community and thereby lose effectiveness in fulfilling any proper law-enforcement role.

However, it could be argued, firstly, that formal procedures to receive and investigate complaints will reduce the efficiency of the security services, in what may be a time of severe internal crisis, by giving weight to propaganda alleging that they have acted illegally and by diverting scarce manpower to the investigation of the security forces themselves. These arguments have some validity. If detainees' allegations are largely propaganda, however, then the expenditure of resources to establish the facts and put them before the public would enhance, not sully, the reputation of the security forces. It is self-evident that there is a potentially gross imbalance of power between a detainee and his or her captors; it is likewise obvious that the state has infinitely more investigative resources than an individual detainee. It follows that a government's determination formally to investigate complaints against its security forces and to report publicly on those investigations would go a long way, albeit after an alleged injury had occurred, to correct that imbalance of power and resources.

Secondly, if some form of official complaints machinery does exist, there may be a reluctance on the part of detainees and former detainees to use it. Victims of torture may fear reprisals from the security forces, and sometimes ill-treatment in custody is not reported because the victim does not believe that it will do any good. They may believe that the word of a security official will be given more weight in court than their own testimony. Also, if detainees have given information against other people during interrogation, they may not wish to draw attention to their "collaboration", even if they "broke" only after being tortured; and if they did not give information, they may not wish to raise fears among colleagues outside that they did. While still in prison they may also wish to protect their families from the fear and anxiety caused by the knowledge that they were tortured. In some societies it is thought undignified to admit to having been tortured. In others, it may be particularly difficult for victims, especially women, to reveal that they have been physically or sexually abused. Just as the existence of allegations cannot be taken as proof of torture, the paucity of official complaints does not demonstrate its absence. Therefore, complaints procedures should provide for an investigation of allegations wherever there is reasonable ground to believe that torture has occurred, even if formal complaints have not been lodged.

Based on its experience, Amnesty International believes that complaints procedures should reflect the following principles.

1. The main *objective* of complaints machinery is to establish, to the degree of certainty possible, whether torture or ill-treatment has occurred. As it is not a criminal inquiry, it should therefore not be necessary to prove beyond reasonable doubt *who* committed the offence in order to conclude that an offence has taken place.

2. The investigating body, however constituted, should be able to demonstrate its formal *independence* from the detaining and interrogating authorities as well as from governmental pressure and influence. In order that its findings prove credible, the government might include among its members persons nominated by independent non-governmental bodies such as the country's bar and medical associations. There is

no strong reason to exclude representatives of the general public, especially in countries with systems involving trials by jury, from serving on a board charged with reviewing complaints against the police.

3. The *terms of reference* of the investigating body should include the authority to subpoena witnesses, records and documents, to take testimony under oath, and to invite evidence and submissions from interested individuals and NGOs. The investigating body should also have powers to review procedures and practices related to the notification of arrest; to visits to detainees by lawyers, family and their own physicians; to medical examinations and treatment; and to the admissibility of statements in court allegedly obtained by coercion.

4. The investigating body should be capable of *acting on its own initiative*, without having to receive formal complaints, whenever there is good reason to believe that torture has occurred. To do so, it must be given the staff and other resources to carry out autonomous investigations. Otherwise, its findings may be limited by the reluctance of some victims to file complaints and it will be dependent on the will of the security forces to investigate themselves.

5. The methods and findings should be *public*. At a minimum, the results and reasoning of any particular investigation should be made public and should be available as evidence in subsequent criminal or civil proceedings. It would serve to reassure the general public if a full record of the hearings and its findings were published.

6. The investigation should be *speedy* if it is to serve the cause of either justice or deterrence. Prompt investigation is also necessary to help ensure that no evidence obtained as a result of the alleged treatment be submitted as evidence in any trial against the complainant.

7. The *right to file a complaint* should be available to all current and former detainees, their lawyers, families and to any other person or organization acting on their behalf.

8. Accurate *records* of complaints filed should be published on a regular basis. These records should include a statistical breakdown by detention centre and by interrogating agency, to facilitate the task of a government seeking to control its own security agents.

9. *Security agents* against whom repeated complaints of ill-treatment are filed *should be transferred*, without prejudice, to duties not directly related to arresting, guarding or inter-

rogating detainees, pending a thorough review by senior officers of their conduct.

10. The investigating body should have available to it the *medical documentation* resulting from an examination by an independent doctor given immediately after the complaint is filed. Records of any post-mortem examination relevant to a complaint should likewise be available.

Other domestic legal remedies

The complaints procedures described above are not a substitute for the proper functioning of the courts. The purpose of this section is to outline several principles worthy of inclusion in the domestic legal system assuming that a government wishes to provide appropriate legal remedies to persons tortured by officials of the state.

1. *The jurisdiction of the courts* should extend to the investigation of complaints of torture against any member of the security forces and to the prosecution of any security agent accused of torture.

2. The *subjects* of judicial investigation and prosecution should include not only those who participate in torture but also all those who incite it, attempt it, consciously cover it up, or are otherwise directly implicated in its use. Commanding officers should be held accountable for torture committed by officials under their command.

3. The principal responsibility to instigate *criminal prosecutions* lies with the state authorities and should be exercised once there is reason to believe that specific agents can be convicted of torture or ill-treatment.

4. A complainant or person acting on his or her behalf should be able to seek damages in *civil proceedings* against individual security agents, the agency, its commanding officer and the state itself. The fact that a previous criminal prosecution on the same charges has not resulted in the conviction of specific agents should not preclude civil actions to obtain damages.

5. *Disciplinary procedures* within the security forces or relevant professional bodies (e.g., the medical authority that licenses doctors to practise) should be pursued promptly and without prejudice to any form of court action.

6. Assistance to torture victims by the state should include *medical rehabilitation* as needed and *financial compensation* commensurate with the abuse inflicted and damages suffered. This assistance should follow from a finding that torture or ill-treatment has occurred and should be awarded to the

detainee without prejudice to any other criminal or civil proceedings.

7. In the event of a detainee's death shown to be the result of torture or ill-treatment, the deceased's family should receive *compensatory and exemplary damages* against the state without prejudice to any other criminal or civil proceedings.

The evidence

To accuse a government of torture is a very serious charge. Accordingly, Amnesty International pays close attention to the verification of testimonies and other evidence of alleged torture. The conclusions about the use of torture and systematic ill-treatment in the countries mentioned in the following pages are based largely on direct evidence: testimonies of people who allege that they themselves have been tortured and testimonies of people who claim to have seen or heard others being tortured or to have seen the marks of alleged torture victims soon after it occurred. Where possible, Amnesty International has drawn on medical evidence given by doctors requested by the victim to provide it, by doctors appointed by the courts or by doctors representing Amnesty International. Sometimes Amnesty International does not have direct access to the victims and instead must assess their allegations at a distance, as they are reported by human rights or political groups in the country concerned or by refugees. In some instances evidence of torture can be inferred from the nature of the government's response when it is confronted with its alleged responsibility for torture.

Torture itself is secretive and is committed by officials who have the power to conceal. Access to the country may prove difficult if the government wishes to impede an independent investigation (all Amnesty International missions are announced in advance to the respective governments). Access to particular people in the country, even if released from prison, may not be possible, or it may be too risky if they are under surveillance or otherwise likely to be endangered by talking to Amnesty International. The lapse of time between a victim's torture and an interview with Amnesty International may in any event be so long as to allow objective physical signs to disappear or at least to change so as to appear to be attributable to one of any of several possible traumas.

Neither the ostensible victim nor the alleged torturers can be said to be impartial witnesses, and their statements must be evaluated in that light. Prisoners or released prisoners may have both personal and political motives for exaggerating so as to justify their own actions or embarrass particular officials or the government itself. The government may deny the validity of the complaints or maintain that any injuries were self-inflicted.

Amnesty International does not make assumptions about the veracity or otherwise of any allegations of torture. This is true even of allegations coming from countries where there is a well-documented pattern of torture. In evaluating the individual allegation Amnesty International must take into account all the information pertaining to the specific case as well as the country and local context within which the allegation is made.

Sometimes the facts come together to indicate beyond any reasonable doubt that the individual was tortured. In other cases, the information is too scant to lead to any conclusion. In very many cases, however, the facts are inconclusive but sufficient to justify a requirement that the authorities conduct their own investigation and make the findings public. In this connection Amnesty International attaches great importance to Article 9 of the UN Declaration on the Protection of All Persons from Torture and Other Cruel, Inhuman or Degrading Treatment or Punishment, which says "Wherever there is reasonable ground to believe that an act of torture . . . has been committed, the competent authorities of the State concerned shall promptly proceed to an impartial investigation *even if there has been no formal complaint* [emphasis supplied]."

Amnesty International's assessments are, in the first instance, based on the demeanour of those who testify and what is known about them individually, on the internal consistency of their testimonies and on whether these testimonies concur with others from the same period and the same place of imprisonment, as well as with any previous pattern of torture in that country that may be known to Amnesty International.

Often the allegations come from a local organization which has conducted its own fact-finding through contacts with prisoners, released prisoners, relatives, lawyers, doctors and others. In evaluating such information too, Amnesty International must take into account the degree of detail and internal consistency, its consistency with other reports, and the record of the group for accuracy.

Medical findings, when available, can add to the credibility of the evidence. Doctors working with Amnesty International over the past 10 years have conducted hundreds of detailed interviews and medical examinations of torture victims. They have systematically analysed the results of these examinations. Based on this experience it is sometimes possible to say that a given physical mark is the kind of mark specifically caused by the type of torture alleged. Certain skin marks are specific to electrical burns as opposed to heat burns. *Falanga* produces specific symptoms and objective signs that have a known average duration in the feet, ankles, legs and back.

Rarely, however, can the medical findings "prove" that torture occurred. There is no test that is so specific as to determine positively that a given mark or symptom is the result of a particular act of torture. Amnesty International's medical research into allegations of torture typifies the way Amnesty International has to examine all the facts about an allegation in order to reach any conclusion.

In order to minimize the possibility of error in its medical assessments, doctors test the consistency of a victim's testimony in a systematic interview of from four to six hours. The interview is conducted in private. On missions to investigate torture, the selection of people to be interviewed and examined systematically is almost invariably made by the Amnesty International representatives, usually after hearing a larger number of witnesses. The questions are not known in advance by the interviewee. The order and type of questions provide a built-in test of veracity in that the same information is sought in different ways. Consequently, answers to similar questions can be checked against each other. The interview is conducted in a professional and sympathetic atmosphere so as to help the person tell what may be a painful story.

If a testimony is consistent with itself and with what others say who witnessed similar events at the same time and place; if the description of early and current symptoms accords with the known pattern of symptoms for the types of torture alleged; and if any physical marks that remain on the person are likewise consistent with their allegations—then Amnesty International can say with confidence that its findings are consistent with the allegations.

Amnesty International will also compare these findings with any available medical evidence concerning the victim's health before torture and with any findings by a doctor consulted by the victim soon after torture or appointed by the courts to conduct an examination.

The facts about the circumstances in which a person was held may also help in evaluating his or her allegation of torture, although they do not constitute proof. The allegation is more likely to be true if the person was held for a prolonged period incommunicado for interrogation, without access being given to outsiders (court, relatives, lawyer).

All too often the alleged victim has died in custody. There can be many causes of such deaths, but if there are allegations that the victim died as a result of torture a number of factors can be taken into account in assessing that allegation: the age and previous health of the prisoner; any pattern of torture in similar places of imprisonment in the country concerned; the credibility of the official explanation of the prisoner's death; whether or not the authorities hand over the body to relatives, thus enabling independent examination of it; whether or not the authorities conduct an open inquiry into the cause of death.

Official government acknowledgements of torture or unofficial statements by government representatives may reveal knowledge of a particular act or of a pattern of abuses and, in some instances, of the government's desire to stop torture. Defectors from several countries' security forces involved in torture have given eye-witness accounts of their personal participation in torture and of how their units were organized to carry it out. Court testimony and decisions in particular cases, especially if those accused of torture give testimony, may help indicate the degree of governmental knowledge and responsibility for torture. Evidence that torture is being inflicted with the approval of the government can also be inferred from such information as the number of security agents involved, the number and location of torture centres, the consistency of methods used in different centres or by different agencies, the apparent rank of any officers involved, the number and repetition of the alleged acts and the official tolerance shown of these abuses of authority.

A government's response to allegations of torture or ill-treatment sometimes provides further evidence of its responsibility. Some governments fail to respond; others deny the allegations in general terms, making no specific rebuttal of the alleged facts. Inconsistencies in some governments' replies in particular cases are all too evident. Further indications of the reliability of a government's response are whether it has investigated the allegations, made public its conclusions and argumentation domestically and internationally, and whether it has brought to justice any officials apparently guilty of torture.

If a government has not investigated past or current allegations; if it has not introduced preventive or remedial measures to combat torture; if it continues to hold prisoners in conditions conducive to torture—then it is fair to infer a lack of governmental concern to stop torture. A continuing pattern of torture must then be seen as attributable to government policy, whether by direct command or by negligence.

This report deals with evidence and allegations of torture between January 1980 and mid-1983. Amnesty International's aim has been to summarize the information available in each country mentioned, but there are other countries where the organization does not have sufficient information to include an entry: this cannot be taken to indicate that torture or other ill-treatment have not taken place. The techniques of torture and other cruelties inflicted on prisoners vary from country to country; furthermore, secrecy and censorship often prevent the free flow of information about such abuses. Amnesty International does not, therefore, attempt comparisons, nor does it grade governments or countries according to their record on human rights. Neither the level of detail nor the length of a particular reference should be used as a basis for comparing or contrasting the extent or depth of Amnesty International's concerns in particular countries.

Since the report has as its primary objective the abolition of torture, entries have also been included on countries where significant steps have been taken to investigate and combat the torture or ill-treatment of detainees since January 1980. In addition, where relatively little information is available on certain countries, brief references have been included at the end of the regional sections. If this report serves to encourage individuals, organizations or governments to provide further information about the treatment of prisoners or steps taken to prevent their torture, one of its purposes will have been well served. Information should be forwarded to the International Secretariat of Amnesty International, 1 Easton Street, London WC1X 8DJ, United Kingdom, and will be treated in confidence.

Torture is a violation of human dignity and international law. In many countries human rights groups have organized protests against its continued use, but those in the front line of the effort to stop torture often take great personal risks.

A demonstration against martial law in Kwangju, South Korea, in May 1980. Following such demonstrations, many protesters were arrested and interrogated under torture, and eight were beaten to death in an army base on the outskirts of the city.

Demonstrators in El Salvador demand the release of people who have "disappeared" after being abducted by security forces. The bodies of many such people, including women and children, have been discovered bearing the marks of torture.

Torture is often inflicted as part of government suppression of dissent.

In the Soviet Union people who have been detained for expressing criticism of the authorities have been confined in Dnepropetrovsk Special Psychiatric Hospital and other psychiatric institutions, some being given pain-causing drugs.

In Chile human rights organizations have identified secret detention centres in which political suspects have been interrogated under torture. A group of nuns, priests and other church members protested outside such a centre at Calle Borgoño 1470 in Santiago in October 1983.

SAYIN DEMiREL BU NEDiR?

Her demecinizde, Türkiye'de "Hürriyetçi parlamenter rejim"in varlığını vurguluyorsunuz. Demokrasinin açıklık rejimi olduğunu söylüyorsunuz. Şimdi soruyor ve açıklama bekliyoruz: FOTOĞRAFINI VERDİĞİMİZ ALET NEDİR?

In many countries the torture of prisoners is systematic and routine. The picture of the machine was first published in the Turkish newspaper *Democrat* in May 1980. The headline asks the Prime Minister just what the machine is: according to *Democrat* it was made in a government-controlled factory and used for electric shock torture.

The evidence suggests that political detainees are most at risk in the period immediately after arrest, with many torture victims subsequently breaking down and signing false confessions.

Sometimes a doctor is present to ensure that the victim cannot escape the torment through losing consciousness or by dying. The corpse is that of a torture victim from Bahrain.

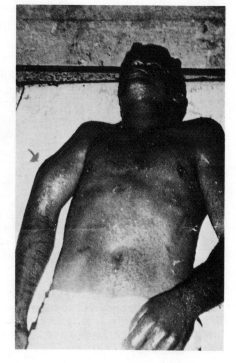

The victims of torture include people from all social classes, age groups, trades and professions.

Women prisoners in Evin Prison, Iran. Reports have been received that children have been forced to witness the torture of their mothers held here. One such mother screamed that she was ready to confess when she could no longer stand the agony of her three-year-old daughter being made to watch.

Edwin López, who was arrested on 26 February 1982 when the offices of the Community Integrated Development Services in Quezon City, Philippines, were raided. He described how he was tortured with electric shocks during interrogation: "I felt a shock of burning heat spread all over my body . . . my whole body trembled because of the high electric charge streaming through it."

Ali Hama Salih, aged 12. He was detained by security forces in Iraq from 25 February to 5 March 1981. His corpse was subsequently handed back to his family badly marked by torture.

Baljit Singh, blinded by the police in Bihar, India, in 1980. Thirty-six suspected criminals suffered the same fate. One of the men said that officers held him down, punctured his eyes with bicycle spokes and then wrapped acid-soaked pads over his eyes.

Independent medical evidence can be vital when assessing allegations of torture or ill-treatment because neither victims nor torturers are necessarily impartial witnesses.

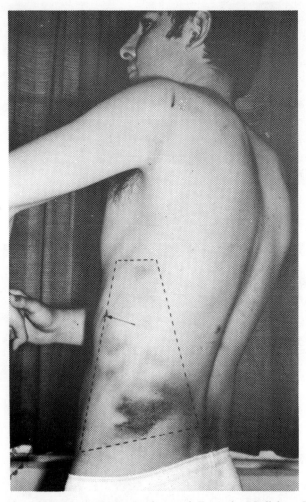

This photo was taken at the Institute of Forensic Medicine, Bogota, Colombia, during an investigation into the claim by Ernesto Sendoya Guzman that he had been tortured over a period of three days by members of F-2 Police Intelligence. The medical evidence of torture was consistent with his allegation that he had been severely beaten.

Although it is rare that medical evidence can "prove" that torture occurred, there is often no reasonable doubt that it has.

Torture and ill-treatment are often inflicted as judicial punishments, sometimes in addition to prison sentences.

In Pakistan since the imposition of martial law in 1977 sentences of flogging can be imposed under both martial law regulations and Islamic law. Many floggings are conducted in public.

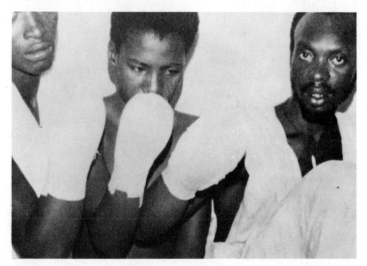

As well as caning and flogging, in a few countries amputations can be inflicted as court-ordered punishments: three convicted thieves, each of whom had a hand amputated in Mauritania in September 1980.

Rosemary Riveros, a Bolivian citizen, was beaten and tortured with electric shocks in a military barracks in Argentina after being abducted by military personnel in Buenos Aires in December 1975. She lost contact with her daughter Tamara in June 1976 and was held without charge or trial until May 1981, when she was released into exile after appeals from Amnesty International.

The Grandmothers of the Plaza de Mayo, an Argentinian human rights group, helped her to find her child, and they were reunited in Lima, Peru, in July 1983. Rosemary Riveros told reporters at the airport: "It's a miracle . . . I still can't believe I'm back with my precious baby . . . the political repression was indiscriminate and I, like many workers, got caught up in it. Now I just want to give my daughter stability and love, the things any mother wants to do for a child."

Global survey

AFRICA

Angola

A number of people arrested on suspicion of belonging to the *União Nacional para a Independência Total de Angola* (UNITA), National Union for the Total Independence of Angola, which is engaged in armed opposition to the government, are alleged to have been tortured. The general incidence of torture appears to have been somewhat less during the period under review than in the years 1977 and 1978, when many allegations of torture were reported involving people arrested following an abortive attempt to overthrow the government by force.

In 1980 the government of Angola created a Ministry of State Security with responsibility for internal security and for both arrests and pre-trial detention of political prisoners. In particular, Ministry officials are reported to have been responsible for interrogating detainees in a new high security prison which opened in Luanda in early 1981, where some detainees are reported to have been tortured.

Victims of torture are reported to have included several teachers arrested in Kwanza Sul province in December 1981. Other prisoners suspected of complicity in acts of violence, for example the sabotage of an oil refinery in Luanda in December 1981, are also alleged to have been tortured.

Methods of torture are reported to have included severe beatings and whippings, inflicted with fists, wooden sticks, belts and special whips, and other techniques, such as the application of electric shocks. Beatings have sometimes resulted in prisoners losing teeth or having their jaws dislocated. Since the beginning of 1981 political prisoners at the new prison in Luanda are reported to have been subjected to electric shocks. A police officer detained there in late 1981, for example, is reported to have suffered burns as a result of electric shocks administered to his head and genitals.

Some detainees who are reported to have been tortured have been subsequently tried and convicted by the People's Revolutionary

Tribunal, a special court set up in 1976 to try cases concerning the security of the state. However, insufficient information is available about the proceedings of such trials to indicate whether confessions and statements made under duress have been accepted as evidence by the court.

Political detainees arrested since 1980 and detained for short periods for offences such as criticizing government housing policy are also reported to have been subjected to frequent beatings while in custody, not only during their interrogation, but throughout their detention, apparently as a form of punishment. Some political detainees have also reported being confined for long periods in small cramped spaces where they could hardly move and being deprived of food and water for several days after their arrest.

In July 1979, Angola's first head of state, President Agostinho Neto, announced that the national security service was being dissolved on account of excesses which it was said to have committed. Unofficial reports indicate that senior security officials had been responsible for both torturing prisoners and committing extrajudicial executions. In August 1979 a number of such officials were apparently placed under arrest. In early 1980 an official inquiry into the service's activities revealed that its officials had committed criminal actions, but did not specify what. The results of a second inquiry which was announced in April 1980 are not known to have been made public. All the officials of the *Direcção de Informação e Segurança de Angola* (DISA), Angolan Directorate for Information and Security, arrested in 1979 are reported to have been released uncharged eventually, although they were not reappointed to their former posts.

Cameroon

Amnesty International received many allegations, including eye-witness accounts, that detainees were routinely beaten in some police stations in Cameroon during the period under review. Beatings were also reported to have been inflicted on prison inmates for infractions of prison rules. Security services specializing in the interrogation of people suspected of subversion reportedly inflicted beatings or, on rare occasions, electric shock torture.

Ill-treatment of suspects by the police was reportedly common at the *commissariat central*, central police station, in Yaoundé, and at some other police stations. In addition, according to eye-witness accounts, prisoners were beaten with truncheons and in some cases deprived of food for up to five days. Similar ill-treatment was reported at the central prison in Yaoundé, where both ordinary criminal and political prisoners were also subjected to beatings on the soles of the feet for alleged infractions of prison rules. One report, in June 1981, stated that prisoners under sentence of death were kept in chains. Following a riot in February 1983 by prisoners at Yaoundé Central Prison in protest against the alleged non-application of amnesty measures, many of them were said to have been beaten and to have had excrement thrown over them, apparently in the presence of senior government officials.

Allegations of torture were also made against the *Brigades mixtes mobiles* (BMM), a paramilitary police force which has responsibility for the interrogation of people held in administrative internment on suspicion of engaging in subversion. Three cases of torture using electricity reportedly occurred in March 1982 at the BMM's headquarters in Yaoundé, where one room, known as *la chapelle*, the Chapel, was said to be used specifically for torture.

Chad

Chad was in a state of insurrection or civil war for most of the period under review. Fighting among rival political and military factions made it difficult to monitor reports of torture, and at times there was no firmly constituted government to whom Amnesty International might address inquiries or appeals. The organization received reports that suspected political opponents were tortured by several of the rival militias during periods of acute unrest. At least 31 members of the *Rassemblement pour l'unité et la démocratie au Tchad* (RUDT), Movement for Unity and Democracy in Chad, were reportedly ill-treated in June 1982 after being detained by the *Forces armées tchadiennes* (FAT), Chadian Armed Forces, led by Colonel Abdelkader Kamougué. Some of the 31 are reported to have been publicly flogged.

In June 1982 Hissène Habré effectively became head of state after the occupation of the capital, N'Djamena, by members of the *Forces armées du nord* (FAN), Armed Forces of the North. He was officially sworn in as President on 21 October 1982.

After President Habré's accession, Amnesty International received reports that suspected ordinary criminals and political opponents of the government were ill-treated by members of the FAN (later renamed *Forces armées nationales tchadiennes* (FANT)). Troops are reported to have inflicted regular beatings and whippings on prisoners in their custody. Among the victims were detained employees of the state cotton company COTONTCHAD, who were suspected of collaborating with the previous administration of Colonel Kamougué. Two such employees, Remadji and Tambaye, are both reported to have been severely beaten and kept tightly bound for long periods during their detention by FAN troops. In March and April 1983 there were reports that a number of villagers in the Doba and Moundou regions were beaten, sometimes to death, on account of their suspected political opposition to President Habré's government. Some were apparently ill-treated in reprisal for a series of atrocities carried out apparently by armed groups opposed to the government.

Comoros

Amnesty International received reports that political detainees were subject to beatings and other ill-treatment in the Comoros at least until May 1981.

Following the overthrow of President Ali Soilih in May 1978, several hundred people associated with his administration were detained by the incoming government of President Ahmed Abdallah. Many of them were reported to have been subjected to beatings while held at Moroni Central Prison and at Voidjou military camp. Although most of these detainees were released gradually, by May 1981 those still in detention were apparently still subject to occasional beatings. Some students arrested in 1979 and 1980 and people detained in February 1981 on suspicion of plotting against the government were also reportedly beaten with fists and sticks.

In May 1981 an Amnesty International delegate visited the Comoros to discuss with the government the detention without trial of members of the previous government and other concerns including allegations of the ill-treatment of detainees. The delegate was granted access to prisoners at Moroni Central Prison and Voidjou military camp, and he was also able to discuss Amnesty International's concerns with the government. After discussions with both government officials and detainees, he reported to the International Executive Committee of Amnesty International that prisoners detained since 1978 were regularly beaten at both Moroni Central Prison and Voidjou camp. Beatings were frequently administered by the security forces. Ahamada M'djassairi, one of the prisoners interviewed by Amnesty International's delegates, detained allegedly on suspicion of plotting against the government, was beaten for six nights in a row. Neither he nor other victims received any medical treatment for their injuries. Amnesty International's delegate reported that 11 detainees at Voidjou camp bore marks of beatings. Two had ear infections, and one suffered from a urinary infection which he thought he had contracted as a result of a beating.

Congo

Amnesty International has received reports that political prisoners have occasionally been tortured in Congo during the period under review, although torture appears to have been used less frequently than during the 1970s. Most reports have concerned prisoners held for questioning by the *Direction générale de la sécurité d'Etat*, State Security Service, at its headquarters in Brazzaville, although detainees are also reported to have been tortured in villas which were originally built on a special estate for African heads of state visiting Brazzaville.

Detainees reported to have been tortured include both Congolese nationals accused of offences against the security of the state and non-Congolese asylum-seekers accused of espionage. In both cases, detainees are reported to have been tortured to make them confess or to implicate other people. In mid-1982, for example, Eugène Madimba, who was one of 10 people arrested and accused of complicity in causing a bomb explosion in a Brazzaville cinema in March 1982, was reportedly subjected to torture, including electric shocks, over a period of three months in order to make him admit his guilt and implicate the other detainees. Later the same year, a Ugandan asylum-seeker is reported to have been arrested, accused of spying and subjected to severe beatings and torture throughout December 1982. In neither case were formal charges subsequently brought against the torture victim.

Detainees are reported to have been subjected to both severe beatings with belts, sticks, and rifle butts, kicks, and more acute forms of torture. The most commonly reported methods are electric shocks, applied either directly to the arms, legs and genitals or else to metal or water with which the victim is in contact, and the suspension of victims from a door-frame to which they are hand-cuffed for minutes or hours while they are sporadically beaten.

Victims have sometimes been transferred to hospital to receive medical treatment after being tortured. In October 1980 a prisoner is reported to have died in hospital as a result of electric burns on his genitals and around his arms.

Djibouti

Amnesty International received reports of the torture of a number of individuals in Djibouti during the period under review. Torture is reported to have been inflicted on both political and ordinary criminal detainees, including people suspected of minor infractions of the law such as traffic offences. An Amnesty International mission visited Djibouti in 1980 and confirmed reports of torture which had been received in previous years.

Torture is reported to have been inflicted by the *Brigade spéciale de recherche de la gendarmerie*, the Gendarmerie Special Research Brigade, the *Service de documentation et de sécurité*, the Documentation and Security Service, and the military security service. Methods of torture were reported to include beatings, immersion in water or the enforced swallowing of soapy water, blindfolding, and a method in which the victim is suspended from a rod placed behind the knees and through the crook of the elbows and beaten. An accountant, Saïd Abdillahi Moumine, is reported to have died on 26 June 1980 as a result of torture. In April 1980 he had been detained and allegedly tortured by officers of the *Service de documentation et de sécurité* for unknown reasons. He was then released but continued to be harassed and threatened, and on 25 and 26 June he was twice taken from the Peltier Hospital by security officers and apparently tortured. On the second occasion he is reported to have been returned to hospital in a coma and later to have died.

There appears to have been no inquest or inquiry into the death despite indications that it may have been caused by torture. In September 1980 it was reported that officers of the Gendarmerie Special Research Brigade inflicted torture as a routine punishment on many suspects held by them. Omar Ousmane Rabeh, a founding member of an opposition political party detained in October 1981, is reported to have suffered from impaired hearing as a result of his treatment in detention. In January 1983 Amnesty International received a detailed personal testimony describing torture allegedly inflicted by members of the *Brigade de recherches et de la documentation*, Research and Documentation Brigade. The victim claimed that the torture included beatings and immersion in water, and that it was inflicted as a result of a personal dispute with officers of the *gendarmerie*. However, Amnesty International was unable to confirm this report.

Ethiopia

Amnesty International received numerous reports during the period under review indicating the frequent torture of political prisoners in Ethiopia. Torture was used as a routine method of interrogating prisoners about their alleged knowledge of or involvement with opposition organizations, particularly those engaged in armed conflict against the government in Eritrea and certain other parts of the country.

Despite the serious nature of the reports of torture during the

period 1980-1983, torture had been much more extensive in the previous three-year period. Particularly during the official "red terror"
campaign of 1977-1978 against alleged counter-revolutionaries,
local security officials of the *kebelles*, urban dwellers' associations,
and peasant associations, were given virtually unlimited powers to
imprison and execute political opponents: tens of thousands of
alleged opponents, including many schoolchildren and students,
were imprisoned and tortured, and as many as 5,000 were believed
to have been killed.

Prisoners held at the Central Revolutionary Investigation
Department headquarters in Addis Ababa, known as "the
third police station", to which those arrested in the capital
and accused of serious political offences were generally taken, were
allegedly tortured as a matter of common practice during the period
under review. Torture was also used at the military police barracks
in Addis Ababa, and other police stations, interrogation centres
and prisons in the capital and in the regions, particularly in Eritrea.

Torture methods included beating on the soles of the feet, with
the victim tied to an inverted chair or hung upside down by the
knees and wrists from a horizontal pole; electric shocks; sexual
torture, including raping of women prisoners or tying a heavy weight
to the testicles; burning parts of the body with hot water or oil; and
crushing the hands or feet.

The victims included members of various "nationalities" or
ethnic groups arrested on suspicion of supporting armed organizations fighting for territorial independence. Torture was regularly
used to interrogate political prisoners in Eritrea, while several
hundred prominent members of the Oromo nationality imprisoned
in Addis Ababa in February 1980 were allegedly tortured for being
suspected supporters of the opposition Oromo Liberation Front.
Reports were also received of incidents of torture or ill-treatment of
members of the Ethiopian Evangelical Mekane Yesus Church
(particularly in Wollega district) and of certain of the smaller
Protestant evangelical or pentecostal churches, who were accused
of obstructing the revolution in various ways; members of the
Falasha community (or "Ethiopian Jews") imprisoned for
refusing to obey restrictions on practising their religion or for seeking
to emigrate without authorization; and a number of students and
others who were seeking asylum in various countries but were
forcibly returned to Ethiopia and reportedly arrested for their suspected links with opposition organizations abroad. In addition,
Amnesty International was investigating reports of torture of
people imprisoned for refusing to join the state militia, for protesting
about their conditions in state farms or in government resettlement
camps for displaced persons, or after being accused of being counter-

revolutionaries while undergoing compulsory political rehabilitation programs conducted at special "re-education" centres.

Gabon

Torture was reported to have been inflicted by several different security agencies in Gabon during the period under review. The alleged victims were political detainees, including people implicated in personal disputes with President El-Hadj Omar Bongo or his most prominent supporters.

Torture was most often reported to have been carried out by the political section of the police force, the *Centre de documentation* (CEDOC), Documentation Centre, which is apparently also known as the *Direction générale de la documentation*, Directorate-General for Documentation, by the army security service, the *Direction de contre-ingérence et de sécurité militaire* (DCISM), Directorate for Counter-Intelligence and Military Security, by sections of the *gendarmerie*, and by members of the presidential guard.

There were indications that people detained or imprisoned on a wide variety of charges were subjected to torture or ill-treatment in prison. One prisoner is reported to have been held in chains for part of his imprisonment after conviction in March 1981 for fraud. A group of 37 political detainees held throughout 1982, 29 of whom were subsequently convicted of crimes against state security and sentenced to long prison terms for criticizing the government and insulting the President, were ill-treated at Libreville's central civil prison, known as *Gros Bouquet* prison, all 37 being held incommunicado in small punishment cells. Some were beaten, apparently on the orders of CEDOC officers. One of the 37 prisoners, Michel Ovono, was reported to have been tortured with electric shocks, again apparently by CEDOC officers. Amnesty International has requested the government to release all of the 29 convicted people who are still serving prison sentences.

There were frequent reports of sometimes severe beatings with fists, clubs or other implements, some being carried out on the direct order of the authorities or even in the presence of senior officials or members of the government. Allegations of torture by electricity, immersion and hooding, which were frequent up to and including the early part of 1980, diminished in the period under review although reports of beatings continued. In most cases the apparent purpose of torture was as a technique of interrogation or to extract confessions.

The evidence of torture includes statements made by defendants at a political trial in November 1982 which was attended by an observer from Amnesty International.

André Angoue Aboghe alleged that he was tortured for five days at the headquarters of the *Brigade de recherches*, Research Brigade, while being interrogated, and Marc Nze Nkoghe alleged that he was similarly tortured at the *Brigade criminelle*, Criminal Investigation Brigade. Defendants were told by the presiding judge that the treatment of detainees was not the responsibility of the court. To Amnesty International's knowledge, no investigation was subsequently made into these allegations of torture or ill-treatment.

Ghana

Amnesty International received reports of ill-treatment, mainly beatings, inflicted by armed forces personnel in Ghana during the period under review. The pattern of ill-treatment appeared to change after 31 December 1981 when the civilian government of Dr Hilla Limann was replaced by the Provisional National Defence Council (PNDC) chaired by Flight-Lieutenant Jerry John Rawlings.

Under President Limann's government the victims of ill-treatment were people associated with the former government of the Armed Forces Redemption Council (AFRC), which had handed over to a civilian government in September 1979. According to information received by Amnesty International, soldiers and former soldiers suspected of sympathizing with the AFRC were harassed and beaten by officers of Military Intelligence, the main security agency. Some victims, such as ex-Captain Kojo Tsikata, were beaten but not detained. However, on several occasions during 1980 suspected political opponents of the government were reportedly arrested and beaten by officers of Military Intelligence while being held at Military Intelligence headquarters or at Nsawam prison. The beatings were apparently intended to secure confessions which would assist the conviction of suspected political opponents of the government.

Since the establishment of the PNDC on 31 December 1981, ill-treatment is reported to have been more frequent. It has apparently only rarely been inflicted on the direct orders of the government. There were widespread reports that people detained in military barracks were subjected to beatings with fists and rifle butts or were forced to do military drill to the point of exhaustion. Those singled out for beatings while in detention were either people suspected of corruption or soldiers suspected of opposition to the government. Dr Joseph de Graft Johnson, a former Vice-President, was reportedly hospitalized after suffering a severe beating at Burma Camp barracks in January 1982. Tata Ofusu, a member of the June the Fourth Movement, a left-wing political organization, was reported to have been tortured with a bayonet at PNDC headquarters after being detained in November 1982. This was apparently done to induce him to provide information about the activities of other members of the movement.

In most cases, beatings were inflicted by soldiers, who appeared to regard them as a routine punishment. Ill-treatment of this sort was apparently less frequent by the end of the period under review.

Guinea

Torture is regularly used in Guinea as a means of intimidating individuals taken into custody and of extracting confessions from them. Reports available to Amnesty International suggest that torture was regularly used in many of Guinea's military camps, prisons and police stations during the period under review and that it was inflicted by the main police and security forces, the army and the militia.

Although individuals arrested on suspicion of having committed ordinary criminal offences are frequently reported to be severely beaten when taken into custody, torture appears to be most commonly used in political cases. In cases known to Amnesty International the apparent reasons for arrest varied considerably. They ranged from alleged failure to comply with the directive of an official of the sole political party, the *Parti démocratique de Guinée* (PDG), Guinean Democratic Party, to alleged participation in a grenade attack apparently intended to kill senior government officials. Arrests for petty political offences reportedly took place on a regular basis in all of the country's major towns during the period under review. Failure to comply with a party directive, or to show enthusiasm for a party-organized collective task, often appeared sufficient reason to justify arrest and subsequent torture. Upon arrival at a police station, militia or army camp or prison, the suspect was usually subjected to severe beatings, often by several guards using rifle butts, sticks or truncheons. In many cases, the suspect was previously bound tightly with rope or metal wire, a practice which often left deep lacerations on the affected limbs and occasionally caused temporary paralysis. In other cases, the suspect was placed on a so-called *diète*, diet, involving deprivation of food, water or both for periods of up to one week and causing acute suffering and distress. Beatings and the *diète* were occasionally used to induce the suspect to sign a confession drafted by the authorities, which customarily contained the denunciation of others for similar offences. Amnesty International has received reports of such methods being used in many Guinean towns, including N'Zerekore, Kankan, Labe, Macenta, Kindia and the capital, Conakry.

Individuals arrested on suspicion of more serious political offences were usually transferred from their place of arrest and initial detention to either Camp Boiro in Conakry or Camp Keme Boureïma in Kindia. As many as 300 individuals were reportedly detained in waves of arrests which followed protests or strikes by students in Kindia and in Kankan between 1980 and late 1982, a grenade attack at the *Palais du Peuple*, People's Palace, in Conakry in May 1980 and an explosion at Conakry airport in February 1981. Amnesty International believes that most of these detainees were tortured. In addition to the use of severe beatings after being bound, and the regular use of the *diète* on arrival at either Camp Boiro or Camp Keme Boureïma, electric shocks were also reportedly applied to the head, limbs and genitals of detainees in these camps to obtain confessions. In such serious political cases, detainees were frequently forced to confess to being members of internal or international conspiracies allegedly aimed at overthrowing the Guinean government, and also to denounce alleged co-conspirators. Interrogations, the preparation of confessions and the application of torture were conducted by so-called *Commissions d'enquête*, commissions of inquiry, composed of high-ranking government officials. In some cases, torture sessions were repeated periodically over a period of two or three months, until a confession was signed or the workings of the *Commission d'enquête* completed.

Amnesty International has repeatedly expressed its concern regarding torture in Guinea in its published documents and has appealed to the government authorities for its cessation when individual cases of torture have been reported to the organization. No replies or comments have been received from the authorities, and there have been no reports of official investigations of torture allegations being launched or criminal proceedings being instituted against alleged torturers. According to the Guinean penal code, illegal arrests and detentions are punishable with imprisonment, and the torturer of any individuals so held is liable to a mandatory death sentence (Articles 295-297). In its Initial Report of August 1980 to the United Nations Human Rights Committee under the terms of the International Covenant on Civil and Political Rights, the Guinean authorities stated that ". . . torture and arbitrary arrest are unknown in the Revolutionary People's Republic of Guinea".

Kenya

There were a number of reports during the period under review of cases of torture and ill-treatment of prisoners while being held incommunicado in police or military custody for interrogation. Methods alleged to have been used to force prisoners to confess to a crime included beatings on various parts of the body including the sexual organs; electric shocks; being held naked for a lengthy period in a cell flooded with water; confinement in a small cell without light; and death threats. The allegations mainly concerned people arrested on suspicion of having committed a serious criminal offence or in connection with an unsuccessful attempt to overthrow the government by force in August 1982.

In Kenya statements proved to have been made under torture or duress are not admissible as evidence in court. In a number of cases since 1980 where defendants sought to retract statements which they alleged were made under torture, their claims were upheld by the court and those accused of being responsible for the torture were subsequently prosecuted and sentenced to imprisonment.

Lesotho

There were allegations of torture or ill-treatment of uncharged political detainees held incommunicado under security legislation in Lesotho. At least three such political detainees died in police custody in suspicious circumstances during the period under review although it was not known whether they had been subjected to torture or ill-treatment. The precise circumstances of their deaths were not revealed by the authorities and no inquests were known to have been held to independently determine the cause of death in each case. In another case, it was reported in July 1982 that Moeli Ts'Enoli, a former detainee, had committed suicide by burning himself alive, allegedly because he feared that he was about to be redetained and subjected to ill-treatment.

The Internal Security (General) Act of 1967 permitted the use of incommunicado detention without trial for renewable periods of 60 days. The act was replaced in September 1982 by new legislation, similarly titled, which reduced the maximum period of detention to 42 days and introduced certain checks and safeguards against abuse of detainees. However, in early 1983, cases were reported to Amnesty International in which detainees were held incommunicado beyond the stipulated 42-day period. The new act also effectively broadened police powers of detention by conferring on all police officers power to detain anyone incommunicado and without charge for up to 14 days. Under the former legislation, the Commissioner of Police was required to give written consent in advance for all detentions, but since the new act came into force responsibility for detentions up to 14 days has been blurred.

In practice, it appears that some people may have been repeatedly subjected to 14-day periods of detention by individual police officers who, by formally releasing and re-arresting them on the 14th day, circumvented the legal requirement that the Commissioner of Police should authorize further detention.

The government faced armed opposition from guerrilla fighters belonging to the Lesotho Liberation Army (LLA), the military wing of one faction of the Basutoland Congress Party (BCP), throughout the period under review. The LLA was responsible for many acts of sabotage and for the assassination of several government ministers and others. The victims of alleged torture and beatings were for the most part suspected supporters of the LLA or people considered likely to have knowledge of its activities. However, according to Amnesty International's information, some of those detained and ill-treated were not in fact supporters of the LLA and its policy of violent opposition to the government, but rather were non-violent critics of the administration.

Amnesty International sent two missions to Lesotho in late 1981, following a series of political killings apparently carried out by government supporters, more than 40 detentions and the death in custody of a political detainee. During the first mission in September 1981, Amnesty International's delegate obtained access to one detainee, Litsietsi Putsoa, a church official, who complained that he had been assaulted during interrogation by police officers. In December 1981, Amnesty International's delegate returned to Lesotho and obtained access to 10 detainees selected at random from more than 40 people then held in incommunicado detention. There was common consent that the detainees had not previously had contact with one another in detention but almost without exception they complained about the same forms of ill-treatment. They said that they had been covered with blankets and partially suffocated, that motor car tyres had been placed over the blankets restraining their arms, and that they had then been beaten through the blankets. The police had refused to tell them where they were held, and had subjected them to prolonged solitary confinement.

Amnesty International's delegate subsequently sought a meeting with Prime Minister Leabua Jonathan in order to put before him evidence of ill-treatment obtained from the detainees. In a letter to the Prime Minister, he drew attention particularly to the "*prima facie* evidence of brutal and potentially fatal systems of interrogation" he had obtained and to evidence of cruel and inhuman conditions of detention. The Prime Minister declined to meet Amnesty International's delegate and did not respond to his letter. Subsequently, reports received in 1982 and early 1983 suggested a similar pattern of torture and ill-treatment of uncharged detainees.

Mali

There were many reported instances of torture and ill-treatment of political detainees in Mali during the period under review, particularly in 1980. Although torture was occasionally inflicted to obtain confessions and information from detainees, its most usual purpose appears to have been to inflict pain and to punish. It was usually inflicted immediately after arrest or in the first few weeks after an individual was brought into custody. According to Amnesty International's information, torture was inflicted by members of the three major security forces in Mali, namely the police, the *gendarmerie* and the army.

In February 1980 a number of schoolgirls suspected of participating in protests by pupils and students in the Segou region were allegedly tortured with beatings and electric shocks. In March 1980, more than 300 students in schools and colleges were detained at the Djikoroni and Kati military camps following demonstrations in the capital, Bamako. These detainees were stripped and beaten with truncheons, sticks and whips; some were forced to run with heavy loads on their backs and were further beaten if they fell or stopped. Many of the detainees received wounds but were denied medical attention, in some cases for several days. Others had their feet and hands bound and were left exposed to the sun for prolonged periods. In their attempts to discover the whereabouts of other students, police arrested and ill-treated their relatives, including young children under the age of 10. On 15 March 1980, the authorities arrested and detained Abdul Karim Camara, nicknamed "Cabral", the leader of the main non-governmental school and college students' union. His death in custody was announced officially on 21 March, but the authorities failed to provide any information on the cause of death or to return his body to his family. According to several reports, Abdul Karim Camara died from injuries received under torture. He was reportedly hung by his feet and beaten with truncheons or heavy sticks as a result of which he sustained many bone fractures. His injuries also reportedly included burn marks. Amnesty International publicly called on the authorities to initiate an inquiry into the circumstances of his death and to provide reassurances about the conditions of several other pupils and students reported to have been tortured. No reply was received from the authorities but all the detained pupils and students were released several days after the appeal.

Between July 1980 and March 1981, more than 50 teachers were arrested in Bamako after the breakdown of negotiations with the authorities over teachers' demands for better pay. Following their arrest, they were detained in one of the police stations in Bamako, where some are believed to have been beaten and tortured with electric shocks. Some were taken to an isolated hut on the outskirts of Bamako, where they were interrogated and tortured with electric shocks applied to the soles of their feet. One teacher arrested in September 1980 was reportedly tortured at the *Brigade d'investigation criminelle*, Criminal Investigation Bureau, in Bamako.

Amnesty International believes that conditions at the Taoudenit Special Re-education Centre, where several political prisoners were reportedly held, were so harsh as to constitute cruel, inhuman or degrading treatment. The extreme temperatures of the Saharan region where the centre is situated as well as the severity of the prison regime make incarceration there a brutal form of punishment. Prisoners are reported to have died from the combined effect of poor nutrition, intestinal and heart complaints from the high salt content of available drinking water and exhaustion due to harsh daily work in salt mines. Prisoners were reported to be forced to march between 20 and 40 kilometres a day, barefoot and without cover. Amnesty International repeatedly expressed its concern regarding conditions at Taoudenit in its public documents and in its appeals to the Malian authorities. No replies or comments by the authorities have been received.

Malian legislation outlaws the use of "acts of violence against detainees" (Article 12 of Law 59-17 of January 1959) and its penal code (Article 186) stipulates that the torture of individuals subject to illegal arrest is punishable with the death penalty. In their report in March 1981 to the United Nations Human Rights Committee (established under the International Covenant on Civil and Political Rights, and acceded to by Mali in July 1974), the Malian authorities stated that they did not know of any proved cases of torture inflicted on detainees, but acknowledged that the "climate and regime were often rigorous" in their Saharan detention centres.

In their response of 6 January 1983 to inquiries from the United Nations Special Rapporteur for Arbitrary or Summary Executions, the Malian authorities stated that the case of Abdul Karim Camara, who reportedly died under torture in March 1980, had been declared "regrettable" by the Head of State General Moussa Traore and that "the Government [had] taken steps to bring to light all the facts in this matter". At the time of writing, Amnesty International had not received any information regarding this reported inquiry into the circumstances of the death of Abdul Karim Camara, nor had it been informed of any criminal proceedings having been instituted against alleged torturers.

Mauritania

In March 1982, as many as 150 suspected "Ba'athists" were arrested in the capital, Nouakchott, and were taken into custody by the police in Mauritania. Among them were civil servants, journalists, and other professionals. According to reports received by Amnesty International, most of these detainees were tortured either by being severely beaten or by being stripped and hung upside down by their feet. Some were reportedly burnt with hot coals. These cases of torture, which were the first in Mauritania to be reported to Amnesty International for many years, apparently took place in several *commissariats*, police stations, and at the *Caserne des Pomniers*, fire station, in Nouakchott.

Amnesty International was also concerned about the cruel, inhuman and degrading punishments imposed by the *Shari'a*, or Islamic law court, established in July 1980 to promote what the authorities termed "good, swift, and effective justice". In September 1980, three individuals found guilty of theft by the court had their right hands amputated in front of several thousand people in Nouakchott. After each amputation, which was carried out without general anaesthetic by a doctor, the amputated hand was held up for the crowd to see and then left tied to a rope. In its appeals to the government and to the medical association in Mauritania Amnesty International called for an end to these penalties and to the participation of medical personnel. Although no response was received from the authorities, it was learned that the medical association had protested vigorously to the authorities about the involvement of a member of the medical profession in the amputations. In June 1981, another individual convicted by the *Shari'a* court had his right hand amputated in front of a crowd at Nouakchott stadium. This amputation, as well as two other less well publicized ones in mid-1982, was reportedly carried out by a medical auxiliary.

The *Shari'a* court has also imposed numerous sentences of flogging for less serious cases of theft. In October 1980, nine people convicted of theft were flogged in public, each receiving between 10 and 30 lashes. In May 1981, 29 others were publicly flogged at Nouakchott stadium. Amnesty International appealed to the authorities to discontinue the use of such cruel and degrading punishment but it appeared that flogging remained in use throughout the period under review.

The conditions of imprisonment under which five convicted political prisoners were reported to be held from March 1982 for about a year at Jereida military camp, some 30 kilometres north of Nouakchott, appeared to constitute cruel, inhuman and degrading treatment. These prisoners, who included former Head of State Lieutenant-Colonel Moustapha Mohamed Ould Saleck and former Prime Minister Sid 'Ahmed Ould Bneijara, were arrested in early February 1982 and accused of plotting to assassinate President Lieutenant-Colonel Mohammed Khouna Ould Haidalla, who took office in January 1980. On 5 March 1982, the Special Military

Tribunal imposed heavy prison sentences on all five accused and ordered that their property be confiscated. At the time of sentencing, the tribunal's President, Major Sow Samba, was reported to have ordered that the prisoners be "subject to a severe detention regime, whereby they never see the light of day and their only contact is with the person who brings their food". According to reports received by Amnesty International, the five prisoners were held in underground cells so small that the prisoners were unable to lie down; the cells were insanitary, without any light and extremely poorly ventilated; food was reported to be very poor and prisoners were denied any exercise, visits or correspondence. In August 1982 and again in January 1983, Amnesty International appealed to the Mauritanian authorities urgently to improve the conditions under which these prisoners were being held but no reply was received. The prisoners were reported to have been taken out of the underground cells in May or June 1983, when their conditions of imprisonment were generally improved.

Mozambique

Amnesty International has received reports that prisoners in Mozambique have been subjected to severe beatings and torture during the period under review. The organization is also concerned that prisoners have been publicly flogged since flogging was introduced as a punishment additional to imprisonment in March 1983.

Reports of severe beatings have mainly concerned prisoners accused of supporting the *Resistência Nacional Moçambicana* (RNM), Mozambican National Resistance, an opposition group which has been engaged in an armed conflict with government forces. Amnesty International received reports during 1982 of public meetings organized by the security forces at which suspected members of the RNM were obliged to make confessions and were then subjected to beatings and physical assault.

Allegations that prisoners have been tortured have been made occasionally. During 1982, for example, a senior member of the National Security Service who sought asylum in South Africa was reported by official and unofficial sources in Mozambique to have been responsible for torturing prisoners. Fewer allegations of torture have, however, been made since 1980 than during the years immediately after independence in 1975.

In November 1981 President Samora Machel made a major speech to mark the beginning of a campaign against arbitrary arrest, torture and other abuses committed by members of the security forces. During this speech he said that torture had taken place and that the government was determined to put a stop to it. He claimed that torture had been used both as a punishment and to extort confessions and bribes. He concluded by stating that torture, beatings and corporal punishment were absolutely forbidden.

Both before and after this speech prison officers and others are reported to have been convicted of assaulting or beating prisoners.

In March 1983 a new law was adopted which provided for the legal use of flogging as a punishment additional to imprisonment to be imposed upon prisoners convicted on a wide range of charges, on the grounds that imprisonment alone was not a sufficient punishment to deter criminals. Under the new law offences punishable by flogging include armed assault, robbery, rape, murder, smuggling and black marketeering and also political offences varying from armed rebellion to "agitation".

Sentences of between three and 90 lashes may be imposed; however, only 30 lashes may be applied at a time and eight days must elapse before further lashes are inflicted. The law stipulates that floggings are to be carried out in public immediately after the sentence is announced. It is unclear whether normal rights of appeal are respected.

Article 8 of the law stipulates that it is applicable to cases not yet tried at the time it came into effect. Three days after it was adopted, 11 prisoners who had already been on trial in Maputo before the Revolutionary Military Tribunal were sentenced to floggings of between 10 and 45 lashes in addition to sentences of up to 12 years' imprisonment. They were convicted on charges of smuggling or black-marketeering, "rumour-mongering", and "agitation".

In April 1983 public floggings were reported in both Maputo and other parts of the country. After the introduction of flogging, Amnesty International repeatedly appealed to the Mozambican Government to repeal the new law and to prevent floggings from being carried out. However, no response was received from the authorities.

Namibia

Torture was used widely by South African security forces in Namibia on people detained on suspicion of supporting or sympathizing with the South West Africa People's Organization (SWAPO), which was engaged in guerrilla warfare against the South African administration throughout the period under review. The purpose of torture appeared to be to obtain information about SWAPO guerrillas and their supporters, and to intimidate the local population. Most torture allegations related to people held in incommunicado detention in northern Namibia, the most populous part of the country and the area in which SWAPO guerrillas were most active. However, there were also some reports of torture involving people detained in other parts of the country, mostly on account of their membership of, or alleged support for, the legal, internal wing of SWAPO. Several such detainees were said to have been held for some months in 1982 at a secret interrogation centre and there subjected to electric shocks and other forms of torture.

Many hundreds of people were believed to have been detained in northern Namibia during the period under review. Such arrests were particularly common in the Ovamboland and Kavango districts, two of nine so-called "security districts" which have been under an effective state of emergency since at least May 1979. In the security districts, all members of the South African security forces who hold either commissioned or non-commissioned rank have wide powers of arbitrary arrest and detention without trial. These are contained in Proclamation AG.9 of 1977, a decree issued by the South African Administrator-General. It empowers appropriate security personnel —both police and military—to detain anyone incommunicado and without charge for 30 days. Thereafter, further detention on an unlimited basis may be authorized by the Administrator-General. Such arrests need not be reported to detainees' relatives and the detainees may be held at any place the authorities decide, whether or not it is within a security district. Members of the security forces have legal immunity for any acts that they commit "in good faith". Detainees are subject to interrogation and are denied visits and access to legal counsel. Many AG.9 detainees were allegedly subject to torture by beatings and the application of electric shocks.

One group of more than 100 men and women detained under AG.9 provisions after being forcibly abducted from Angola by South African soldiers in May 1978, received better treatment. They were held at a camp near Mariental and were permitted visits from delegates of the International Committee of the Red Cross (ICRC). They were reportedly not liable to torture, although some of them are said to have been tortured in 1978 in the first months of their imprisonment. The ICRC was first granted access to them in 1979, by which time they had been moved to Mariental from inter-rogation centres in the north. However, similar provision for independent inspection of detention conditions by the ICRC was not extended by the authorities to places other than Mariental, in particular to the security police interrogation centre at Oshakati where many AG.9 detainees were said to have been tortured.

Two delegations of foreign clergy who visited Namibia in late 1981 both subsequently alleged that the use of torture and beatings was common and widespread. In a report published in May 1982, the Southern African Catholic Bishops' Conference (SACBC) said that its representatives had received allegations of electric shock torture, physical assaults, blindfolding and partial suffocation of detainees. It stated that it was "common knowledge" among clergy and others in Namibia that "detention and interrogation in any part of the country are accompanied by beating, torture, spare diet and solitary confinement". In the northern districts, many civilians were said to have been taken from their homes, blindfolded and beaten or killed by South African soldiers. Many women were said to have been raped. They and other victims of abuse often sought no redress because reporting irregularities or atrocities to military commanders was considered "a dangerous or fruitless exercise".

Before publication, the SACBC report was submitted to the South African Prime Minister for comment. He dismissed the allegations of torture but claimed that the authorities were prepared to act against security forces personnel who committed offences. Following publication, the SACBC report was banned by the South African Government and it was reported that its authors might face prosecution.

A British Council of Churches (BCC) delegation which visited Namibia in November 1981 found similar evidence of torture. It alleged that detainees had been beaten and given electric shocks and reported the widespread beating and rape of civilians. Like the SACBC, the BCC delegation found that victims of such abuses were afraid to make complaints or felt that they would receive no attention from the responsible authorities. Further allegations of torture were made in early 1982 by journalists who interviewed former detainees in the Kavango area and by the head of the local administration in Ovamboland.

As a result of these allegations, the South African authorities established a board of inquiry to investigate allegations of torture and other abuses of human rights. At least 40 complaints were investigated over the next few months: a few were reportedly substantiated but it is not known whether any of these related to torture. One is believed to have led to the prosecution of two soldiers for killing a civilian. A liaison committee was also established to investigate complaints in Ovamboland. It comprised representatives of the local administration, police and military officers but church leaders declined to participate on the grounds that it would not be impartial.

In late 1982, Amnesty International received information about the existence of a secret interrogation centre in which several AG.9 detainees had been tortured with beatings and electric shocks. The detainees concerned had been taken blindfold to and from the secret centre and had been permitted no contact with one another, nor any exercise outside their cells. They had each been held for several months but were ultimately released uncharged.

In November 1982, there were renewed allegations of torture following a wave of arrests in Kavango carried out by a special police counter-insurgency unit known as *Koevoet*, Crowbar. Two of the detainees, Jona Hamukwaya and Kadumu Katanga, died within hours of being taken into custody. It was alleged that they had been severely assaulted. The police announced that there would be an investigation but its outcome had not been disclosed by the end of May 1983. A number of other detainees, all of whom had been held under AG.9 provisions, were also allegedly assaulted. Several were later reported to be bringing court actions for damages against the responsible South African authorities.

Detailed allegations of torture were made in the Windhoek Supreme Court in early 1983 by former detainees in the Kaokoland area. They appeared as witnesses in a case brought by relatives of Johannes Kakuva, who had "disappeared" after being detained by security police in August 1980. The security police claimed that he had been released after agreeing to act as an informer, but several former detainees who had been held with him testified that he had died in detention as a result of torture. They described how they had been blindfolded, subjected to severe beatings and electric shocks and had heard Johannes Kakuva screaming when he too was assaulted.

In November 1982 Amnesty International appealed to South African Prime Minister P.W. Botha to take immediate steps to protect detainees in Namibia. Amnesty International called publicly for the repeal of Proclamation AG.9 of 1977 and for the establishment of an impartial judicial commission of inquiry into allegations of torture, alleged "disappearances" and extrajudicial executions. The South African Prime Minister did not respond to this appeal.

Rwanda

Amnesty International received detailed information about the torture of several people detained for political reasons in 1980 and 1981 and also about the extremely harsh conditions to which some political prisoners were subjected in Rwanda. Some reports also indicated that ordinary criminal suspects have been subjected to severe beatings and torture.

The *Service central de renseignements* (SCR), Central Intelligence Service, which is directly responsible to the President, was reported by a number of detainees to have been responsible for torture. The SCR interrogates detainees at its headquarters in Kigali and is also reportedly responsible for a special section in Ruhengeri prison, in the northwest of the country, where political detainees have allegedly been subjected to ill-treatment.

During the mid-1970s more than 30 political detainees in the custody of the SCR in Ruhengeri prison and other places are reported to have died in custody, as a result of torture, deprivation of food and water or extremely harsh conditions of imprisonment. Although these deaths have never been publicly acknowledged by the government, it does appear that from 1979 onwards steps were taken to control the service's activities and limit the use of torture.

In April 1980 the former SCR director, Théoneste Lizinde, was arrested and accused of planning to kill the head of state. During the following year more than 50 other people were arrested and accused of complicity in Lizinde's alleged plot. In about April 1981 Théoneste Lizinde and two other people are reported to have been subjected to torture, apparently to make them sign confessions of guilt. Another detainee, Stanislas Biseruka, is also reported to have been tortured: this apparently resulted in his suffering from partial paralysis of the hands and a dislocated hip. After seeking asylum in Uganda in 1980, he was kidnapped from Kampala in September 1981 and forcibly repatriated by Rwandese security agents. He was also reportedly tortured to make him confess to complicity in the plot.

The confessions and other information obtained from these four detainees was subsequently used as evidence at a trial before the State Security Court which lasted from September until November 1981. Although Stanislas Biseruka appeared in court using crutches, the court did not accept the allegations made by the detainees that they had been tortured while in custody, ruling that they did not show obvious marks of torture.

The most commonly reported forms of ill-treatment of detainees in the custody of the *gendarmerie* are severe beatings; detainees have reported being pushed to the ground and both hit and kicked. Some have apparently sustained bone fractures and other serious injuries as a result. Detainees held by the SCR have also reported being threatened with pistols and whips. More sophisticated methods of torture are reported to include electric shocks applied through either a special belt or electrodes placed on the genitals or on other parts of the body, and the insertion of needles under the victim's finger- and toe-nails.

In addition to receiving reports about individual acts of torture, Amnesty International has also been concerned about the prolonged confinement of political detainees in *cachots noirs*, dark cells, which have no windows and into which no light penetrates. Political prisoners arrested in 1980 and 1981 were sometimes held individually or with one other prisoner in such cells in Ruhengeri prison for periods varying from a few months to a year or more. Detainees are also reported to have been held in such cells in Kigali central prison. As a direct consequence of long-term imprisonment in total darkness some prisoners suffered from deterioration of their eye-sight and other health problems. Imprisonment in dark cells is explicitly prohibited under the terms of Article 31 of the United Nations Standard Minimum Rules for the Treatment of Prisoners.

During 1982 and 1983 Amnesty International appealed to the authorities to both prevent torture and transfer prisoners out of *cachots noirs*, and to improve such conditions of imprisonment as constituted cruel, inhuman or degrading treatment. In June 1983 President Juvénal Habyarimana denied that prisoners were held in inhuman conditions. However, in 1982 and again in 1983 he ordered inquiries into the reports of harsh conditions. In early 1983 several detainees were also transferred from *cachots noirs* to ordinary cells.

Somalia

Amnesty International received reports of the torture of a number of individuals arrested on political grounds in Somalia during the period under review. They were allegedly tortured by National Security Service (NSS) officers in the NSS headquarters in Mogadishu or in the maximum security prisons of Lanta Bur and Labatan Jirow. Torture methods alleged included beatings while tied in a contorted position, electric shocks, rape of women prisoners, being held naked in a dark cell, simulated execution and death threats.

Certain long-term political prisoners, including prisoners of conscience, were subjected to ill-treatment in Lanta Bur and Labatan Jirow prisons. They were held in prolonged solitary confinement, some in cells which were permanently dark, and others in cells which were permanently lit. Several of these prisoners suffered as a consequence from eye complaints, hypertension, and in some cases, nervous breakdowns.

South Africa

There was considerable evidence to show that political detainees were commonly tortured and ill-treated during interrogation by security police in South Africa during the period under review. Until July 1982 those concerned were for the most part people held uncharged under Section 6 of the Terrorism Act of 1967. In July

1982 this provision was repealed and effectively replaced by Section 29 of the Internal Security Act of 1982. Like Section 6 of the Terrorism Act, Section 29 of the Internal Security Act effectively provides the security police with the power to detain anyone incommunicado and without charges being laid for an unlimited period. Detainees held under both these provisions were held in solitary confinement, often for periods of many months, and were denied access to relatives or legal counsel. Many were reportedly subjected to lengthy periods of continuous interrogation by security police officers during which they were tortured or physically assaulted. Several detainees required treatment in hospital after becoming psychologically disoriented or physically unwell apparently as a result of their treatment and conditions of detention. At least six political detainees died in security police custody during the period under review, three of whom were held by security police in one or other of the four African "homelands" declared "independent" by the South African Government but not recognized internationally. Despite substantial evidence of torture in some of these cases, only one resulted in official action being taken against those allegedly responsible for torture. In this case, in the Venda "homeland", the two security police officers said by an official inquest to have tortured to death Isaac Tshifhiwa Muofhe, a political detainee, in November 1981, were acquitted by the Venda Supreme Court when brought to trial for his murder.

Many allegations of torture were made before the courts both by defendants and by detainees who appeared as witnesses for the prosecution in political trials. It was frequently alleged that detainees were tortured during pretrial interrogation by security police in order that they should either confess to offences which they had not committed or implicate other people in the commission of political offences. In the majority of cases, the courts appeared to accept police denials of torture at face value and to give insufficient consideration to the problems detainees faced, as a result of their incommunicado detention in solitary confinement, in proving that they had been tortured perhaps many months before. However, in some cases there was judicial acceptance that torture had been inflicted. One notable case was that of Linda Mario Mogale, a Soweto student leader whose seven-year prison sentence imposed two years before was revoked by the Appeal Court in June 1981. The Appeal Court accepted that he had been convicted largely on the basis of a confession which he agreed to make only after he had been subjected to electric shocks and had had some of his teeth pulled out with a pair of pliers by his security police interrogator. He had then been held for seven months so that there should be less evidence of torture and because a six-month limit existed beyond which victims of torture could not initiate legal actions for damages or redress. Following the Appeal Court judgment, it was reported that the authorities would take no action against the security police officer who had tortured Linda Mario Mogale because the latter had not laid a complaint against him within the specified time.

Detailed allegations of torture were made in 1982 by a number of former detainees who appeared as witnesses at the inquest into the death in detention of Neil Aggett, a white official of a black trade union. He had been arrested in late November 1981 together with other black and white trade union officials, students and political activists. He was reportedly found hanged in his cell at the Johannesburg security police headquarters on 5 February 1982, the first white detainee to die in security police custody. Prior to his death, Neil Aggett had twice complained of torture, alleging that he had been assaulted and subjected to electric shocks and sleep deprivation. At the inquest, detainees who had by chance seen or heard Neil Aggett while he was in detention testified in support of his torture allegations and about their own torture or ill-treatment at the hands of security police interrogators. It was also disclosed that shortly before his death Neil Aggett had been interrogated continuously for more than 60 hours. Nevertheless, the inquest magistrate accepted police denials of torture and ruled that Neil Aggett's death had not been induced by ill-treatment in detention.

In September 1982, the Detainees' Parents Support Committee (DPSC), a support organization formed to assist detainees, published a *Memorandum on Security Police Abuses of Political Detainees*. Based on 70 affidavits obtained from former detainees and already submitted to the authorities for investigation, this *Memorandum* alleged that "systematic and widespread torture is an integral feature of the detention system". It reported that common methods of torture included hooding and partial suffocation, the infliction of electric shocks, beatings with fists, sticks and other implements, and enforced suspension with the victim handcuffed in a crouching position and suspended by means of a pole inserted between the legs and arms. Detainees were said to have been made to stand for long periods sometimes holding heavy objects above their heads, to have been exposed to severe cold and subjected to prolonged sleep deprivation. They had been exposed to threats against their relatives or themselves and to deliberate humiliation and degradation through denial of toilet or washing facilities and by being interrogated while naked.

The DPSC said that it published the *Memorandum* because it was dissatisfied with the government's response to evidence of torture already submitted by the DPSC. It called for the introduction of adequate safeguards to protect detainees from ill-treatment and for an enforceable code of interrogation practice. In November 1982, the government issued new guidelines for security police treatment of detainees, stipulating that they must not be tortured or ill-treated, but these constituted little more than a restatement of earlier guidelines which had proved ineffective.

Torture and ill-treatment of ordinary criminal suspects was also reported and there was a high rate of deaths in custody—more than 300 between the beginning of 1980 and the end of 1982—among people arrested for questioning about criminal matters. It was not known, however, to what extent some of these may have been the result of torture or ill-treatment. A number of cases did lead to the prosecution of police officers allegedly responsible for assaulting or killing ordinary criminal suspects apparently while attempting to extract confessions from them.

Amnesty International took action on behalf of many detainees who were torture victims and made public its concerns in a number of documents. In late 1982 the organization campaigned against torture in South Africa and called both for the establishment of an impartial inquiry into allegations of torture and for the repeal of legislation permitting indefinite incommunicado detention without trial.

Uganda

There were many reports during the period under review indicating the extensive infliction of torture in Uganda on large numbers of people arrested on political grounds or on suspicion of supporting armed opposition movements, and detained illegally in military custody. Many people held in these circumstances died as a result of torture or "disappeared".

Torture and killing of prisoners had been widespread and systematic during the military government of President Idi Amin from 1971 to 1979. The security agencies principally involved in committing these abuses were the State Research Bureau, the police Public Safety Unit, and certain army units, in particular those based at Makindye barracks in Kampala, where many suspected opponents of the government were tortured and killed.

In the year following the overthrow of President Amin in April 1979 by the Tanzanian army and Ugandan guerrilla organizations, torture appeared to have become routine again in certain establishments of the new Ugandan army, the Uganda National Liberation Army (UNLA), notably in Makindye military barracks. In late May 1980 Amnesty International expressed concern to Paulo

Muwanga, who chaired the Military Commission which had recently taken power, about the reported torture in military custody of James Namakajo, a former presidential press officer, and Roland Kakooza, a journalist. Amnesty International received further reports in 1980 of civilians detained illegally and incommunicado in Makindye barracks and beaten with rifle butts and sticks, whipped with barbed wire, denied food for days at a time, wounded with bayonets, or shot dead. Amnesty International's appeal to the Military Commission in August 1980 to establish an inquiry into the reports of torture at Makindye and Malire barracks received no response.

President Milton Obote's government took office in December 1980 as a result of his party, the Uganda People's Congress, winning the parliamentary elections. New reports of torture were received by Amnesty International in 1981. A prisoner detained in Makindye Barracks in mid-January 1981 stated that he was beaten unconscious with gun butts and metal wire, denied food and water for three days and routinely beaten along with numerous other prisoners.

On 6 February 1981 two opposition guerrilla organizations, the People's Revolutionary Army (later re-named the National Resistance Army) and the Uganda Freedom Movement, launched attacks on several military, police and prison establishments. In response the Ugandan army arrested hundreds of officials and members of opposition political parties—the Democratic Party and the Uganda Patriotic Movement in particular—including several members of Parliament. Further widespread arrests took place later in the year following renewed guerrilla activities. Those arrested were mostly held illegally in military custody without official acknowledgment. Many were tortured under interrogation as suspected guerrillas while being held in incommunicado detention, although it appeared that some people were arrested with the objective of forcing them or their relatives to pay large ransoms for their release.

Torture took place in the Nile Mansions military intelligence offices in Kampala; Makindye, Malire and Mbuya barracks in Kampala; Kireka barracks near Kampala; Katabi barracks in Entebbe; and certain private houses and offices in Kampala (such as the Milton Obote Foundation offices) which were under the control of military intelligence or security officers. Torture methods included beatings with sticks, electric cables, hammers, iron bars and guns; bayoneting and shooting in the limbs; rape of women prisoners; and burning of the sexual organs. Many prisoners were killed or died of their injuries.

Following a guerrilla attack on Malire barracks in Kampala on 23 February 1982, over 100 people were arrested by the army in the adjoining Rubaga Cathedral area, from where the attack was made. Amnesty International received reports that the bodies of several people taken for interrogation to Makindye barracks were later found bearing marks of torture. Amnesty International submitted to the government the names of some of the prisoners who were allegedly tortured and killed at Makindye barracks but the government claimed that all those arrested had been released.

During March and April 1982 thousands of people were arrested in security operations in Kampala, and many were detained on suspicion of having guerrilla sympathies. In April 1982 Amnesty International publicly appealed to President Milton Obote to investigate reports of torture and killings of some of these prisoners in Katabi barracks in Entebbe. However, no independent inquiry has been established to investigate these allegations of torture or others made later.

Detailed testimonies of torture were received from prisoners who had been held during 1981-1982 in Makindye, Mbuya and other barracks, Nile Mansions military intelligence offices, and a private house in Kampala. Amnesty International also learned of torture in military barracks in other parts of the country, for example in Bombo, Masaka, Tororo and Soroti, although the practice was said not to be so extensive as in military establishments in or near the capital. In contrast, prisoners held in police custody or in civil prisons such as Luzira Upper prison, who were either charged with ordinary criminal offences and were awaiting trial or detained indefinitely without charge or trial under the Public Order and Security Act, were apparently not tortured.

An Amnesty International mission visited Uganda in January 1982 and raised with President Obote and government officials the organization's concerns about human rights violations. The government denied the allegations of torture.

In a memorandum to the government in August 1982, Amnesty International referred to numerous reports of the systematic use of torture in certain military establishments and urged the government to take effective measures to protect all prisoners, particularly those held in military establishments, from torture or ill-treatment. The organization called on the government to affirm publicly that torture or complicity in torture were serious criminal offences, and to investigate all allegations of torture and bring to justice those found to be responsible for torture. The organization also called for a special inquiry into torture in Makindye and Kireka barracks and the military interrogation offices in Nile Mansions in Kampala.

The government's reply of 1 September 1982 made no substantive reference to the subject of torture. The government provided no information on any investigations into reports of torture by military personnel, and gave no specific undertaking to investigate such allegations in the future.

Amnesty International subsequently reiterated its recommendations and appealed to the government to take measures to give force to its stated commitment to the rule of law and the protection of human rights. The organization continued to receive frequent allegations of torture in early 1983.

Zaire

Amnesty International received detailed reports concerning more than 100 prisoners who were reportedly tortured during the period under review, indicating that political detainees in particular were subjected to torture and beatings while in the custody of various branches of the security forces in Zaire. Prisoners of conscience were among those allegedly tortured.

Reports were also received concerning torture and beatings of ordinary criminal suspects, which appeared to be frequent. For example, during the first two months of 1983, 11 people accused of theft or armed robbery were reported to have died in the Kinshasa area as a result of torture and ill-treatment.

Various branches of the civilian security services, the armed forces and the *gendarmerie* have authority to carry out arrests and are said to have been responsible for torturing prisoners held uncharged in incommunicado detention at special detention centres. Investigating judges are also occasionally reported to have threatened suspects or ordered them to be beaten while questioning them.

Severe beatings were the most regularly reported form of ill-treatment. They were inflicted with soldiers' belts, rifle butts and truncheons and sticks of various sorts. Detainees were often beaten at the time of arrest and were sometimes subjected to daily beatings throughout their detention by the security forces. In mid-1982, for example, political detainees at a detention centre in Bukavu were said to be woken in the morning, often made to drink their own urine and then beaten by guards on their backs and shoulders.

Among methods of torture used by the various branches of the security forces the following have also been reported: the infliction of electric shocks to the body, particularly to limbs and genitals; the administration of drugs, apparently to debilitate detainees; the insertion of sticks between the victim's fingers, which are then crushed together; and tying prisoners up extremely tightly and sometimes exposing them in the sun for long periods. Many detainees were also held for several days immediately after their arrest without receiving food or drink. On several occasions during 1982 women arrested for political reasons are reported to have been raped by their guards.

After an indefinite period of detention by the security forces, prisoners may be charged and transferred to a civil or military prison where they are no longer held incommunicado. Torture is not reported to take place, in such prisons, nor are convicted prisoners held at such prisons known to have been tortured. However, in some prisons prisoners are reported to have been punished by being deprived of food for long periods, by being held in leg-irons or by being held in total darkness.

Most newly arrested people who remained in the custody of the security forces while their cases were investigated appeared liable to beatings, but it seems that two particular categories of prisoner, political detainees and people arrested on suspicion of involvement in armed robberies, were most frequently subjected to ill-treatment as a form of punishment and in order to obtain confessions.

Most of the evidence of torture received by Amnesty International comes from the testimonies of former political prisoners. In some cases Zairians who have left their country have been examined by doctors working on behalf of Amnesty International. For example, in 1980 doctors in Europe examined 80 Zairians who had apparently been detained. The doctors found that 60 of them bore marks on their bodies which appeared consistent with their allegations of torture and beatings. Other reports of torture have been sent to Amnesty International from Zaire itself, sometimes from people still in prison and sometimes from others in Zaire who have themselves obtained detailed reports of the use of torture.

Amnesty International has repeatedly called on the authorities to take steps to prevent torture from occurring and has also appealed on behalf of individual victims of torture. During 1980 and 1981, before and after representatives of the organization visited Kinshasa for talks in July 1981, Amnesty International submitted three separate communications to the government, all of them containing details of the organization's concern over torture. Amnesty International urged the authorities to institute safeguards against torture and recommended particularly that the practice of holding detainees incommunicado for long periods should be discontinued. However, reports received subsequently indicate that detainees continue to be held incommunicado and to be tortured and still have no effective means of redress. Even when allegations have been formally reported by victims to court authorities, in most cases reported to Amnesty International no official investigations of the allegations are known to have taken place.

The government's response to Amnesty International has been to draw attention to Article 13 of the constitution, which specifically prohibits torture, and generally to deny that torture takes place. It seems, however, to have failed to promote official investigations of torture allegations or to have taken any significant steps to reduce the opportunities for such abuses to occur.

From time to time, junior members of the *gendarmerie* have been accused of abusing detainees and prosecuted. However, the number of such cases has been extremely small in relation to what Amnesty International perceives to be the extent of the problem. Members of the civilian and military security services whose names have appeared regularly in detainees' torture allegations do not appear to have been subject to investigation and seem to be virtually immune from prosecution.

Zambia

Several people arrested in connection with an alleged plan to free 13 defendants in a treason trial were reported to have been tortured in mid-1981 in Zambia while detained incommunicado by security personnel. Six of the seven treason trial defendants who were ultimately convicted and sentenced to death in January 1983 also alleged in May 1983 that they had been ill-treated when they were moved to Kabwe maximum security prison after their death sentences had been imposed.

In October 1980, President Kenneth Kaunda announced that a plot to overthrow the government by force had been discovered and thwarted shortly before it was due to be put into effect. A number of arrests were made but it was not until May 1981 that 13 people were eventually charged with treason. A few weeks later, before the trial had begun, the authorities carried out further arrests and announced that those detained had been planning to help the treason trial defendants escape from custody. Those held included both civilians and junior-ranking members of the armed forces. In most cases, the detainees were initially held incommunicado under police detention orders of up to 28 days' duration and then served with presidential orders of unlimited duration. None of those detained had been charged in connection with the alleged escape plan by the end of May 1983 although they had by then been in custody for almost two years.

Those detained in mid-1981 included two lawyers, one of whom, Nkaka Chisanga Puta, was legal counsel to Valentine Musakanya, a leading defendant in the treason trial. Nkaka Chisanga Puta was arrested on 2 July 1981 at Ndola. He was then taken to Lilayi police training camp near Lusaka where he was allegedly threatened and tortured during three days' interrogation. His relatives were not informed of his whereabouts. In December 1981, the Lusaka High Court awarded him damages for "inhuman treatment" after accepting that he had been stripped naked, made to do strenuous physical exercise and beaten about the face and back with a stick while being interrogated at Lilayi. However, the court refused to declare his detention unlawful and order his release.

Ronald Chansa, an army major, was also arrested in connection with the escape plan. He too was allegedly beaten at Lilayi and threatened with death by security officers who questioned him. He was then reportedly blindfolded and taken to a secret interrogation centre where he was subjected to electric shocks and tortured by having objects inserted into his penis and anus. He was said to have suffered permanent injuries as a result.

Faustinos Lombe was also allegedly tortured. He was arrested in July 1981, having been released from more than two years' detention without trial only four months earlier. He was allegedly subjected to ill-treatment similar to that of Ronald Chansa and other detainees.

In May 1983, six people who had been sentenced to death for treason four months earlier took court action in an attempt to improve the allegedly inhuman conditions they had been subjected to in Kabwe Prison. They complained that their treatment had been deliberately severe and that prison authorities had harassed them constantly, denied them adequate medical treatment and not permitted them to receive visits to which they were entitled. They alleged that tear-gas had been fired into one cell and that they had been beaten by prison staff. The case was still in progress at the end of May 1983.

Torture and the infliction of "inhuman or degrading punishment or other treatment" is prohibited under the constitution. On a number of occasions in the 1970s, there was judicial acceptance that detainees had been tortured or ill-treated under interrogation and in several cases the Appeal Court ordered the state to compensate the victims concerned. However, no action appears to have been taken by the government in the light of those cases, or other allegations made during the period under review, to investigate the use of torture or to discipline members of the security services allegedly responsible for torturing political detainees.

Zimbabwe

Amnesty International received no reports of torture for almost two years after Zimbabwe achieved independence in April 1980, but allegations were received with increasing frequency from early 1982. They coincided with a period of serious political instability which reached its height in the first months of 1983 when many hundreds of people were detained, tortured or killed in the Matabeleland area.

Torture was used extensively throughout the 1970s under the Rhodesian administration headed by Prime Minister Ian Smith. The government led by Prime Minister Robert Mugabe which came to power in 1980 retained emergency powers providing for detention without trial and renewed the national state of emergency in force since 1965 at six-monthly intervals throughout the period under review. However, in November 1980, the government repealed the Indemnity and Compensation Act which had effectively denied torture victims access to the courts to seek redress since its introduction by the previous Rhodesian administration in 1975. It was repealed after a cabinet minister invoked it successfully to obtain his acquittal on a murder charge. Subsequently, following new allegations of torture, the former Indemnity and Compensation legislation was reintroduced in July 1982, virtually unchanged, by government decree.

Allegations of torture or ill-treatment were made in early 1982 following the arrest in December 1981 of suspected opponents of the government. Wally Stuttaford, a white member of parliament, was held incommunicado for the first month after his arrest and was assaulted during interrogation. He was kicked and punched, made to do strenuous physical exercise although aged over 60, and had his hair pulled violently, apparently in an attempt to make him confess to conspiring against the government. Pencils were inserted between his fingers and his hands were then squeezed. When his lawyers gained access to him, they arranged for a medical examination which found evidence of his having been ill-treated.

In June 1982, Wally Stuttaford brought a civil action for damages against the government as a result of his ill-treatment. The authorities ordered that the action should be heard *in camera* and that the outcome should not be disclosed for reasons of security. However, unofficial sources indicated that the action had been successful and that the High Court had awarded Wally Stuttaford substantial compensation. It was shortly after judgment in this case that the former Indemnity and Compensation legislation was reintroduced under the Emergency Powers Regulations.

In February 1982 the government announced the discovery of arms caches on farms owned by the Patriotic Front (PF) party and dismissed Joshua Nkomo and other PF leaders from the cabinet. There was an outbreak of violence apparently by supporters of the PF. These included former guerrilla fighters, some of whom had deserted from the national army and some of whom had earlier been demobilized. Acts of banditry were committed, some civilians were killed and there was sabotage of government property. Many people were arrested by government security forces, particularly in Matabeleland, the PF's political stronghold. A number of detainees, including in particular alleged army deserters, were reportedly beaten or tortured during interrogation by members of the Central Intelligence Organization (CIO), which is responsible to the Prime Minister's Office. Unconfirmed reports suggest that several detainees may have died in custody as a result of torture or ill-treatment: they were said to include Collen Mhlanga, an army lieutenant arrested in April 1982.

Further arrests and allegations of torture were made following incidents in mid-1982. In June shots were fired at the residence of Prime Minister Mugabe; in July six foreign tourists were abducted by anti-government rebels and aircraft at the main air force base at Gweru were destroyed through sabotage. The tourists' abduction led to an intensive search of Matabeleland North province by the security forces. In all, hundreds of people were said to have been detained for questioning by police or army units, and many were reportedly assaulted. Journalists and others who visited the area witnessed beatings of civilians by soldiers.

In October 1982 lawyers representing three out of at least 11 air force officers detained following the sabotage incident at Gweru alleged publicly that they had been subjected to torture by CIO interrogators. Hugh Slatter and Peter Briscoe were said to have been threatened, hooded and subjected to electric shocks while detained incommunicado under the Emergency Powers Regulations. The third officer, Philip Pile, was also said to have been threatened and, like Hugh Slatter and Peter Briscoe, to have become psychologically disoriented as a result of ill-treatment. A doctor called in to examine the three detainees found evidence corroborating their allegations. The lawyers who made these disclosures were subsequently charged with making subversive statements and contempt of court. In November 1982 the Justice Minister announced that the torture allegations would be investigated if they were accepted at the air force officers' trial.

After a new outbreak of killings by anti-government rebels in late 1982, the government deployed the army's Fifth Brigade in

Matabeleland North in late January 1983. It immediately embarked on a policy of brutal repression which resulted in many hundreds of civilians being killed or seriously injured. Local officials of the PF and former members of its military wing during the pre-independence period were particular objects of attack, but there were also widespread allegations of indiscriminate beatings, bayonetings and summary killings. These continued for several weeks despite growing protests from church leaders, representatives of non-governmental agencies and PF political leaders. By mid-1983 the situation had become calmer but the government had not responded to appeals for the withdrawal of the Fifth Brigade. An internal government inquiry was promised soon after the first allegations were made and, while the Matabeleland situation was the subject of international publicity, appeared to have produced no results by the end of April 1983.

* * * *

In addition to the countries mentioned above, Amnesty International received allegations of some cases of torture or ill-treatment from Benin, Burundi, the Gambia, Guinea-Bissau, the Ivory Coast, Liberia, Madagascar, Niger, Nigeria and Sudan during the period under review.

From Benin, Amnesty International received information that severe overcrowding regularly occurred at the *Commissariat central*, central police station, in the capital, Cotonou, where up to 30 detainees were held in a cell known as *la grille*, the cage, approximately three metres wide by four metres long. During the period under review, as many as eight detainees were at various times held in cells measuring only three metres by one and a half metres. Only a few detainees had room to lie down and others were forced to remain standing. Detainees experienced these grossly overcrowded conditions for periods lasting as long as several months. Some detainees held on political grounds were reportedly subjected to a form of ill-treatment known as *le rodéo*, the rodeo, in which they were forced to run or crawl carrying heavy weights until exhausted.

In Burundi, it was reportedly common for people suspected of ordinary criminal offences to be beaten and sometimes tortured during interrogation while being held in the Central Police Commissariat or the cells situated at the *Palais de Justice* in Bujumbura. These beatings were allegedly inflicted with a variety of blunt instruments, including iron bars. In a few cases, it was reported that suspects had been deliberately wounded with knives and subjected to electric shocks on their hands and genitals with an electric cable tied to the end of a stick.

In the course of a mission to the Gambia in August 1982, Amnesty International representatives expressed concern to the authorities over reports that 36 prisoners sentenced to death in trials since December 1981 were being held in leg-irons, a form of treatment which is specifically banned by international standards. In subsequent meetings during the mission, the authorities informed Amnesty International's representatives that they had carried out an investigation which had confirmed these reports; the authorities announced, however, that the use of leg-irons would not be discontinued, for reasons of security. In December 1982, following new appeals from Amnesty International, the authorities informed the organization that they had ordered the total abolition of the use of leg-irons in the Gambia.

In Guinea-Bissau prior to the coup in November 1980 it was reported that political detainees had been tortured at the headquarters of the Second Police Squadron, next to the Ministry of the Interior in Bissau. Since November 1980 Amnesty International has received further allegations of beatings of political suspects, some of whom have also been held in harsh and degrading conditions, particularly at the *Prisão de Marinha*, Naval Prison, in Bissau. Three detainees arrested at the time of the November 1980 coup are known to have died in prison. In one case, official sources claimed that the body of a former police inspector, who died at Brá detention camp in May 1982, bore marks of torture.

In the Ivory Coast, Amnesty International was concerned about the ill-treatment of detainees who were among several hundred people arrested on 6 March 1981 in the course of a police operation to suppress urban crime. Forty-six people died of suffocation in a cell at the *gendarmerie* barracks at Agban, having apparently been crowded into a cell built to hold no more than five prisoners. There were no reports of proceedings being instituted against the *gendarmerie* officials responsible. Amnesty International was also concerned about reports that migrant workers from the Upper Volta and Ghana had apparently been singled out by the Ivory Coast authorities for arbitrary arrest and ill-treatment in detention at the time of the March 1981 operation and on subsequent occasions. Many of these detainees were allegedly given repeated beatings at the *Commissariat central*, central police station, and *Ecole de Police*, Police Training School.

Immediately following the April 1980 coup in Liberia, several hundred former officials of the overthrown government and relatives or associates of the late President William Tolbert were arrested and detained. In the first three months after their arrest, many of them were reported to have been regularly beaten by soldiers while being held in the Post Stockade and South Beach prisons in Monrovia. These beatings were allegedly inflicted with sticks, whips and car fan belts. It was also reported that people suspected of ordinary criminal offences were subjected to whipping by police officers as a matter of routine throughout 1981 both in the street and in police stations.

In Madagascar, several political prisoners were reported to have been tortured, usually at the headquarters of the political police in Ambonibao. One prisoner was allegedly burnt with an electric cattle prod, and another was allegedly forced to drink acid. Beatings and the use of psychological pressure were also reported. At the beginning of the period under review there were reports that prisoners were ill-treated in some prisons under the authority of the civilian prison service. Amnesty International has received no reports of torture or ill-treatment since early 1982.

In Niger, two political detainees were alleged to have died as a result of ill-treatment at the hands of the security forces in May 1982. Siddo Hassane, a former trade union leader, and another detainee, a former *gendarme*, were alleged to have died of suffocation when held in a small, poorly ventilated cell in Tillabery prison. Amnesty International appealed to the authorities to confirm these reported deaths in detention and to establish an official inquiry to determine responsibility for them. No answer was received from the authorities.

Amnesty International received no reports of torture in Nigeria during the period under review. However, in March 1980 one incident of ill-treatment occurred which resulted in some 50 deaths. The victims were among 68 people who had appeared in court in Lagos on vagrancy charges and had been remanded in custody. The police responsible for their transfer to Ikoyi prison forced all of them into a vehicle designed to hold no more than 20 people with the result that, on arrival at the prison, 47 of them were found to have died of suffocation. Three others subsequently died in hospital. After these deaths, President Shagari is reported to have ordered a judicial inquiry, but it is not known whether those who conducted the inquiry made a report or whether any of their recommendations were enforced.

In Sudan, the treatment of some prisoners accused of seeking to overthrow the government gave cause for concern. Some prisoners held in military custody were allegedly ill-treated while under interrogation. Such allegations concerned prisoners in the State Security Service headquarters in Khartoum and the Dabak military camp near that city.

In Tanzania, prosecutions of alleged torturers were among a number of measures taken by the authorities which led to some improvements in the protection of prisoners from torture and ill-treatment during the period under review. In two separate trials in 1980/1981, 12 senior security and police officers were sentenced to prison terms ranging from five to eight years for causing the death by torture of prisoners arrested in Mwanza and Shinyanga during 1976. They had led a security operation, acting on the instructions of a special high-level security committee headed by the then Prime Minister, Rashidi Kawawa, which was inquiring into a wave of unsolved murders in the two regions. According to evidence produced in court, over 800 men and women had been arrested and systematically tortured by police and security officers. Torture methods included beatings and floggings, particularly on the genitals; deprivation of food and water; and the insertion of hot pepper into the bodily orifices. Medical treatment for the victims was denied. The prosecutions related to the deaths of four of the prisoners, but several more were said to have died as a result of the torture.

THE AMERICAS

Argentina

Both political and ordinary criminal suspects were routinely tortured in Argentina during the period under review. Throughout the country local police forces have resorted to torture as an habitual method of criminal investigation in order to extract signed confessions to alleged criminal acts. It is, however, in the sphere of politically-motivated detention that torture has been most extensive.

In 1975 the Armed Forces established a secret repressive structure to counter "subversion" with the policy of massive planned "disappearance" as its principal weapon. These illegal procedures were consolidated and extended after the coup of 24 March 1976 and, as a result, thousands of people entered the world of the *detenidos-desaparecidos* ("disappeared" detainees). From 1976 to 1979 "disappearances" virtually replaced formal arrest and detention procedures. Without legal guarantees and with all contact with families and friends broken, there was no check on torture or ill-treatment, to which the "disappeared" were invariably subjected. Amnesty International had collected evidence about these conditions from more than 100 individuals who were held for varying periods in one or more of the 47 secret camps identified by human rights groups and situated throughout the country, in barracks, military outbuildings, police stations and safe-houses. Some of these "disappeared" prisoners were transferred to official prisons and their detention was acknowledged; others were simply released.

These testimonies show that torture was used as an instrument of policy. Furthermore, the "disappeared" prisoners were held in degrading physical conditions: they were hooded and chained and kept in filthy cells. They were refused washing and toilet facilities, poorly nourished, and subjected to frequent threats, verbal abuse and mock executions. According to Amnesty International's own records 5,000 people who were abducted by the police, military or security forces between 1975 and 1981 are still not accounted for and it is feared that many have been killed and their bodies buried in unmarked graves.

Since 1980, as the number of abductions has diminished, the scale of torture has been reduced but the practice has not been eradicated. Torture was usually inflicted during the initial stage of detention, even when the arrest has been officially acknowledged. The most common methods of torture during the period under review were the following: electric shocks applied to all parts of the body with the *picana eléctrica* (electric cattle prod); *"submarino"*: immersion in water with the head covered by a cloth hood—when this becomes wet, it sticks to the nose and mouth and when the victim is taken out of the water breathing is practically impossible; beatings with fists, truncheons, rifle butts and sticks; kicks; cigarette burns; plunging victims into ice cold baths; keeping victims hooded; forcing prisoners to stand in awkward positions for hours; depriving prisoners of food, drink and sleep.

Amnesty International has issued urgent appeals on behalf of more than 30 people who were abducted allegedly by the police or security forces. In 15 of these cases Amnesty International has received reliable reports that the victims were tortured, most commonly with the *picana eléctrica* while in custody in police stations or military barracks. In nine cases, two of which occurred on 14 May 1983, the victims were subsequently killed.

Amnesty International knows of no instance in which the judicial authorities have instituted an investigation into allegations of torture inflicted on people detained for political motives. However, as a result of the public outcry at the kidnapping and killing of Osvaldo Cambiaso and Eduardo Pereira in May 1983 three agents of the Buenos Aires Provincial Police were arrested and accused of homicide.

Following the visit to Argentina by the Inter-American Commission on Human Rights (IACHR) in 1979, some of the worst abuses were checked but Amnesty International continues to receive reports of torture and the arbitrary ill-treatment of political prisoners for alleged infractions of minor prison regulations.

In March 1982 the Buenos Aires Bar Association deplored the judiciary's failure to guarantee the right to life, liberty and physical integrity of detainees and stated that, "the existence of torture as a system of police investigation is a notorious and indisputable fact". The Bar Association recommended a number of measures to prevent extrajudicial confessions resulting from ill-treatment and torture and to regularize detention procedures.

Some efforts have been taken by the judiciary to curb the torture of ordinary criminal suspects. In the course of 1982,

35 police officers were subjected to criminal proceedings for alleged ill-treatment of detainees. In Mar del Plata a court is to investigate the case of five police officers accused of torturing, in October 1982, five youths aged between 14 and 17.

On 6 October 1982 the Court of Appeals in La Plata ordered the release of a prisoner who had served four years' imprisonment after being convicted of homicide on the grounds that the confession of the accused had been extracted under torture. In November 1982 the Supreme Court, following allegations that a judge, Laura Damianovich de Cerredo, had condoned the torture of prisoners, called for an investigation into her conduct.

On 10 September 1982 the Minister of the Interior, General Llamil Reston, ordered provincial governors to take steps to eliminate the use of torture or brutality by provincial and municipal police, and to take severe measures against officers found guilty of excesses.

However, the Argentine *junta* has persistently refused to account for the thousands of "disappeared" detainees and has failed to bring to justice members of the police, military and security forces who have been accused of torture and other human rights violations in connection with these "disappearances". Repeated requests for information on these cases by the United Nations Working Group on Enforced or Involuntary Disappearances and by the Inter-American Commission on Human Rights of the Organization of American States have gone unanswered.

At the time of writing (June 1983) an amnesty law is under consideration in Argentina. There are fears that should this law be passed it will further impede judicial investigations into the history of repression in the country, including the practice of torture.

Bolivia

Although the civilian government of Lidia Gueiler, which took office in January 1980, took measures to defend human rights and the rule of law, isolated incidents of torture were reported during the period under review. Such incidents did not occur in official detention but at the hands of paramilitary groups linked to sectors of the military which later supported the July 1980 military coup. On 22 March 1980 such a paramilitary group reportedly tortured and killed Father Luís Espinal, a Jesuit priest and editor of the magazine *Aquí*.

After the military coup in July 1980 led by General Luís García Meza, Amnesty International began to receive persistent reports of the torture of political prisoners held in incommunicado detention. Moreover, it became apparent that the military authorities sanctioned or even encouraged irregular detention procedures in violation of the constitution and other guarantees protecting individual rights and freedoms. The right of *habeas corpus* was effectively suspended. In Amnesty International's view, such a situation facilitated torture and ill-treatment both on arrest and in detention.

Widespread arrests occurred after the coup throughout the country, partly as a result of the ban imposed by the military on all political and trade union activities. The most common targets of arrest were trade unionists, union leaders, journalists, church workers, lawyers, politicians, human rights activists and students. Several thousand individuals were detained during the period the military were in power from July 1980 to September 1982, the majority during the government of General García Meza. In most cases detention was short-term and the prisoners were released on condition that they went into exile.

Testimonies of former prisoners indicated that torture of political prisoners immediately after arrest during incommunicado detention was routine. A number of detention centres were used, including the basement of the Ministry of the Interior, the headquarters of the *Servicio Especial de Seguridad* (SES), Special Security Service, the national and regional offices of the *Departamento de Orden Político* (DOP), Department of Political Order, as well as the *Estado Mayor*, Army High Command, in La Paz and military installations throughout the country. Prisoners arrested outside La Paz were normally transferred to the capital after a few days, although relatives were not always informed of such transfers.

Political detainees were generally held apart from ordinary criminal suspects after arrest. They shared cramped cells with other political suspects or were deliberately kept in isolation for long periods. Frequently they were denied food and water for many days in unlit cells. It was reported that they were regularly kicked and beaten by the guards and were forced to sleep on wet floors and eat off plates on which the guards had urinated.

Interrogation sessions lasting several hours were carried out over a period of days. The most common forms of torture used during interrogation included the following: the *picana eléctrica* (electric cattle prod) was applied to the victim's mouth, ears, genitals, breasts and soles of the feet—during such torture the prisoner was tied to a metal bed or had his or her feet immersed in water; beatings with rifle butts, clubs, and horse whips on the head and sometimes other parts of the body; suspension by the wrists or feet for long periods; the *chancho*, where prisoners lie parallel with the floor supported only by the head and the tips of the toes—if they fall or move, they are beaten; sexual abuse including rape; burns with lighted cigarettes applied to the palms and the soles of the feet; constant threat of physical abuse including castration and amputation of limbs; mock executions. Prisoners further testify to having had their finger-nails pulled out and pins or nails forced under finger- and toe-nails.

The main purpose of interrogation seemed to be to obtain information about the suspect's political affiliation and activities and in particular to secure the names of colleagues or associates. On some occasions prisoners were tortured to obtain confessions or to sign statements attesting to their correct treatment in detention.

Paramilitary agencies set up after the coup of July 1980 under the auspices of the then Minister of the Interior, Colonel Luis Arce Gómez, were most frequently named as those responsible for torture. Regular military personnel reportedly witnessed or supervised the torture sessions and sometimes participated in them. Amnesty International has received reliable reports alleging that Argentine advisers participated in the torture of prisoners after the 1980 coup.

Between July 1980 and September 1982 Amnesty International intervened on behalf of approximately 600 individuals to try to protect them from the possibility of torture after their arrest.

In November 1980 an Amnesty International delegation visited Bolivia and raised the organization's concerns with the authorities. In a memorandum subsequently submitted to the Bolivian authorities, Amnesty International concluded that torture was widespread and recommended a number of measures for the protection of prisoners. These covered: formalizing arrest and detention procedures, permitting regular visits and medical examinations and establishing an independent complaints machinery to investigate torture allegations. As far as Amnesty International is aware, these recommendations were not acted on by the military authorities.

Further evidence about the scale of torture in Bolivia was included in a report published in 1981 by the Inter-American Commission on Human Rights of the Organization of American States.

In May 1980 the United Nations Commission on Human Rights appointed a Special Envoy to study human rights violations in Bolivia. The Special Envoy in his report concluded that the government of General García Meza had failed to meet its obligations to prevent torture and ill-treatment. Amnesty International continued to receive reports of torture and ill-treatment during the governments of Generals Celso Torrelio Villa and Guido Vildoso Calderón (September 1981 to September 1982).

In a second report published in December 1982, the Special Envoy commented on the positive steps taken since October 1982 by President Hernán Siles Zuazo's government for the protection of human rights. These included the abolition of state security agencies established by the military authorities, including the SES, DOP and the *Departamento de Inteligencia del Estado* (DIE), State Intelligence Department, "since these organisms have committed a series of acts and actions denigrating to the human condition by lending themselves to the service of instruments of repression and torture".

Amnesty International remained concerned about the slowness of both the official investigations into human rights violations committed under the military government and the latter's bringing of those responsible to trial.

Brazil

The Brazilian constitution exhorts those in authority to respect the physical and moral integrity of those in custody, yet Amnesty International received reports indicating that torture was widespread in Brazil during the period under review. The victims have tended to be ordinary criminal suspects from the most disadvantaged sectors of society: the urban poor, landless peasants and Indians. During the period under review, Amnesty International has also received allegations of torture of individuals arrested for political reasons, such as a number of journalists and leading trade unionists charged under the law of National Security. For example, in July 1982 Amnesty International received reports that five people who were arrested in Salvador da Bahía after attending a public meeting about the "disappearances" in the early 1970s of members of the illegal *Partido Comunista do Brasil*, a Maoist Communist Party, were allegedly tortured by military police.

The methods of repression built up during the 1960s and 1970s to combat political opposition to the military remained largely intact even after the policy of *abertura*, controlled liberalisation, was introduced. However, the torture techniques developed over this period were later used more frequently against ordinary criminal suspects, including minors. Persistent, well-documented allegations have been received by Amnesty International from many different sources during the period under review: the Roman Catholic Church, the Brazilian Bar Association, trade union and human rights organizations, politicians and the press. In a handful of cases these allegations have been the subject of criminal prosecutions which have resulted in police officers and other state officials being convicted of torture and ill-treatment of detainees. Amnesty International has received reports of torture from all states of Brazil although the greatest number of cases would appear to occur in the large metropolitan areas of Rio de Janeiro and São Paulo.

The methods of torture most commonly referred to by former prisoners during the period under review were: electric shocks, beatings and the *pau de arara*, parrot's perch, used for suspending the victim upside down from a rod placed under the knees, while the hands are bound to the ankles. Torture has most often been inflicted in local police stations in order to extract signed confessions from suspects.

After receiving dozens of complaints from former prisoners, an official commission of inquiry, in Rio de Janeiro, consisting of members of the state legislature, a judge and a forensic doctor, carried out a spot check on one police station in Benfica and discovered a torture room equipped with a machine for applying electric shocks and a blood-stained *pau de arara*.

Nor has torture been confined to the period immediately after arrest. Amnesty International has also received reports of the torture of convicted prisoners. In August 1982 the Governor of Ilha Grande prison in Rio de Janeiro and three other prison officials were found guilty of the torture and abuse of inmates and given sentences ranging from two years nine months' to five years' imprisonment. At the time of writing they were appealing against the conviction.

Amnesty International has received similar reports from prisons in other parts of the country. In May 1983 three prison guards were transferred from the Central Prison of Pôrto Alegre after a tape-recording of them beating a prisoner was broadcast on a local radio station.

Prisoners who have tried to protest about their treatment have been threatened and sent to punishment cells. In May 1983 a prisoner, who had been held in prison in Rio de Janeiro for almost a year after completing a sentence for robbery, was released and is now seeking compensation in the courts for paralysis in his legs which, he claims, is a result of the torture. In 1980, while in pre-trial detention, he was allegedly put on the rack—the victim's arms and legs are strapped to a metal frame which is gradually extended causing the limbs to be stretched to the limit. He had been too afraid while in prison to denounce his treatment.

In the interior of the country a similar pattern of arbitrary behaviour by those in authority, the Federal police or army, emerges. The targets of torture in the countryside are often Indians and peasants claiming squatters' rights to land. Over the last 10 years both groups have tried to organize themselves in order to resist being forced off the land by large companies or landowners, who have sometimes hired gunmen to intimidate and harass them.

Increasingly priests working in these remote areas and members of the expanding rural trade union movement have accused the police and the military of condoning or even actively supporting these illegal actions.

In September 1982 in the state of Mato Grosso do Sul Roman Catholic priests claimed that members of the Caiovas tribe, accused of stealing from landowners, had been tortured with electric shocks by local police and that although several similar complaints had been lodged with the authorities, no steps had been taken to afford the Indians effective protection. Such allegations have brought priests and rural trade union officials into conflict with the authorities. A group of peasants arrested in 1981 after the shooting of a hired gunman in the Baixo Araguaia region of the Amazon were allegedly tortured while in the custody of the federal police in order to try to make them implicate two priests in the killing.

Chile

Torture of political detainees by members of the security forces has been reported regularly since the present military government under General Augusto Pinochet Ugarte seized power in 1973 and has continued during the period under review. Although most of the information available to Amnesty International refers to cases of a political nature, allegations of torture and ill-treatment of detainees accused of ordinary crimes have also been widespread.

No political party has been allowed to function legally since 11 September 1973 and those who were detained and tortured on account of their alleged political activities came from a broad spectrum of sectors and professions of Chilean society—teachers, students, peasants, doctors, lawyers, trade unionists, workers, and shanty-town dwellers.

Although torture and ill-treatment (especially of detainees suspected of ordinary crimes) was reportedly used by both *Carabineros*, uniformed police, and *Investigaciones*, plain-clothes police, in police stations, it was the *Centrál Nacional de Informaciones* (CNI) which was by far the most frequently cited as responsible for torturing people suspected of political activity. The CNI was created in 1977, taking over the personnel and functions of the *Dirección de Inteligencia Nacional* (DINA). People detained by, or handed over to, the CNI for interrogation were usually taken to secret detention centres where they may be held in incommunicado detention for up to 20 days. It was during this period of incommunicado detention that torture was used, apparently to obtain information and self-incriminatory statements from political detainees, to intimidate them and, in some cases, to obtain their collaboration with the security forces.

According to Transitory Provision 24 of the 1981 constitution, the President may order the detention of political suspects for up to 20 days. Although the text of the law restricts the 20-day period to cases of people suspected of being involved in "terrorist activities with serious consequences", the executive and the courts have taken a very broad view of the scope of its application. In fact, most of those detained for up to 20 days have not been charged with any offence related to terrorism.

Amnesty International has gathered information on torture in Chile from a wide variety of sources: directly from victims, lawyers, victims' families, and human rights groups working in Chile.

The most common physical tortures described in testimonies available to Amnesty International (some collected by an Amnesty International mission to Chile in 1982) were: beating; administration of electric shocks and burns on the head and sensitive parts of the body; rape and other sexual abuse of women; non-therapeutic use of drugs; sleep deprivation; use of a form of torture known as *el teléfono*, the telephone, consisting of blows with the palms of the hands on both ears simultaneously; *la parrilla*, the metal grill, consisting of electric shocks on the most sensitive parts of the victim's body (usually the genitals, mouth, temples, toes, wrists) while he or she is tied to a metal bed frame; the *pau de arara*, parrot's perch, in which the victim is trussed into a crouching position, with the arms hugging the legs, a pole being then passed through the narrow gap between the bent knees and the elbows, the ends resting on two trestles or desks—with the victim in a position in which the head hangs downwards, electric current is then administered to sensitive parts of the body, and water squirted under high pressure into the mouth and nose until the victim is on the verge of suffocation; the *submarino* or *bañera*, in which the victim's head is held under water almost to the point of suffocation.

The Chilean courts have not taken effective action to prevent detainees from being tortured: they have usually failed to respond to *recursos de amparo*, similar to petitions for *habeas corpus*, within the 48-hour period stipulated by law. When detainees have filed complaints before the courts, and military personnel were suspected of being involved, they were normally dealt with by military tribunals which have consistently failed to charge or convict any member of the security forces for the torture or ill-treatment of detainees. This was true of the several hundreds of complaints filed with the courts since 1980.

Amnesty International has frequently issued appeals in cases since 1980 where the organization feared that detainees faced the possibility of torture after arrest. The organization has published numerous testimonies of torture victims and sent documentary evidence to the United Nations Commission on Human Rights and the Inter-American Commission on Human Rights.

In 1983 Amnesty International published its report *Chile: Evidence of Torture*, describing the use of torture in that country as systematic and widespread. This report was based on the findings of an Amnesty International delegation which visited the country in 1982 and included two doctors who carried out in-depth medical examinations of 19 people, 18 of whom alleged they had been tortured. They found that the results of the medical examinations were consistent with the allegations of torture. Documentary evidence collected by Amnesty International included formal complaints by the victims submitted to the courts, medical certificates both from independent doctors and from the official Institute of Forensic Medicine in Santiago, and reports from autopsies of people who died allegedly as a result of injuries sustained during torture. One of the more disturbing findings in the report was that medically trained personnel—probably doctors—had taken part in the torture of detainees.

The report concluded that, based on its information, the organization regards it as beyond reasonable doubt that the use of torture has been a constant feature of the security forces' practice over the past nine years. The report recommended, among other measures, that the Government of Chile institute promptly a public, open and independent inquiry into the allegations of torture filed before the courts—more than 200 were pending in the courts in mid-1982—the results of which should be made public and redress and compensation secured for the victims. No response was received from the government.

Colombia

Under a state of siege in force for most of the past 30 years in Colombia systematic torture was found to be a practice in all military interrogation centres known to Amnesty International. During the period under review civilians were detained and interrogated both by military and police intelligence in military detention centres and in the course of field operations against suspected insurgents in rural areas. Since the lifting of the state of siege in March 1982 and a change of government in August 1982, some significant improvement has been observed in the pattern of reported treatment of political prisoners, and measures have been taken by the Colombian Attorney General's office to investigate specific allegations of torture.

An Amnesty International report based on a mission to Colombia from 15 to 30 January 1980 was published in September 1980. It concluded that torture was inflicted on a regular basis during periods in which political prisoners were held incommunicado prior to initial court hearings and transfer into the custody of the national prison system. Torture was reported to have been inflicted both in police and military centres, although not within the national prison system, by military personnel, in particular members of the Army Intelligence Service, known as B-2, and of the National Police Intelligence Service, F-2.

Evidence of torture cited in the report included the findings of medical examinations of alleged torture victims by a doctor on the delegation, and detailed accounts describing torture by former prisoners and by many of the over 400 prisoners met by the mission delegates. Some testimonies were corroborated by the findings of the medical examinations and documentary medical evidence provided to Amnesty International by Colombian medical professionals. The report cited more than 600 individual cases of alleged torture or ill-treatment, and included extracts from the testimonies of prisoners detained in 1979 and early 1980 describing torture. Similar cases continued to be reported in 1981 and 1982.

The pattern of torture procedures and techniques reported from military detention centres was generally similar. Interrogation usually lasted from five to 10 days, during which time prisoners were generally stripped naked and blindfolded or hooded. A combination of physical and psychological coercion was involved, the latter including threats to kill, mutilate or to sexually molest, and threats to harm victims' friends or relatives. The range of techniques of torture included: systematic beatings; near drowning; near asphyxiation; electric shocks; sexual abuse; the use of drugs to induce pain or disorientation; enforced standing; deprivation of sleep, food and sometimes water; exposure to sun or rain or cold; and suspension by the arms while bound or handcuffed behind the back.

Most of the victims of torture during the period under review were prisoners suspected of collaboration with Colombia's active guerrilla opposition groups; they included hundreds of peasant farmers, trade unionists, students, intellectuals and others from virtually all walks of life.

In the course of 1980 and 1981 the question of torture was the subject of great public attention in Colombia. Human rights and political party organizations, and groups of legal and medical professionals, students and intellectuals, trade unionists and others held public discussions on the problem. This was accompanied by a reduction in reports of torture from the cities. However, reports of torture of prisoners detained in the course of counter-insurgency operations in isolated rural areas continued. These prisoners were tortured on the spot in temporary army bivouacs or in safe-houses during unacknowledged detention rather than in the urban military detention centres. The methods required no special equipment or technical sophistication: captives were bound to trees or handcuffed to posts, exposed to the sun by day and insects and cold by night; forced to remain standing for days on end; hung by the arms while beaten with rifle butts; heads were submerged in dirty water. A new feature after 1981 was a requirement that prisoners sign a form stating that they had received "good treatment" while undergoing interrogation. In some cases these forms were presented for signature before the interrogation started.

The infliction of torture in militarized zones appears to have been intended both to get information on the identities and movements of guerrillas and their sympathizers, and to intimidate or deter the general population from cooperating with guerrilla groups. Most of the reported victims have been peasant farmers and members of Indian populations in some remote areas. In November 1981 random detentions by army troops in which prisoners were stripped naked, strung up from trees, beaten with clubs and whips, and nearly suffocated with cloths repeatedly soaked with water placed over their faces caused leaders of the Coreguaje Indian communities in Caqueta department to lodge protests with the regional authorities.

Following the lifting of the state of siege in March 1982 and change of government in August 1982, the National Police Intelligence Service, F-2, took over many of the duties previously undertaken by military intelligence personnel. Some F-2 agents were reported to have inflicted torture. Withdrawal of the legal powers of the military to arrest, interrogate and try civilians under the state of siege did not, however, mean an end to the direct involvement of the military in interrogations in which torture was alleged to have occurred, either in the military detention centres or in the course of the rural, anti-guerrilla operations that were to continue. Moreover, there was some evidence to suggest that some military interrogators previously responsible for torture had been transferred to serve in F-2 after the lifting of the state of siege.

In a letter to the Colombian Government in February 1983

Amnesty International noted the efforts of the government to investigate reports of torture by Colombian military personnel, but expressed concern about recent evidence of torture having been inflicted in the army's intelligence division in Bogotá, the *Brigada de Institutos Militares* (BIM), the Military Institutes Brigade. Amnesty International noted that it had observed a significant reduction in reports of torture from permanent military detention centres during the previous two years. It said that the evidence indicated that torture continued on a regular basis in isolated rural areas, and expressed concern about evidence that a group of prisoners held incommunicado in the BIM in December 1982 had been interrogated under torture, including near drowning and suspension by cords. The letter noted that documents had been sent to Amnesty International concerning medical examinations of the prisoners in the BIM carried out on the orders of the Attorney General by the government's *Instituto de Medicina Legal*, Institute of Forensic Medicine, which confirmed there had been physical injuries consistent with allegations of torture made by seven prisoners.

Since August 1982 the Colombian Attorney General's office has undertaken a series of investigations into allegations of torture made by prisoners formerly in military or police custody, some of which have led to the opening of criminal investigations under the civilian courts. Amnesty International has, at the request of Colombian courts, provided documentation on a number of cases of alleged torture.

El Salvador

Amnesty International has received regular, often daily, reports identifying El Salvador's regular security and military units as responsible for the torture, "disappearance" and killing of non-combatant civilians from all sectors of Salvadorian society. Such reports have been received with respect to the period following the October 1979 coup, when El Salvador was ruled by a series of governing *juntas*, as well as for the period since the elections for a Constituent Assembly in March 1982.

These abuses have occurred in the context of civil conflict between government and armed opposition forces, but Amnesty International has concluded on the basis of the available evidence that the vast majority of the victims, both Salvadorian and foreign nationals, were characterized by their association, or alleged association, with peasant, labour or religious organizations, with human rights monitoring groups, with the trade union movement, with refugee or relief organizations or with political parties. Journalists, church workers and teachers have been subjected to such abuses, as have other non-combatant civilians, including women and children living in areas targeted for security operations because the authorities suspected local inhabitants of sympathizing with the guerrilla forces. A number of patients have allegedly been removed from their beds or operating theatres and tortured and murdered. On a number of occasions, Salvadorian military and paramilitary units linked to the official military and security units have reportedly crossed into neighbouring Honduras. In some cases these units have allegedly tortured, abducted and sometimes killed Salvadorian refugees there, including women and children, with the cooperation of their Honduran counterparts. Honduran nationals who were assisting with relief operations or who lived near the Salvadorian refugee camps have also allegedly been tortured and ill-treated.

Testimonies obtained by Amnesty International provide convincing evidence that prisoners were routinely tortured during the initial phase of incommunicado interrogation in security force or military installations. Torture has also allegedly taken place after detentions have been acknowledged and detainees have been transferred to prison. Security units have also reportedly raided the prisons where political detainees are held, beaten up the prisoners, and taken some of them back to security corps installations for renewed torture.

The torture of prisoners while they are in unacknowledged detention has occurred in the context of Decree Law 507, of 3 December 1980, which came into force in January 1981 and revised the administration of justice and eliminated guarantees of fair trial procedures.

Article 7 of Decree Law 507 permits a secret six-month period of investigation at the pre-trial stage. This pre-trial stage itself only begins when the detainee is placed in the custody of the examining judge. Amnesty International considers that this legal incommunicado detention period facilitates the use of torture in the interrogation of detainees.

Types of torture reported to Amnesty International by those who have survived arrest and interrogation included beatings, sexual abuse, use of chemicals to disorient, mock executions, and the burning of flesh with sulphuric acid. The units responsible for these abuses have included El Salvador's regular armed forces, naval as well as land forces, and special security forces such as the National Guard, the National Police and the Treasury Police.

The Salvadorian countryside was patrolled both by regular military and security forces and by members of nominally civilian paramilitary units formerly known as ORDEN, the *Organización de Defensa Nacional*, National Defence Organization, but now operating as the *Frente Democrático Nacionalista*, National Democratic Front. These groups operated in conjunction with regular army and security units and have frequently been named in reports of human rights abuses, including torture. Many of their members were thought to be off-duty or retired security service personnel.

Recently, reports have been received of the involvement of local *Brigadas de Defensa Civil*, civil defence patrols, formed by the Minister of Defence, or of *patrullas cantonales*, canton patrols, in abuses including torture. Salvadorian officials maintained that acts carried out by such groups were actually the work of "death squads" which it was unable to control.

In response to appeals by Amnesty International, the Salvadorian authorities have occasionally produced a previously unacknowledged detainee on Salvadorian television in an apparent effort to assure concerned international organizations that the person had not been tortured in custody. On other occasions Salvadorian officials have maintained in response to allegations of ill-treatment of prisoners that international propagandists were responsible for the dissemination of misinformation.

An Amnesty International mission to the country in July 1983 found convincing evidence that torture continued to be widely used by all branches of the Salvadorian military, paramilitary and security apparatus. The Amnesty International delegation met the government-formed Human Rights Commission which began to operate earlier in 1983.

Amnesty International was concerned to learn that the commission did not intend to investigate the many thousands of human rights abuses which have occurred in recent years, including the widespread use of torture, before the commission had been established.

Amnesty International has submitted its concerns to relevant international organizations during the period under review. In 1981 the United Nations Commission on Human Rights recommended the appointment of a Special Rapporteur to investigate the human rights situation in El Salvador, who later delivered a series of reports to the United Nations General Assembly in which he confirmed the persistence of grave violations of human rights in the country. The General Assembly passed several resolutions requesting, among other things, that the Salvadorian authorities ensure respect for the articles of the Geneva Conventions which govern the actions of parties to conflicts not of an international nature, and expressed its grave concern that the judicial authorities in El Salvador were unable to carry out their responsibility of maintaining the rule of law through prosecuting and punishing those responsible for murders, torture and other forms of ill-treatment.

The Inter-American Commission on Human Rights of the Organization of American States also maintained an active program of investigation into the human rights situation in El Salvador, which it repeatedly described as giving rise to grave concern. Early in 1983 the Salvadorian Government asked the commission to send an observer delegation to the country.

Numerous other delegations from intergovernmental as well as national bodies and legislatures visited El Salvador during the period under review and published information concerning the human rights violations they had verified, including the use of torture during the interrogation and detention of political detainees, and to terrorize civilian populations in areas of conflict.

Guatemala

The use of torture and ill-treatment in an attempt to control all forms of dissent has been a long-standing problem in Guatemala. Under successive regimes during the period under review, opponents or suspected opponents of the government have been systematically seized without warrant, tortured and murdered. All of the country's military and security units have been cited as implicated in such abuses. The authorities frequently blamed the abuses on paramilitary "death squads", allegedly operating out of government control. In fact, the "death squads" operated with government tolerance under some presidents, and were intimately linked with the government under other administrations.

A 1981 Amnesty International report entitled *Guatemala: A Government Program of Political Murder* showed how the selection of victims for detention, torture and murder and the deployment of official forces for extralegal operations was organized at that time under the direct control of the President of the Republic (President Romeo Lucas García 1978-1982).

Few of the many thousands abducted during the Lucas García period survived. In many cases, they simply "disappeared". Some had survived initial attacks and were abducted from their hospital beds, or as they were being transferred from one prison to another. In other instances, mutilated bodies of abducted people were later found by the side of the road, frequently at some distance from the place of their original arrest without warrant, bearing clear evidence of torture. Such evidence included cigarette burns, castration, traces of insecticide in the hair indicating the use of a *"capucha"*, hood, impregnated with noxious chemicals, allegedly used to the point of suffocation, multiple slashing often inflicted with machetes, sometimes severing entire limbs. Mutilated bodies of socially prominent victims were sometimes left in public places accompanied by notes signed in the name of the "death squad", stating that the torture and death of the individual should serve as a warning to others not to engage in opposition to government policies.

In other cases, bodies of people detained during popular demonstrations, at their homes or on the streets were later found in secret cemeteries, frequently with their hands bound, and their throats enclosed in a primitive garotte (a string round the throat tightened by turning a stick).

It was often impossible to identify the corpses—some had been mutilated and left at some distance from the place of abduction in an apparent effort to make such identification impossible. Others had badly decomposed in the secret cemeteries where they had been hidden.

Testimony obtained from the few who were abducted and survived torture during this period indicates that in addition to terrorizing the population, the torture was also intended to assist in interrogating people suspected of "subversion".

A number of cases became known to Amnesty International during 1981 in which torture had apparently been used to obtain public recantations from well-known popular leaders or church figures.

In the context of an increasing level of confrontation between the government and armed opposition groups in 1980-1981, Amnesty International began to receive reports of torture being used to extract information about guerrilla movements from villagers in contested areas, to terrorize the population in such areas so that they would deny support to the guerrillas, and to clear certain areas of the civilian population in order to isolate the guerrillas and combat them more effectively.

In March 1982 elections were held in Guatemala which were widely denounced as fraudulent, and shortly afterwards a new government seized power in a near bloodless coup. Upon taking power, the new three-man *junta* declared that it intended to ensure a return to the respect for human rights in Guatemala. New legislation was passed to replace the suspended constitution; the so-called *Estatuto Fundamental de Gobierno*, Basic Statute of Government, provided, among other things, for the establishment of all necessary machinery for the effective and unqualified observance and maintenance of human rights (Article 5), and stipulated that state authorities at all levels were to act scrupulously and assiduously by all lawful means available to them to ensure that the guarantees and rights of individuals were strictly observed and were safeguarded as effectively as possible (Article 23).

However, in July 1982, Amnesty International issued a special briefing paper entitled *Massive Extrajudicial Executions in Rural Areas Under the Government of General Efraín Ríos Montt*, which concluded that both before and after General Ríos Montt assumed sole control of the country in June 1982, government troops or newly formed "civil defence patrols" under their command continued, as under previous administrations, to attempt to control opposition, both violent and non-violent, through the widespread use of torture and the killing of large numbers of rural non-combatant civilians including young children, as well as people suspected of sympathizing with violent or non-violent opposition groups.

During the period under review foreign church and relief workers reported a number of cases involving the torture of refugees in Mexico and as they were being forcibly returned to Guatemala by Guatemalan regular and paramilitary troops who had crossed into Mexico. Such abuses have also been inflicted on Mexican nationals by Guatemalan troops operating on Mexican territory.

In the months following the March 1982 coup Amnesty International also received reports of the torture of people in custody, including both Guatemalan and foreign Protestant church workers. The agency implicated in these instances was the army secret police unit.

Other prisoners who had initially "disappeared", but were later acknowledged to be in detention following the expression of high levels of international concern on their behalf, appeared dazed and seriously underweight when visited in prison by relatives. The use of drugs and torture in their interrogation has been alleged. Several such people were later released into exile.

Amnesty International has also concluded, on the basis of testimony obtained from relatives, legal counsel and other prisoners, that several of the individuals executed since Decree Law 46-82 was passed in July 1982 had been convicted on the basis of information extracted under torture during the period when they were held in incommunicado detention at security corps headquarters or at various government "torture houses" in Guatemala City. Amnesty International has received evidence strongly suggesting that a number of people detained under this Decree Law had also been subjected to torture during their interrogation.

In addition to its major publications issued on Guatemala during the period in question (the 1981 report and the July 1982 briefing paper), Amnesty International has addressed the government directly on a number of occasions. The government has never responded to the substance of Amnesty International's concerns, suggesting that Amnesty International was leading a political campaign of defamation against the Guatemalan Government and that independent "death squads" were actually responsible for the abuses which Amnesty International said it ought to investigate and bring to a halt.

Amnesty International has also continuously submitted material on its concerns in Guatemala, including reports of torture, to relevant national, regional and international bodies.

In December 1981 a 134-page report prepared by the Inter-American Commission on Human Rights of the Organization of American States described violations of the right to life, liberty, security and personal integrity and concluded that "an alarming climate of violence" had prevailed in Guatemala in recent years, "either instigated or tolerated by the government". The Organization of American States sent delegations to investigate human rights concerns in Guatemala in 1982 and 1983; a visit had first been requested by the organization in 1973.

In March 1982 the United Nations Commission on Human Rights called for the appointment of a Special Rapporteur to make a thorough study of the human rights situation in Guatemala. The Special Rapporteur eventually agreed to by Guatemala visited the country in the course of 1983.

In August 1982 the Working Group on Enforced or Involuntary Disappearances of the United Nations named Guatemala among 22 countries where it had found that "disappearances" "served as a euphemism for terror campaigns often led by police, military or paramilitary forces". The report said that "The victims are either simply never heard of again, reappear bearing the scars of torture, or are found dead, often with their bodies mutilated beyond recognition."

Guyana

Amnesty International received reports of the torture or ill-treatment of a number of people in police custody during the period under review in Guyana. They concerned alleged political opponents of the government as well as people held on suspicion of ordinary criminal offences. In November 1982 Amnesty International sent an observer to the trial of a defendant charged with treason who alleged that he had signed a confession after a prolonged period in police custody in June 1980, during which he was beaten, deprived of food and sleep and denied access to his lawyer for several days. At the trial his confession was excluded on the grounds that it was not voluntary and he was acquitted.

Amnesty International received reports of the deaths in custody of three people during 1982 which were alleged to have occurred as a result of ill-treatment by the detaining authorities. In January 1982 a prisoner was found dead in a police cell by relatives after being held for four days in Brickdam police station, Georgetown, on suspicion of theft. A subsequent post mortem found the cause of death to be internal bleeding from a punctured lung caused by broken ribs.

In April 1982 two prisoners died in Mazaruni Prison, shortly after their recapture by guards following their escape from prison. Cause of death was given in one case as "(a) haemorrhage and shock (b) fracture of the ribs with haematoma of the left lung by lateral subpleural haemorrhages". Four prison warders were subsequently charged with murder of the two prisoners. These charges were later reduced to manslaughter and the warders were released on bail.

In April 1983 Amnesty International wrote to the Minister of Home Affairs expressing concern at reports of the deaths from malnutrition of five prisoners in Camp Hill Prison since August 1982 as a result of an inadequate prison diet. A number of other prisoners from Camp Hill Prison alleged to be suffering from the symptoms of severe malnutrition had been hospitalized during the same period. Amnesty International said that the prolonged deprivation of a minimum diet necessary for the prisoners' basic health constituted cruel, inhuman or degrading treatment in contravention of Article 5 of the Universal Declaration of Human Rights.

Haiti

Torture and ill-treatment of detainees in Haiti has been regularly reported to Amnesty International since *Président-à-vie*, President for life, Jean Claude Duvalier took office in 1971.

Although torture and ill-treatment have reportedly been inflicted on people from a wide range of sectors of Haitian during the period under review, Amnesty International has mainly documented cases of people suspected of political activities. No political parties are tolerated in Haiti. Trade union confederations have not been allowed to function. The rights to freedom of speech, association and assembly are severely restricted.

Among those who have reportedly been tortured since 1980 are Sylvio Claude, leader and founder of the *Parti démocrate chrétien haïtien*, Haitian Christian Democrat party, whose members are periodically arrested or expelled from the country; Yves Richard, Secretary General of the unofficial *Central autonome des travailleurs haïtiens*, Autonomous Congress of Haitian Workers; Evans Paul, a radio journalist; and Gérard Duclerville, a lay priest and radio journalist whose reported torture by the police in January 1983 caused him to be hospitalized. In August 1982, Amnesty International made known its concern to the Haitian authorities following the death in prison of Robert-Marc Thélusma. The prisoner is said to have been denied proper medical care and hospitalization by the authorities, and to have died as a result.

Torture reportedly took place following detention, usually without any legal formality, in military barracks. In Haiti the army also functions as a police force. Most testimonies available to Amnesty International mention the *Casernes Dessalines*, military barracks, in Port-au-Prince, as the place where torture was inflicted. Reports of torture and ill-treatment have also referred to military barracks or police stations in other places, such as the town of Cayes in the southern part of the country, and Croix des Bouquets on the outskirts of Port-au-Prince. Furthermore, it was generally believed that *Chefs de Section*, local police chiefs, ran small detention centres, sometimes even in their own homes, where ill-treatment allegedly took place.

Methods of torture described in testimonies received by Amnesty International during the period under review include beatings on the head or other parts of the body with sticks, obliging detainees to remain standing still for very long periods, and the so-called *pau de arara*, parrot's perch, known in Haiti as the "Jack".

Political detainees were normally arrested without any arrest warrant by the *Service détectif* (SD), a form of plain-clothes police, or by the *Volontaires de la sécurité nationale*, more commonly known as the *tontons macoutes*, an armed militia created by the late President François Duvalier to supress any manifestation of political opposition in the population. Long-term incommunicado detention, unacknowledged by the authorities for months or years, and sometimes never acknowledged, without access to lawyers, relatives or doctors, has become the pattern of political detention in Haiti. Only on rare occasions, usually following vociferous expressions of international concern, are detainees brought before a tribunal. On such occasions, international observers have reported that in no cases were international legal standards adhered to.

Amnesty International has not been able to record a single instance in which a complaint made by a detainee about torture and ill-treatment has been investigated by the Haitian authorities.

Since 1980 most opposition lawyers, journalists and intellectuals have either been imprisoned or expelled from Haiti. Human rights activists have been forced almost to halt their work of documenting instances of abuses of human rights in Haiti, and disseminating information about them, and this had made it difficult to obtain information about torture and ill-treatment from most parts of Haiti. However, testimonies received from former detainees or their families, and from ex-members of the Haitian army or security forces who have sought asylum in other countries have provided information which portrays a disturbing picture of continued use of torture and other forms of ill-treatment of prisoners in Haiti.

Since 1980 Amnesty International has made frequent appeals on behalf of people arrested in circumstances in which the organization believed they were in danger of being tortured, but no substantive response has been received from the government.

Honduras

Amnesty International has received reports at an increasing rate during the period under review of the torture in Honduras of both Honduran and foreign nationals, believed by the authorities to be in opposition to the Honduran Government or linked to the Salvadorian opposition. Victims have included trade unionists, medical professionals, students, teachers, Salvadorian peasant refugees housed in camps on Honduran territory and Honduran and foreign nationals working with relief and assistance programs for these refugees.

These abuses have continued in the context of regional unrest and the inauguration in February 1982 of Honduras' first civilian president in a decade. They have been carried out by the Honduran military and regular security forces including the *Departamento Nacional de Investigaciones* (DIN), National Department of Investigations, the *Cobras*, a plain-clothes intelligence unit, the *Cuerpo Anti-Subversivo*, anti-subversive police corps, the *Fuerzas de Seguridad Pública* (FUSEP), Public Security Forces, Honduran paramilitary "death squads" which were proclaimed during the period under review, as well as a number of new special anti-terrorist groups, such as the *Tropas Especiales para Selva y Nocturnas* (TESON), Special Troops for Jungle and Night operations. Techniques reported include beatings, the use of electric shocks, phychological torture and confinement in spaces too small for the victims to stand, sit or lie down.

Such treatment has occurred at military and security squad installations in Tegucigalpa and other cities, as well as in the presence of witnesses in small villages where the army has publicly interrogated victims using torture. Foreign delegations who have visited the country have collected photographic evidence and testimonies indicating the probable use of torture. An Amnesty International mission which visited Honduras in 1981 conducted similar interviews with victims who testified that they had been tortured while in custody at army barracks in the Honduran countryside. Following this mission, Amnesty International has continued to receive credible testimony indicating that the use of torture continues to be a regular technique both for the interrogation of political suspects and the intimidation of Honduran and foreign nationals living in border areas where confrontations between the Salvadorian military and its armed opposition have taken place. Information has been made available to Amnesty International suggesting that the Honduran military have cooperated in actions with their Salvadorian counterparts on both Salvadorian and Honduran territory during which indiscriminate attacks, including the use of torture and mutilation, were made upon fleeing Salvadorian refugees, including women and children. Information in the possession of Amnesty International suggests that on a number of occasions torture has led to the deaths of prisoners in custody, as well as of non-combatant civilians killed by soldiers carrying out counter-insurgency operations in areas near the Salvadorian border.

Such abuses have occurred both before and after the passing by Congress of a new anti-terrorist law in May 1983. Known as Decree 33, the measure is a modification of Law 206 of 1956 which defined a large number of acts such as distributing political propaganda, association with foreigners, joining groups considered subversive, damaging property or destroying documents, as subversive acts against the state. Under Decree 33 for example, invasion of land was henceforth to be considered a terrorist activity.

In response to Amnesty International appeals, the Honduran authorities frequently denied that the individuals in question were in custody, although subsequently, a number of those on whose behalf Amnesty International had appealed, were later established to be in custody, and were eventually released.

In a February 1983 response to the report prepared by the United Nations Special Rapporteur on Summary or Arbitrary Executions, the Honduran Government replied that with respect to one incident where a "disappeared" person was tortured and then murdered by the Honduran military, and another person physically abused, the appropriate detention order had been issued against five soldiers, and the trial was following its appropriate course. With respect to other cases of the "disappeared", however, who had subsequently been found murdered with obvious marks of torture, the government replied that it had no knowledge of their whereabouts, despite the fact that the finding of their bodies had been widely reported in the Honduran press.

Mexico

During the period under review Amnesty International has frequently received reports of the torture of people either awaiting trial in police cells or in the temporary custody of the police or of parapolice groups. Such parapolice groups allegedly operated under the order of, or with the tacit approval of, governmental and local authorities. The evidence gathered by Amnesty International about torture in Mexico has been based on the detailed testimonies of torture victims, complaints published by the victims or their relatives in Mexican newspapers and press reports.

Torture has reportedly been used mostly for obtaining confessions prior to detainees' first appearance in court. However, the use of torture to intimidate has also been reported. Most of the torture allegations received by Amnesty International have related to people detained as a result of their political or trade union activities or in connection with local conflicts in rural areas, particularly over land ownership. Cases have also been reported where torture has been used apparently as a means of extracting confessions to obtain convictions for ordinary crimes, such as robbery. Torture victims have included members or suspected members of left-wing political parties and groups, and members of trade unions and peasant organizations which have been established independently of the official government-sponsored bodies. Numerous reports have been received of the arbitrary arrest and torture of Indian peasants in the context of local political, trade union and land disputes. While detailed information on such incidents is difficult to obtain, members of indigenous Indian communities have frequently been the victims of abuses perpetrated by gunmen hired by *caciques*, local strongmen, against whom state authorities have failed to take effective action. In many such cases the direct involvement of local police and government authorities has been alleged.

Methods of torture which have been reported include severe and repeated beatings, including beating with cupped hands over the ears; submersion in water; the introduction of carbonated water into the nasal passages; electric shocks applied to the most sensitive parts of the body; burning with cigarettes; and sexual violation and abuse.

The most frequent and consistent allegations have been made against members of the *División de Investigaciones para la Prevención de la Delincuencia* (DIPD), Division of Investigations for the Prevention of Delinquency, a plainclothes police unit based in Mexico City which has carried out illegal abductions of suspected opposition political militants, the most recent being in January 1983. Another Mexico City police body frequently accused is the *Dirección Federal de Seguridad* (DFS), a security police force under the control of the *Secretaría de Gobernación*, Ministry of the Interior, which has also carried out illegal arrests and abductions. Members of both the DIPD and the DFS are believed to have belonged to a paramilitary group, known as the *Brigada Blanca*, which has been accused by Mexican human rights groups of responsibility for the kidnapping of some of the more than 500 people reported to have "disappeared" in Mexico over a 10 year period. The Mexican Government has consistently denied the existence of this brigade, although some "disappeared" people who later reappeared gave highly detailed testimonies about their detention and ill-treatment by this unit in a clandestine detention centre on the outskirts of Mexico City, known as *Campo Militar No. 1*, Military Camp No. 1.

Reports have also been received of the infliction of torture by members of the *Policía Judicial Federal*, Federal Judicial Police, and of the local police forces, *Policía Municipal*, municipal police, in the states of Sinaloa, Oaxaca, Chiapas, Guerrero and Hidalgo. These allegations are best documented as regards the state of Sinaloa, where there is evidence of the systematic ill-treatment of detainees held on ordinary criminal charges and torture by members of the local police forces. One such incident was witnessed by a local journalist, whose evidence resulted in penal action against a group of police officers accused of the sexual abuse of three detainees in November 1982. A survey conducted in 1982 by the Lawyers Association of Culiacán, Sinaloa, based on interviews with 457 prisoners, showed that the majority claimed to have been ill-treated or tortured while in the custody of the Federal Judicial Police following their arrest.

In rural areas, torture appears to have been most frequent in local police stations and prisons, whereas in Mexico City many of the reports refer to the occurrence of torture in clandestine detention centres apparently equipped for the purpose of interrogation.

In June 1980 the Mexican Government made a unilateral declaration of its intention to comply with the Declaration against Torture and to implement the provisions of the declaration. In July 1980 the government responded to the United Nations' questionnaire on torture by providing information on legal guarantees and measures taken to prevent torture in the Mexican constitution, the criminal procedural codes and legislation governing the prison system. It was, however, unable to provide any information on whether, since the adoption of the declaration, any investigations had been carried out or proceedings instituted with regard to allegations of torture. The case referred to above is the only one on which Amnesty International has information in which criminal proceedings were instituted against police officers for alleged abuse of authority, but it is not known if a conviction was obtained or if any compensation was made to the victims. Defence lawyers have claimed that in practice it is difficult to establish medical evidence of torture. It appears that such evidence is often not accepted by the judge as a basis for the retraction of the confession obtained during the early stage of interrogation. Amnesty International has details of several trial proceedings in which the defendants have alleged that the charges and subsequent conviction were based on statements obtained as a result of torture.

In January 1983 the DIPD was dissolved by the incoming government of President Miguel de la Madrid Hurtado, as one of a series of measures taken against corruption and criminality in the police forces. Many of its estimated 1,500 agents were reassigned to the Federal Judicial Police and the *Policía Judicial del Distrito Federal*, Federal District Judicial Police. Amnesty International has continued to receive reports of arrests made without regard for due process, and concern has remained about the lack of effective control of the activities of the police forces.

Paraguay

A state of siege has been renewed in Paraguay as a matter of routine every three months for the past 29 years, although since 1978 it has been limited to the Central Department. The judiciary has ruled that people arrested in other parts of the country may be transferred to Asunción, the capital, and held there under Article 79 of the constitution, which provides for the state of siege and gives the President the right to keep people in indefinite detention without charge or trial. In Amnesty International's view the state of siege, combined with the wide powers of the police and the inability of the judiciary to achieve independence from the executive, has facilitated the persistent torture and ill-treatment of political prisoners.

In 1980 Amnesty International submitted information to the United Nations Division of Human Rights about the secret disposal of three tortured bodies in the River Paraguay, one of which was identified as being that of Derlis Villagra, a Communist Party member who "disappeared" after his arrest in 1975.

The government's failure to acknowledge arrests promptly and to give information regarding place of detention put prisoners at particular risk of torture during early stages of detention. Amnesty International has received frequent reports of prisoners tortured in unacknowledged detention for days or even weeks before being transferred to official detention and being allowed visits. During this period prisoners are kept incommunicado in cramped cells in the *Departamento de Investigaciones de la Policía* (DIPC), Police Investigations Department, without natural light, access to fresh air, medical attention and with scarcely any food.

The principal centres for torture in Paraguay known to Amnesty International were the DIPC and its *Dirección de Vigilancia y Delitos*, Vigilance and Crime Division, and the *División Técnica de Represión del Comunismo*, Technical Division for the Repression of Communism, all of which are in Asunción. According to

Amnesty International's information, torture sessions usually took place at night in an annex to the DIPC which is euphemistically called the "laboratory".

The methods of torture most commonly alleged to have been used were the following: *picana eléctrica* (electric cattle prod); *pileta*, where the victim's head is plunged into a tank of water, which is sometimes polluted with excrement, until a sense of asphyxiation is induced; beatings, particularly on soles of feet with truncheons; *cajones*, prolonged confinement in a box or other restricted space—positions used are: *feto*, in which the victim is forced to remain for hours at a time in foetal position; the *guardia*, where the victim is placed upright in a large box with holes to enable him or her to breath; *secadera*, in which the victim is wrapped in a plastic sheet and placed in a metal cylinder; and *murciélago*, suspending the victim by the ankles.

Although victims were usually forced to sign false confessions, the main purpose of torture was apparently to discourage any opposition to the government.

During the period under review Amnesty International interceded on behalf of over 400 individuals—students, peasants, journalists, lawyers and teachers—fearing that they might be subjected to torture after having been arrested. Most at risk were those suspected of being members of the Communist Party or other left-wing or Marxist groups, which are banned in Paraguay, and members of the peasant organization, *Ligas Agrarias*, Agrarian Leagues. The worst treatment was apparently received by those regarded by the authorities as leaders of such groups.

In May 1983 following the arrest in Asunción of about 30 people connected with the *Banco Paraguayo de Datos*, a non-profit research body, Amnesty International received reliable reports that three people whom it had adopted as prisoners of conscience, Enrique Goossen, Roberto Villalba and Ruben Lisboa, had been tortured while in incommunicado detention. All had allegedly been severely beaten and two had been subjected to the *pileta*. Roberto Villalba was reported to have suffered a heart attack during interrogation and Ruben Lisboa required surgery to repair damage to his intestines.

It would seem that torture was routine during the period under review. Ordinary criminal suspects were almost invariably tortured, but in political cases much may depend on the prisoner's identity and on the place and length of detention. There is no information to suggest that anyone responsible for the torture of prisoners has ever been punished.

Although the Paraguayan Government agreed in principle in 1977 to an on-site investigation by the Inter-American Commission on Human Rights, it has not permitted the visit to take place.

Peru

Amnesty International has received persistent reports of the torture or ill-treatment of prisoners held both for political and ordinary criminal offences between January 1980 and April 1983, the period under review. Reports have been received from most parts of Peru, both before and after a change of government in July 1980. Torture has been most widely reported from isolated mountain areas of the country in which special security measures have been taken to combat a guerrilla opposition movement active since 1980. In these areas torture has occurred in the context of a regional state of emergency, under which some constitutional guarantees have been suspended for most of the period since October 1981. The use of torture increased considerably, with hundreds of cases reported after 29 December 1982, when areas already under a state of emergency were placed under the administration of a Peruvian army political-military command based in the city of Ayacucho. Since that time torture has in many cases been reported to have occurred before extrajudicial executions.

Torture generally occurred before prisoners appeared before a court and while they were held incommunicado in the custody of the security services. Although a constitutional provision requires prisoners held for ordinary criminal offences to be brought before a court within 24 hours of detention, most political prisoners were held under Decree Law 046 which defines the crime of terrorism and which allows prisoners to be held in incommunicado detention for up to 15 days before appearing before a court. Although Decree Law 046 provides for the detention of prisoners to be acknowledged to the respective court immediately after they are taken into custody this does not always occur in practice. Under state of emergency conditions prisoners have reported being held in secret, incommunicado detention for up to 30 days during which time their detentions have been denied, *habeas corpus* petitions have been refused, and prolonged interrogation under torture has taken place. Although brutal treatment, severe beatings and arbitrary shootings by guards have been regularly reported from Peruvian prisons, systematic torture and ill-treatment for purposes of interrogation, punishment or the intimidation of prisoners' relatives or associates has not been frequently reported after prisoners have appeared before a court and been remanded to a formal prison establishment under the administration of the Ministry of Justice.

The victims of torture and ill-treatment have included people from all walks of life who have been accused of ordinary criminal offences and faced interrogation in local police stations, although the pattern indicates that greater brutality is prevalent in the cases of those prisoners from the largely Indian peasantry, or from sections of the urban poor. Although not all political prisoners have been subjected to torture, Amnesty International has received detailed reports of the torture of members of lawful left-wing opposition parties elected to local government; leaders of or activists in teachers', mineworkers', construction workers', or peasant trade unions detained in the course of labour disputes; students, including minors as young as 13; intellectuals accused of collaboration with guerrilla groups; and lay Roman Catholic catechists and church workers participating in development and consciousness-raising programs in isolated rural areas. By far the largest number of political prisoners reported to have undergone torture have been peasant farmers detained in the course of land disputes, or during counter-insurgency operations in rural areas where guerrilla groups were active.

Security services which have reportedly inflicted torture included divisions of the *Policía de Investigaciones del Peru* (PIP), Peruvian Investigative Police, which are concerned with criminal investigations without political connotations, and its political branches, *Seguridad del Estado*, State Security, and *División Contra el Terrorismo* (DICOTE), Anti-Terrorism Division. Detailed testimonies received from prisoners charged with ordinary criminal offences ranging from theft to drug trafficking have described systematic torture during interrogation in many parts of Peru, including the northern coastal city of Chimbote, the highland cities of Cuzco in the south and Cajamarca in the north, and the capital, Lima, where several cases of death under torture during PIP criminal investigations were reported in 1980.

Prisoners interrogated by the PIP and later released, including both ordinary criminal and political suspects, have made statements which indicated that there is a consistent pattern of torture in all parts of of Peru. A characteristic routine of torture described in testimonies from Ayaviri in Puno department, Chimbote in Ancash, and in the city of Ayacucho, independently described by former prisoners, indicates that prisoners were blindfolded or hooded, sometimes for prolonged periods, and held without food for up to six days. Prisoners were stripped naked during interrogation, regularly drenched with cold water, and systematically beaten with leather or fabric implements filled with sand. Two particular methods described in testimonies from Ayacucho, Lima, Chimbote, Cuzco and elsewhere in the country appear to be characteristic of PIP interrogations, and are described by the same name throughout the country: *La Tina*, "the tub", involves near drowning by immersion of a suspect's head in a tub of water; *La Pita* involves binding or handcuffing hands behind the back—victims are then lifted by their wrists by a rope thrown over a beam or pulled through a ceiling-mounted pulley, while at the same time breathing is obstructed by wet rags placed over the nose and mouth. Blindfolding for periods as long as 16 days in PIP cells of the Lima Prefecture has been reported, and since 29 December 1982 hooding for up to 30 days has been reported in Ayacucho detention centres. In some cases the use of electric shock torture by the PIP has been reported.

The treatment of prisoners not accused of political offences by the Civil Guard is not believed to have included systematic torture, although ill-treatment of alleged offenders, such as beatings at the time of arrest, has been reported. Political cases in which Civil Guard forces have been reported to have inflicted systematic torture or ill-treatment have frequently occurred in the context of provincial strike action by peasant or trade union organizations and conflicts over land tenure, or as measures to disrupt the organizational activities of political opposition parties. Ill-treatment of prisoners in these cases appears to have been intended both to intimidate the victims into abandoning further involvement in such organizations, and as a means of interrogation.

The most widespread reports of torture by the Civil Guard have come from areas in which major efforts were underway to combat insurgency, and frequently involved its special counter-insurgency forces known as *sinchis*, "the valiant ones". Torture by these forces has reportedly been carried out most frequently in isolated rural areas. In October 1982 in Quillabamba, La Convención Province, prisoners were reported to have been tortured with electric shocks; nearly suffocated with plastic bags; forced to eat sand; and submerged in the Vilcanota River while tied into hemp bags. In Cocairo, Andahuaylas province, bound prisoners were slashed with razor blades in January 1983 by Civil Guards who then smeared the prisoners' blood on their own faces, apparently in order to terrorize villagers who witnessed the interrogation of the prisoners. In areas under military administration, evidence of torture on the bodies of people reported detained and then killed included marks from burning with cigarettes, slash wounds, and the removal of finger-nails.

Amnesty International has regularly reacted to cases in which there was a fear of torture, and has appealed for medical attention to be provided for reported victims of torture. The organization has received no information indicating that the Government of Peru has initiated independent investigations into the many reports of torture raised with it by Amnesty International, domestic human rights groups, and such bodies as the Roman Catholic Church, *Comisión Episcopal de Acción Social*, Episcopal Commission for Social Action, and the *Comisión de Derechos Humanos*, Human Rights Commission, of the Chamber of deputies of the Peruvian parliament. Amnesty International knows of no cases in which members of the security services accused of torture have been prosecuted.

Suriname

There have been frequent reports of torture or ill-treatment of prisoners in Suriname during the period under review. In most cases the victims were either civilians or military officers arrested on suspicion of involvement in attempted counter-coups against the military-backed government, or were members of political or professional groups considered to be hostile to the government's policies.

The reported ill-treatment usually occurred shortly after the prisoners' arrest, while they were detained in military custody. The alleged torture included severe beatings, threats, deprivation of sleep (sometimes while being made to maintain an upright position), deprivation of food and drink, and, in some cases, mutilation.

This treatment was allegedly carried out by military personnel. Since August 1980 the military police have had the same powers of arrest and interrogation as ordinary police. The most frequent allegations of ill-treatment received by Amnesty International concerned people held incommunicado for interrogation at Fort Zeelandia military headquarters. Arrested people are commonly held incommunicado for several days following their arrest.

One of the most serious incidents reported to Amnesty International concerned the shooting to death of 13 civilians and two former army officers while in military custody on 8/9 December 1982. The civilians, who included lawyers, former politicians, journalists, university professors and a trade union leader, were arrested at their homes in the early hours of 8 December 1982 and taken to Fort Zeelandia barracks for interrogation. They were held incommunicado for the following 24 hours. On 9 December, Lieutenant Colonel Desi Bouterse, leader of Suriname's government, announced on Suriname state television that a number of people arrested on suspicion of plotting a coup had been "shot while trying to escape from custody". However, reliable sources indicated to Amnesty International that all 13 were summarily executed and that they had been severely tortured. Eye-witnesses who subsequently identified the victims' bodies in a city mortuary testified to their injuries. These included severe bruising and cuts on the face, smashed jaws, broken teeth and fractured limbs. The victims also had multiple bullet entry wounds in the face, chest and abdomen. Amnesty International expressed its concern to the government regarding the reported executions and torture of these 15 people and issued several international appeals calling for an inquiry into the deaths.

Amnesty International has also written to the Suriname authorities on a number of occasions since February 1980 expressing concern about reports that people in military custody had been subjected to torture or ill-treatment. Amnesty International raised these and other concerns with the authorities during a mission to Suriname in January 1981. In March 1981 Amnesty International drew the government's attention to reports it had received that Frits Ormskerk, a former member of the Surinamese army, who had been arrested after an attempted coup in May 1980, had been beaten to death while in military custody, and urged the government to ensure that all complaints of torture were subject to impartial investigation.

To Amnesty International's knowledge, the government has not undertaken any investigation into the circumstances of the alleged summary executions and torture of the 15 people in December 1982, nor has there been any judicial investigation into any of the previous allegations of ill-treatment or deaths of people in military custody.

Uruguay

During the 1970s Amnesty International received reports indicating that the great majority of political prisoners arrested in Uruguay were tortured. The systematic use of torture as a means of obtaining information and confessions leading to prosecution under Uruguayan security legislation has remained a major concern of Amnesty International during the period under review.

Since 1980 individuals detained for political reasons have continued to be held for long periods incommunicado, without access to lawyers, doctors, or their relatives, before formal charges have been brought against them. Amnesty International has continued to receive reports of the torture of such people during interrogation. The vast majority of the victims were detained on suspicion of illegal political or trade union activities or of membership of proscribed political parties and trade union organizations. Many were subsequently sentenced by military courts to long terms of imprisonment for alleged offences under the Law of State Security and Internal Order (1972).

The police force and all three branches of the armed forces have continued to engage in political intelligence work directed at opposition political parties and groups, which include previously legal political parties forced to become clandestine by legislation banning their activities. The most frequent allegations of torture have concerned units of the army, navy and police force, and intelligence coordinating bodies, such as the *Organismo Coordinador de Actividades Anti-Subversivas* (OCOA), Coordinating Body for Anti-subversive Activities.

Safeguards against torture or ill-treatment of detainees are lacking, due to the common practice of the authorities of failing to acknowledge arrests officially when they occur, or of not informing relatives of the place of detention. In most cases, the prisoner is allowed to receive visits from relatives only after a confession or other incriminating evidence has been obtained and formal charges have been made. This period of incommunicado detention, without safeguards or guarantees, often lasts for several months.

Reports of torture after prisoners have appeared before a court or have been transferred to a penal establishment under the jurisdiction of the armed forces have been rare. Cases were reported in 1980, however, in which convicted political prisoners were summarily transferred from a regular military prison to an army barracks where they were reinterrogated and allegedly tortured, either to obtain information leading to their indictment on new charges, or to gain information about other political suspects. Amnesty International has continued to receive reports of the ill-treatment and torture of a group of nine leading members of the *Movimiento de Liberación Nacional—Tupamaros*, National Liberation Movement, who have been held separately in military barracks in the interior of the country since 1973, when they were removed from *Penal de Libertad*, Uruguay's high security military prison.

Reports received since 1980 suggest that torture took place with the greatest frequency in military barracks, although allegations of torture in police stations have also been received.

Testimonies of prisoners released after serving prison sentences, supported by information supplied by former serving members of the armed forces have provided details of the torture techniques commonly employed in Uruguay. These include forcing prisoners to wear hoods for prolonged periods (in some cases for more than a month); severe and repeated beatings; *plantón*, enforced standing for prolonged periods; hanging from the wrists, knees and ankles; *picana eléctrica*, electric shocks administered to the most sensitive parts of the body; *submarino*, near asphyxiation by submersion of the head or upper part of the body in tanks of water, sometimes polluted by excrement; *caballete*, forcing prisoners to sit straddling iron or wooden bars which cut cruelly into the groin;

burns; simulated executions; rape and other sexual abuses.

Consistent allegations have been made that medical staff at military barracks have routinely assisted in or advised over torture by conducting preliminary examinations of the victims, reviving and treating them following torture sessions, and advising officers when their life appeared to be in danger.

Since 1980 Amnesty International has issued frequent appeals when it feared that detainees faced the possibility of torture after arrest. It has asked the Uruguayan Government to carry out an independent inquiry into the death in custody of three prisoners in December 1980, April 1982 and June 1982, when it was feared that the prisoners in question might have died as a result of torture. In the first of these cases, that of Hugo Haroldo Dermit Barbato, the Human Rights Committee set up under the International Covenant on Civil and Political Rights, which considered the case in October 1982, found the Uruguayan Government responsible for a violation of Article 6 of the covenant for failing to take adequate measures to protect his life while in custody. In nine other cases considered by the committee since August 1979 (the date of its first ruling), it found that Article 7 of the covenant had been violated.

The Uruguayan authorities have consistently maintained that rigorous measures are taken to prevent the torture and ill-treatment of detainees in the custody of the police and military units. In its report to the Secretary-General of the United Nations under Article 40 of the International Covenant on Civil and Political Rights, submitted in February 1982, the government provided a list of 16 cases in which officials had been convicted of abuses against detainees. However, the cases all dated from 1977 or earlier, although Amnesty International has continued to receive allegations of torture since that date, and no details were given of the incidents to which the convictions related, of the people involved, or of the sentences passed by the courts.

Strict controls on the press and the effects of widespread self-censorship have prevented the publication inside Uruguay of allegations of torture and ill-treatment, and even complaints made to military magistrates have been rare, due to their widely attested lack of impartiality and failure to investigate or act on such complaints. In many cases details of the alleged torture of detainees can only be obtained after their release from prison on the completion of a prison sentence, when many are obliged to go into exile. In July 1983, however, a Montevideo human rights organization issued a statement which received publicity in the Uruguayan press, denouncing the alleged torture of a group of students, 25 of whom were subsequently committed for trial on accusations of membership of the *Unión de Juventudes Comunistas*, Union of

Communist Youth. Amnesty International obtained independent reports which corroborated this statement. Some of the prisoners were said to have been tortured with electricity, beatings and semi-asphyxiation by immersion in water, and several women were raped, one of them in front of her husband. One prisoner, a student of agronomy, was reported to have been transferred to the main military hospital as a result of injuries caused by torture, including the administration of electricity to the genital area. According to information obtained independently by Amnesty International, another of the detainees, a female medical student, was tortured repeatedly over a 15-day period by the methods described above, including being hung naked by the wrists in an outdoor patio in winter temperatures. Committal proceedings against the 25 were instituted by a military court, allegedly on the basis of confessions obtained as a result of this treatment, and they were subsequently transferred to regular military prisons to await sentence.

* * * *

In addition to the countries mentioned above, Amnesty International has received some reports of torture or ill-treatment from Canada, Costa Rica, Cuba, Dominica, Grenada, and the United States during the period under review.

An Amnesty International mission visited Canada in April 1983 to investigate allegations that prisoners in Archambault Prison, Quebec, had been ill-treated following a riot in the prison in July 1982. The most serious allegations concerned the treatment of prisoners placed in the segregation unit of the prison and included beatings; the spraying of teargas directly into prisoners' mouths; keeping prisoners naked in cells for up to three weeks; deprivation of sleep and adulteration of food; and in three cases the alleged "choking" of prisoners by wrapping a wet towel tightly round the prisoners' heads. In June 1983 Amnesty International submitted a memorandum to the Canadian Government. The organization collected enough evidence to conclude that the government was obliged under its international human rights commitments to conduct an impartial investigation into the allegations. In August 1983 the government announced that it had asked the Correctional Investigator of Canada to conduct an inquiry into the allegations contained in Amnesty International's memorandum. At the time of writing the results of the inquiry were not known.

In Costa Rica Amnesty International was concerned about reports that medical examinations of a group of detainees arrested in

March 1982 on politically-related charges found that at least two had bruises inflicted after arrest. The Minister of Justice promised an investigation. The court inquiry concluded that although there was documented proof that two of the prisoners had been beaten, the contradictory nature of the prisoners' evidence made it difficult to continue proceedings against the 10 agents of the *Organismo de Investigación Judicial* (OIJ), Judicial Investigation Organization, accused of ill-treating the detainees. The case was closed. Amnesty International has also received allegations of the torture of other people arrested on political charges in Costa Rica during the period under review. Most were subsequently freed on bail after periods in untried custody far exceeding those permissible under Costa Rican law. Government officials have strenuously denied that any torture has occurred in Costa Rican prisons or detention centres, and maintain that the allegations have been made in an effort to discredit the OIJ.

In recent years, Amnesty International has repeatedly expressed concern about reports of ill-treatment of political prisoners in Cuba, particularly those prisoners serving long sentences, known as the *Plantados*, a category of prisoner known for their refusal on political grounds to take part in the government's "rehabilitation" programs, and to wear the prison uniform worn by ordinary (as opposed to political) prisoners. Alleged ill-treatment included beatings and the withdrawal of medical attention, as punishment for infringing prison regulations.

Amnesty International received allegations that a number of Rastafarian youths were beaten in custody by the police during 1981 in Dominica. Amnesty International raised these allegations with the government, asking, in particular, if an inquiry had taken place into the death of John Rose Lindsay, who was found dead in June 1981 at the foot of a cliff the day after his arrest. A coroner's inquest subsequently returned a verdict in the case of "death as a result of physical injuries received in the police station by unknown police personnel". In December 1981 the government announced its intention to conduct an inquiry into the matter, the result of which is not known to Amnesty International.

Amnesty International received allegations during the period under review that some political detainees and others arrested on suspicion of politically motivated violence in Grenada were ill-treated by members of the People's Revolutionary Army shortly after their arrest. The allegations included beatings and, in two cases, the administration of electric shocks. Most of the allegations refer to the period 1979/1980. Amnesty International raised the allegations with the Grenadian Government during a mission to Grenada in January 1981 and was told that there had been some cases of ill-treatment in the past and that four members of the People's Revolutionary Army had been tried and given suspended sentences. The confessions of two defendants at a trial in October 1982 were excluded after they told the judge that they had been ill-treated following their arrest in June 1980.

Amnesty International made several inquiries of state penal authorities in the United States about allegations that prisoners were ill-treated by guards. The most widespread allegations were of beatings, kickings and the spraying of mace (teargas) directly into prisoners' faces. There have also been reports of police beatings and other forms of brutality towards suspects in police custody in towns throughout the country. Alleged victims of ill-treatment may sue police or prison officials directly in the federal courts for violations of their civil rights (which include the freedom from "cruel and unusual treatment"). Such actions have in some cases resulted in payment of damages to victims or the imposition of fines or prison sentences on officials convicted of carrying out ill-treatment.

ASIA

Afghanistan

Amnesty International received reports of the torture and ill-treatment of people taken into custody by Afghan military personnel, and more especially by the *Khad*, state information police, during the period under review. Prisoners are alleged to have been subjected to beatings, deprivation of sleep and electric shock torture. Prisoners interviewed by Amnesty International, and other reports the organization has received, indicate the widespread use of such torture techniques in as many as eight interrogation centres belonging to the *Khad* in Kabul.

In a memorandum to the Afghan Government in March 1980 Amnesty International stated that it was concerned at reports that many people associated with past atrocities under the governments of Noor Mohammad Taraki and Hafizullah Amin, overthrown in December 1979, continued to hold official positions. Amnesty International's specific recommendations included the institution of a full, impartial investigation into past torture practices and "disappearances" and the institution of criminal or disciplinary proceedings against the individuals concerned if such allegations were substantiated. It was further recommended that detainees should not be kept in places of interrogation such as existed under the previous governments of Presidents Taraki and Amin, in which torture was regularly inflicted, but should be kept in regular prisons.

In April and May 1980, following demonstrations and strikes at Kabul University, several hundred students, who included school children in some cases as young as 12, were detained. Testimonies and other reports received by Amnesty International indicated that the students were taken to Block 2 at Pul-e-Charchi Prison where they were deprived of sleep and food for three to four days and kept in incommunicado detention. The students testified to systematic beatings, many with electric shock batons. Other students, accused of being leaders of the demonstrations, were taken to the headquarters of the *Khad* where they were beaten, subjected to electric shocks and reportedly in at least two cases had nails ripped out.

Other testimonies and reports that Amnesty International has received during the period under review indicate that torture is regularly inflicted during interrogation at the headquarters of the *Khad*, situated in the Shash-darak district of Kabul, close to the presidential palace. Detainees who have been interrogated there have testified to beatings and torture with electric shocks during interrogation, involving the use either of electric shock batons or of electrodes wired to a telephone. In most cases reported to Amnesty International it appears that torture has been used to extract information and in order to force prisoners to make a confession.

Besides the headquarters of the *Khad* and Pul-e-Charchi Prison, Amnesty International has also received allegations of torture in the Central Interrogation Office attached to the Prime Minister's office, usually referred to as the *Sedarat*. Other interrogation centres known to Amnesty International where torture has been reported are *Khad-i-Panj*, *Khad* Office No. 5, in Darullaman, *Khad-i-Nezami*, the office of the military *Khad*, several private houses near the *Sedarat* building, including the Ahmad Shah Khan house and the Wasir Akbar Khan house as well as the house of Howzai Barikat in Nahridarson. Other former prisoners have reported being ill-treated inside the Ministry of Internal Affairs building itself.

It is reported that in some cases prisoners have suffered serious physical and mental injuries as a result of their ill-treatment, including permanent deafness and dumbness. Some cases have been reported to Amnesty International of prisoners dying as a result of injuries incurred during torture.

In December 1982 Amnesty International received the detailed testimony of Farida Ahmadi, a 22-year-old medical student who was detained for six months in 1981 in a *Khad* detention centre in Kabul. Farida Ahmadi said that during her detention she was continually interrogated, denied sleep for up to a week, and subjected to electric shock torture. She also alleged that she witnessed the torture of other political prisoners. Other former prisoners interviewed by Amnesty International report disturbingly similar experiences. Those tortured have included women as young as 16 and people in their early 60s.

Although many of those reportedly tortured appear to have been involved in armed resistance to the government of President Babrak Karmal, other victims include civil servants, teachers and students who have been detained merely on suspicion of opposition to the government. Many of those arrested claim not to have been involved in politics at all but to have been arrested as a deterrent to others. In some areas it was reported that regional governors summoned people to a meeting and then had them all arrested and detained for questioning about possible contacts with insurgents. Other people have been arrested and tortured solely for having relatives in the West and even for being in possession of Western or "counter-revolutionary" literature. Frequently people are arrested on the basis of reports by *Khad* informers.

Arrests take place for the most part without warrant or even identification of the arresting officer. These arrests usually take place at night. No reasons are given for the person's arrest and the family is not informed of where the prisoner is taken. Torture often takes place in front of other prisoners, and, in some cases reported to Amnesty International, even before family members. Deprivation of sleep and food for prolonged periods during interrogation was widely alleged, as was the complete absence of medical care.

No prisoners known to Amnesty International have been allowed access to family or lawyers during interrogation, which in many cases continues for several months. Prisoners are also denied fresh clothing and access to washing facilities.

In September 1982 the Afghan Government promulgated a "Law on the Implementation of Sentences in the Prisons". Article 3 of this law reinforces prohibition of torture in Afghan prisons. At the same time, the Afghan Government reported in a statement that a number of police officers were being tried for allegedly torturing prisoners. No further details are known. Amnesty International is concerned that reports of torture continue to be received from Afghanistan, and that effective measures to counter the practice or to implement the provisions of the Declaration against Torture have not been undertaken.

Bangladesh

Amnesty International has received reports of torture, ill-treatment and deaths in custody allegedly as a result of torture under the two military administrations holding office during the period under review in Bangladesh. Some allegations concerned abuses at the hands of the army of civilian as well as military political suspects while being interrogated in order to obtain confessions prior to their trial by military tribunals. There have also been more general reports of army brutality in the remote Chittagong Hill Tracts. Other allegations concern several cases of death in police custody and in prison, reportedly as a result of torture. Many reports have been difficult to verify.

Amnesty International knows of several cases where political prisoners accused of attempting to overthrow the government have been held incommunicado and denied access to lawyers for weeks or months. Ill-treatment and torture allegedly took place during this period. An Amnesty International observer in Dhaka in April 1981 attending the trial of five men charged with attempts to overthrow the government in June 1980 found that two of them had been held incommunicado for two months and that they had made statements in court to the effect that confessions had been extracted under duress and torture in the Dhaka Army Cantonment. The methods used allegedly included threats of being killed and prolonged interrogation while blindfold and tied. These allegations were not denied by the prosecution. Amnesty International also received reports that 12 soldiers, who were sentenced to death after a military trial *in camera* in July and August 1981 found them guilty of the killing of former President Ziaur Rahman, had been tortured in order to sign confessions. It was impossible for Amnesty International to obtain further details since outsiders were denied access to the men until the start of the trial *in camera* and they were executed shortly afterwards.

Amnesty International has also received several reports that detainees have died in police custody and that convicted political prisoners and prisoners being tried have died in prison, allegedly as a result of torture or ill-treatment. In some cases prosecutions of officials involved are reported to have followed. On 12 January 1981 a prisoner awaiting trial on charges of theft was reported to have died in Kushtia Jail, the jail superintendent saying he was "admitted to jail hospital with marks of physical torture". His death was reported in the Bangladesh press. Cases were filed against the sub-inspector of the police station involved under Section 302 of the Bangladesh penal code for the alleged torture of the man who died. The outcome of the proceedings in this case is not known to Amnesty International. On 25 August 1982 a man died in Chittagong Medical Hospital following alleged torture during interrogation by the Chittagong harbour police on a theft charge. He was admitted to hospital in an "unconscious state and with both legs fractured". Amnesty International knows of two political prisoners, both members of the left wing *Jatiyo Samajtantrik Dal* (JSD), National Socialist Party, who died in prison allegedly as a result of torture. One died in Kushtia Jail hospital on 30 November 1982, and was allegedly beaten to death in prison and, the JSD allege, was buried without a post mortem examination. The other report concerns the death of a man in the custody of the police in Rashahi District in late 1982. Amnesty International has no independent information confirming these serious allegations; a post mortem examination was held in the latter case and two police inspectors reportedly suspended, but the final outcome of these investigations is not known.

In some cases reported in the Bangladesh press, police officers have been ordered to appear in court for their alleged participation in torture. On 25 April 1982 a Dhaka magistrate was reported to have ordered two police officers to appear before him for allegedly torturing a student to extract a confession after an earlier magistrate's inquiry had found "truth in the allegation" of the student's father that he "found the police officers assaulting his son mercilessly with rollers". The outcome of these proceedings is not known.

Amnesty International has received many reports that since the late 1970s members of the armed forces and of the police, as well as tribal people in the Chittagong Hill Tracts have been killed in the course of guerrilla activities. International organizations and foreign press reports have given frequent accounts of assaults on and shootings by the armed forces of villagers thought to be sympathetic to the *Shanti Bahini*, Liberation Army, guerrilla group. Tribal sources have alleged the wide-spread detention of people without trial—sometimes in holes dug underground, covered with bamboo—and torture during interrogation on a large scale, the methods including rape, breaking of limbs, withholding food and prolonged beatings, sometimes resulting in death. These allegations have, however, been extremely difficult to verify.

In one case, Amnesty International has received details of the torture of a journalist while in army custody at Rangamati in the Chittagong Hill area. The organization received detailed reports that he was tortured by members of the Defence Forces Intelligence, whose identities are known to Amnesty International, during the several months he was held in incommunicado detention following his arrest in June 1981. The allegations include the pulling out of hair, electric shocks and burning with cigarettes. He was denied contact with the outside world during the first six months of his detention, when the torture allegedly occurred.

Recent reports of torture in army custody reached Amnesty International following the arrest of opposition leaders and students in February 1983 during a series of protests against the continuation of military rule. Whereas Amnesty International has not been able to verify these allegations, students and opposition parties (the Awami League and the JSD) have alleged that during interrogation by the army in Dhaka Army Cantonment detainees were beaten, suspended from the ceiling and were threatened with further torture. The government did not respond to Amnesty International's inquiries in a letter of 31 March 1983 asking the government to investigate the seven individual cases mentioned. One of those arrested during the demonstrations in February, the student leader Moshtaque Ahmed—the ex-President of the Dhaka Medical College —was allegedly tortured to death in the Dhaka Army Cantonment, but there are no further reports to confirm the circumstances of his death.

China

Amnesty International has received reports that some detainees were ill-treated in detention centres administered by public security (police) officers during the late 1970s and early 1980s in the People's Republic of China. Such ill-treatment included beatings, the use of shackles and other means reportedly used to punish prisoners or to put pressure on them during interrogation. Liu Qing, a prisoner of conscience held in mid-1980 in Beijing's main detention centre, reported having been beaten, forced to wear a gas mask which made breathing difficult and being handcuffed with tight manacles for refusing to obey a regulation ordering detainees to observe an attitude of humility when walking. He was also held in solitary confinement in a cold and wet cell for several months after his arrest. Zhang Wenhe, another political detainee held at the time in the same detention centre, is also reported to have been ill-treated for indiscipline; he was reportedly beaten on many occasions, forced to wear a gas mask and handcuffed with manacles behind his back continuously for several months. His mental health is reported to have been affected as a result.

Amnesty International is also concerned about the use of solitary confinement for prolonged periods during investigation or for prisoners the authorities consider could exert a "dangerous" influence on others. Wei Jingsheng, a prisoner of conscience sentenced to 15 years' imprisonment in October 1979, is reported to have been held in solitary confinement in Beijing Prison No. 1 since then. In 1980 he was reported to be held in the block of the prison where prisoners sentenced to death are held. In mid-1983 it was reported that he was being allowed out of his cell for exercise only once a month and not permitted to meet other prisoners or to receive visits from his family.

The use of torture and other means to extract confessions has been prohibited by Chinese law since the 1950s. However, despite efforts made in recent years by the authorities to publicize and denounce cases where public security personnel had ill-treated prisoners, detainees still have inadequate protection from such abuse. The official media also show that confessions and admission of guilt still play a dominant role in judicial work.

India

Police brutality and torture have long been common and widespread in India and have continued during the period under review. Such methods are frequently used when people suspected of ordinary criminal offences are interrogated, in order to extract confessions or for purposes of intimidation. Each year, these police practices have resulted in the deaths of dozens of victims held in police custody. Torture also reportedly continues to be used on political prisoners suspected of involvement with armed opposition to the government, especially on members of the Communist Party of India (Marxist-Leninist), commonly referred to as "Naxalites". Torture is reported to have taken place in police stations although a few cases of beatings in prisons have also been reported. The Indian army has been accused of torture in those Indian states where its forces are engaged in suppressing armed insurrection against the government, particularly Nagaland and Mizoram. On a few occasions the army has also reportedly used torture during investigation into such offences as spying, conspiracy and theft.

In India, torture is not prohibited by the constitution but the Ministry of Home Affairs has claimed that Indian laws contain adequate provisions for safeguarding human rights and that sufficient safeguards against police brutality and torture exist. Although the Prime Minister is reported to have condemned police brutality on several occasions, there appears to be some official acceptance of the use of ill-treatment by the security forces among officials at both the state and central government level. For example, on 27 October 1980 the Union Home Minister—who is in charge of the administration of justice—was reported as saying: "Though a shameful thing, third degree methods had to be applied because there were hardened criminals who would not otherwise come out with the truth."

The alleged methods of torture include hanging people upside down, severe beatings (sometimes until the victim's limbs are broken), burnings and applying heavy rollers to the victim's legs. In some cases the use of electric shocks has been reported. Such methods were particularly common during the investigation of ordinary criminal offences, such as theft, and are most widely used against the poorer sectors of Indian society, notably the *Adivasis*, tribals, and *Harijans*, "untouchables". But other methods of torture have also been employed when deterrence appears to be an element of police torture: 36 suspected criminals in Bhagalpur Jail in the state of Bihar were deliberately blinded by the police between October 1979 and November 1980 by having their eyes pierced and soaked in acid. In early 1981 the Indian press reported detailed accounts of people suspected of ordinary criminal offences whose legs had been broken and then twisted by the police in Varanasi and Ghazipur in Uttar Pradesh.

The use of brutal interrogation methods frequently resulted in the death of suspects in police custody: for example, between January and September 1980 at least 27 deaths in police custody occurred in India, and during 1981 at least 21 prisoners were reported to have died in police custody. Such cases have been reported from the states of Bihar, West Bengal, Madhya Pradesh, Uttar Pradesh, Karnataka, Gujarat, Maharashtra, Rajasthan, Haryana, Tamil Nadu, Tripura and New Delhi territory. The police usually cited "suicide", "disease", "shock" or "injuries received prior to arrest" as causes of death but post mortem reports in most cases indicated the victims had died of multiple injuries sustained while in detention.

The police named low pay and strong pressure to produce evidence in a large number of cases as reasons for resorting to illegal methods of interrogation. Whereas nearly all allegations of torture by the police concern its use in police stations, often on people who have not been formally arrested, some reports of beatings and the prolonged use of iron fetters leading to disability concern prisoners in jail following arrest or conviction.

Guerrilla tactics employed by Naxalite groups since the early 1970s provoked stern police reaction and counter-insurgency measures frequently accompanied by torture. Amnesty International continued to receive reports of the torture of political prisoners during the period under review from the states of Andhra Pradesh, Kerala, Tamil Nadu, Bihar and West Bengal. In several Indian states, especially in Andhra Pradesh and Tamil Nadu, torture of political suspects is reported to have preceded their killing in staged "encounters" with the police.

Cases of torture and deaths in custody are widely reported in the Indian press, and in a number of instances have been investigated by civil liberties organizations, although there have been few official inquiries. Although the establishment of magisterial inquiries into instances of death in custody is mandatory, such inquiries were often not held, or held only after strong public or local pressure. Of the 21 deaths in custody reported during 1981, Amnesty International knows of only six cases in which the holding of magisterial inquiries was subsequently announced. Such inquiries, when held, often failed to be conclusive because the magistrate must depend on the police to investigate members of its own forces. When magisterial inquiries found that deaths in custody were due to police brutality—as was the case in at least three instances during 1981—the responsible police officers were usually suspended from duty or transferred. When criminal charges followed, conviction on these charges was rare. Sometimes, police were later reinstated. For example, of the 15 police officers originally suspended for involvement in the Bhagalpur Jail blinding case, at least 12 were subsequently reinstated, while some police and officials reportedly responsible were even promoted. The Chief Minister of Bihar State officially stated that the blindings had "social sanction". The Superintendent of Bhagalpur Jail, in which the blindings occurred, who was directly responsible for exposing the blindings, was suspended from duty without pay. A similar attitude was displayed by the Tamil Nadu government. After evidence of police torture and killings of political activists in staged "encounters" had been presented by civil liberties organizations, the Chief Minister publicly urged the police "to put down anti-social elements with a strong hand without worrying about criticism in the press or any quarter".

The Supreme Court of India in particular has taken an active role in seeking to protect detainees and prisoners from torture. In a number of cases it has treated letters written by detainees as *habeas corpus* petitions, ordering judicial investigations into the allegations or itself investigating reported violations of human rights. However, the Bihar state government has frustrated the Supreme Court's investigations by withholding relevant documents.

During the period under review Amnesty International repeatedly wrote both to the central government and to the Chief Ministers of certain states asking officials to institute independent investigations into these allegations of torture and deaths in police custody. Only rarely did Amnesty International receive a reply from the state governments. Those authorities which did reply stated that magisterial inquiries had been instituted, but did not give further details of their findings, as Amnesty International had requested.

In 1977 the Indian Government co-sponsored United Nations General Assembly Resolution 32/62, which requested the drafting of a convention against torture and other forms of ill-treatment. In 1977 it was also the chief sponsor of Resolution 32/64, which called on member states to reinforce their support for the Declaration against Torture by making unilateral declarations against torture and other ill-treatment. In 1979 India made such a unilateral declaration. At the national level the Prime Minister of

India is on record as having said in early 1980 that there must be "basic faults in police training to make them so inhumane", calling for changes in the police manual. However, as far as Amnesty International is aware, this commitment has not been translated into effective action to protect Indian citizens from the widespread use of torture. Amnesty International urged the government to establish a totally independent and effective body, functioning openly and subject to public scrutiny, to investigate complaints of ill-treatment, torture and deaths in custody, and to protect suspects from such abuses by introducing a set of detailed legal measures, including investigations into the record and conduct of police officials and a detailed code of conduct for police officials to be included in the training of police personnel. Successive Indian governments did not reply to these recommendations, claiming that there were already sufficient safeguards against police brutality and torture.

Indonesia and East Timor

There were persistent reports of the torture and ill-treatment of people arrested on suspicion of belonging to groups opposed to the government, particularly groups engaged in violent opposition to the government of Indonesia during the period under review. In December 1981, the government introduced a new code of criminal procedure which offers pre-trial safeguards for ordinary criminal suspects. Amnesty International continued to receive reports of the torture, sometimes leading to death, of ordinary criminal suspects held in police custody, even after introduction of the new code. People accused of subversion and other political offences were explicitly excluded from the protection of the new code.

Amnesty International learned of instances of torture occurring in areas where there is considerable opposition to the government, including armed resistance, such as Aceh, North Sumatra, Irian Jaya, West Papua, and East Timor, and against people allegedly engaged in violent efforts to create a Muslim state. Amnesty International believes that units of the armed forces—principally *Intel*, army intelligence; the elite *Resimen Para Kommando Angkatan Darat* (RPKAD), Army Paracommando Attack Regiment; the *Laksusda*, the branches of the *Kommando Operasi Pemulihan Keamanan dan Ketertiban* (KOPKAMTIB), Command for the Restoration of Security and Order, attached to the local commands, and the military police—have tortured people suspected of membership of, support for or simply knowledge of insurgent groups active in these areas.

In Irian Jaya, suspected supporters of the *Organisasi Papua*

Merdeka (OPM), Free Papua Organization, have reportedly been subjected to severe ill-treatment after arrest. Six women, arrested in Jayapura in August 1980 allegedly for raising a Free Papuan flag, were reportedly raped and beaten after being taken into detention by the military police. Several people believed to have been prominent members of the OPM are reported to have died in detention as a result of ill-treatment. Marthen Tabu, who had been arrested in April 1980 after reporting to the authorities under an amnesty guaranteeing his freedom, reportedly died as a result of ill-treatment following his transfer in September 1981 to a special army camp after an attempt had been made to rescue him from the prison where he was held.

Because of the remoteness of many of the areas from which they commonly emanate, Amnesty International often receives such reports only after a delay. In 1983, for example, Amnesty International received credible testimony indicating that members of the Aceh National Liberation Front arrested in 1977 and 1978 had been tortured while in the custody of *Intel* and the military police.

Muslims detained for alleged involvement in movements engaged in violent efforts to create an Islamic state have also reportedly been treated with great brutality. Prisoners held by the *Laksusda* in Mlaten prison, Semarang and Wirogunan prison, Yogyakarta, both in Central Java, were reported in February 1982 to have been subjected to a variety of brutalities and indignities including: having matchsticks inserted under their fingernails and lit; being put in a cell tied up and without food for two days; being interrogated with a pistol aimed at the head; being given electric shocks; near drowning; being beaten repeatedly on the head. They were subjected to some forms of treatment which offended their religious beliefs, such as not being allowed to pray and being confined with people of the opposite sex. The health of those in need of treatment for injuries and diseases contracted in detention was also reportedly ignored, leading in at least one case to the death of a detainee. At least two members of one Muslim group, the *Imran* group, who had been arrested in connection with an aircraft hijacking in March 1981, are believed to have died as a result of ill-treatment while in military custody.

Amnesty International has continued to receive reports of torture and ill-treatment from East Timor. Torture is most commonly reported to occur during interrogation following the surrender or capture of suspected supporters of the *Frente Revolucionaria do Timor Leste Independente* (Fretilin), Revolutionary Front of Independent East Timor. Amnesty International has received extensive reports of the torture of people suspected of involvement in an attack on a broadcasting station on the outskirts of the capital Dili in June 1980 and of another group of about 100 people arrested in January 1981 for alleged involvement in a conspiracy to abet a Fretilin attack. Amnesty International has been able to identify two houses in Dili used for interrogation by *Intel* and the RPKAD respectively and where torture is reported to have been inflicted routinely. Amnesty International has on several occasions requested the Indonesian Government to investigate allegations of torture and ill-treatment in East Timor but no such investigations have been conducted. Indeed there is strong evidence that torture is officially condoned. A secret Indonesian military document issued in July 1982, of whose authenticity Amnesty International is confident, contains guidelines on the interrogation of captives which clearly condone the use of torture and death threats.

Attempts to gain redress in cases of alleged torture and ill-treatment have generally been thwarted. In 1982 Haji Fatwa, a well-known Muslim teacher, brought a civil suit against a number of military personnel including the Minister of Defense and the commander of KOPKAMTIB for damages allegedly arising from ill-treatment he suffered while in detention in October 1980. In the weeks leading up to the opening of the case, Haji Fatwa and his lawyers reported that they had been subjected to various kinds of intimidation including, in the case of Haji Fatwa himself, physical assault. As a result the lawyers withdrew from the case citing an unfavourable atmosphere and the suit subsequently lapsed.

In a few cases involving the ill-treatment of ordinary criminal suspects by the police, Amnesty International knows of prosecutions, usually in well-publicized instances where ill-treatment has resulted in the death of the suspect. The new criminal procedure code introduced in December 1981 provides for pre-trial judicial investigation; maximum periods for detention without charge or trial; conpensation for wrongful detentions or conviction; and access to legal assistance including during interrogation. However, these safeguards do not apply to people held under certain "special laws" including those cases involving national security. The security agency KOPKAMTIB is still empowered to make arrests without reference to the new procedures. Amnesty International knows of no prosecutions brought against police officers for violations of the new code. Cases of severe ill-treatment and deaths in custody continue to be reported.

Korea (Republic of)

Torture and ill-treatment of political prisoners was prevalent in

1980 when martial law was in force in South Korea. It continued to be inflicted on political and ordinary criminal suspects during the period under review in spite of its prohibition under the constitution promulgated in October 1980 and government promises that it would take steps to eradicate such abuses.

At least 200 students, journalists and others involved in a movement for democracy and human rights, which gathered strength after the assassination of President Park Chung-hee in October 1979, were arrested after the nationwide imposition of martial law on 17 May 1980. Their interrogation, in most cases allegedly under torture, was carried out by the military in military as well as civilian facilities. In Seoul, the capital, these included Suh Bingo, the interrogation centre of the Defence Security Command, and the National Police Headquarters. In Kwangju, an estimated 1,000 people were rounded up after violent disturbances at the end of May 1980 and taken to an army base on the outskirts of the city, where eight were reportedly beaten to death by Special Forces troops. Others were held incommunicado in the security division of Kwangju Police Headquarters. In Pusan, one cleric, Rev. Im Ki-yun, died in July 1980 after one week of interrogation by the army. According to accounts received by Amnesty International, most prisoners held for violations of martial law were physically assaulted; a few, well known at home or abroad, were not, although they were subjected to sleep deprivation.

Reports indicate that after the lifting of martial law at the end of January 1981, torture continued to be used regularly in the cases of people who were suspected of pro-communist or socialist sympathies and anti-state activities and were arrested and interrogated by the Korean Central Intelligence Agency (renamed Agency for National Security Planning in January 1981) or by the security or anti-communist section of the National Police at its local, provincial or national headquarters.

Between 100 and 200 students were detained each year for illegal demonstrations or leafleting during the period under review. Reports received by Amnesty International indicate that they were routinely subjected to beatings at police stations. Less information is available about the torture or ill-treatment of prisoners in ordinary criminal cases. South Korean newspapers publicized at least four cases where torture was inflicted on criminal suspects. One of them, a business person, Kim Kun-jo, was reported to have died as a result of torture in March 1983.

Torture and ill-treatment seem to have been used for two purposes: as a means of intimidation, in cases where no charges were brought, and to obtain confessions. Most prisoners appear to have been initially subjected to up to several days of beating, threats of secret execution etc. to break their resistance; later on, during interrogation, beatings or other methods of torture were used to obtain factual information or the suspect's signature on a false confession. Methods of torture often used included water torture (forcing water through the nostrils of a prisoner suspended upside-down); suspending the prisoner, whose hands and feet are tied together, with a club put into the crook of the knees ("roast chicken" torture); twisting of limbs with wooden sticks, and banging the head backward and forward. Beatings were sometimes inflicted by special teams. Electric shocks were reportedly inflicted in one case at the Detention Security Command interrogation centre at the end of May 1981 and, in another case, at the National Police Headquarters in Seoul in the summer of 1981.

In most cases where torture was alleged, the prisoners were detained without a warrant of arrest and the legal limits of the length of detention (48 or 72 hours) were not respected. Although a suspect is legally entitled to meet counsel, in most cases this right was not respected until the indictment. In all cases known to Amnesty International relatives were also prohibited from meeting prisoners before indictment. Under martial law, a military doctor has occasionally been available for the examination of prisoners but even in these cases this did not prevent ill-treatment.

Physical ill-treatment also took place when individual prisoners or groups of prisoners protested, often by going on hunger-strike, against prison conditions. Amnesty International received detailed reports of such incidents where prisoners were beaten in various prisons in 1981, 1982 and 1983. In 1982, two prisoners held in Kwangju prison died: one, Kee Jong-do, reportedly from the after-effects of torture and lack of medical attention; the other, Park Kwan-hyon, died in October 1982 after he had led a hunger-strike protesting against his torture and other ill-treatment in the prison. He was reportedly ill-treated during his hunger-strike.

During the period under review, several prisoners suffered broken limbs, back injuries and nervous disorders as a result of torture or ill-treatment, and many suffered from the long-term effects of torture. Claims that prisoners had been tortured to extract false confessions were made in court or in written statements of appeal by prisoners tried on charges of anti-state activities. Often these claims were publicized by their families and also supported by Protestant and Roman Catholic clergy. In spite of a constitutional guarantee that evidence obtained under torture shall not be accepted by the courts, confessions obtained by such means were accepted as evidence in several political trials without proper examination of their validity or of the defendants' claims that they had been improperly obtained. However, in three separate non-political cases in the period August 1981 to June 1982, the prosecution released a suspect without charges and two defendants were acquitted by the courts because it had been found that their confessions had been obtained under torture.

In repeated communications to the government, Amnesty International asked that it investigate specific reports of torture and ill-treatment and make the results of such investigations public. The organization did not receive replies, nor did it subsequently learn that independent investigations were made.

At the end of October 1981, after the South Korean press publicized two cases of torture of ordinary criminal suspects, the Director of the National Police announced the establishment within the National Police of a department to protect the human rights of suspects held in custody. Amnesty International asked the authorities for further information about this announced measure, but received no reply.

In October 1982 the Minister of Home Affairs gave assurances before the National Assembly that no suspects would be assaulted or tortured and that the government would step up the education and training of police officers. Two cases where assault on suspects was officially investigated are known. After the death in March 1983 of Kim Kun-jo, a business person held for questioning by police in Seoul, a police officer was tried, convicted of assault and sentenced to seven years' imprisonment. The National Police Headquarters issued a statement in which it said it regretted the incident and would take measures to prevent "police violence" and the Director of the National Police resigned, taking responsibility for the incident.

Pakistan

Amnesty International has received detailed reports during the period under review which indicate the frequent torture of prisoners in Pakistan. Prisoners who have been subjected to torture include political party workers, trade unionists, teachers, students, journalists and lawyers, as well as prisoners held for ordinary criminal offences.

Amnesty International was also concerned about the widespread use of flogging as a punishment for ordinary criminal and, to a lesser extent, political offences, as well as for offences under Islamic law. In addition, under both martial law provisions and Islamic law, mutilation through amputation is available as a punishment for theft.

Torture was inflicted by police and military agencies, in particular by the army's Field Investigation Unit (FIU) and the police's Special Branch and Criminal Investigation Agency (CIA), in army camps, special interrogation centres and regular police stations throughout the country. Political prisoners are known to have been tortured in Shahi Fort in Lahore, which is regularly cited as a place of interrogation where torture is used, at Attock and Bala Hissar Forts, Warsak Camp (Peshawar), Much Jail in Baluchistan, the military interrogation centre at Malir Cantonment, Clifton Police Station in Karachi and the Baldia Interrogation Centre near Karachi.

Methods of torture reported to Amnesty International have included: hanging prisoners from the ceiling, sometimes upside down, for hours at a time while beating them; severe and prolonged beatings, including on the soles of the feet, ankles, knees and on the head; electric shocks; burning the body with cigarettes; placing the prisoner on a wooden bench fitted with wooden rollers which are forced over the upper legs; deprivation of sleep for periods of up to five days and threats of execution and threats to the safety of relatives. Amnesty International believes that several hundred prisoners may have been tortured since 1980.

Amnesty International has received detailed signed statements by former prisoners who have allegedly suffered torture and has also been able to make medical examinations of some released prisoners. The medical report on one released prisoner, allegedly tortured by army personnel in 1981, concluded that the scars left on the body "are so strongly suggestive of being caused by torture that they should be accepted as confirmatory evidence". Amnesty International has also received detailed reports of torture in the form of affidavits from the lawyers of political prisoners and accounts published in the Pakistan press.

Torture has often taken place during prolonged interrogation in preventive or pre-trial detention, which has frequently lasted for weeks or even months. The majority of prisoners who have alleged torture have been held in incommunicado detention. Relatives of prisoners are frequently unable to establish the prisoners' whereabouts during the period of interrogation. Amnesty International believes that the incommunicado detention of political prisoners has increased since 1981 and that this practice, together with other deficiencies in legal safeguards for prisoners, has facilitated torture. Martial law authorities have wide powers of preventive detention and prisoners may be held for 12 months without any requirement that they be informed of the grounds of arrest. Constitutional changes introduced in March 1981 have resulted in political prisoners losing the right to *habeas corpus* and the judiciary may no longer examine the actions of the martial law authorities.

Torture of prisoners during interrogations has often been used in an attempt to extract information about political activities, to extract confessions to acts of violence against the government, or to implicate others suspected by the authorities of such activity. Amnesty International has received reports that prisoners' statements extracted under torture may have been used as evidence during court proceedings.

Since the imposition of martial law in July 1977, several hundred prisoners have received sentences of flogging. Sentences may be imposed by military and Islamic courts. Amnesty International is unable to compile complete statistics, but has recorded that during 1980 alone at least 155 prisoners were sentenced to be flogged, largely for ordinary criminal offences. In early 1981 the incidence of flogging of political prisoners increased markedly, and the flogging of both political and ordinary criminal prisoners continued during 1982. During the first half of 1983 the incidence of flogging rose considerably and the number of lashes regularly imposed increased. Between 15 and 17 April 1983 at least 216 men were flogged in Karachi Central Jail, having been convicted by a summary military court of participation in sectarian riots in Karachi earlier that year. In addition to a sentence of one year's imprisonment, they were subjected to between 10 and 18 lashes, which were administered to the buttocks with a cane five feet long and half an inch thick. Some prisoners are reported to have collapsed after these floggings. Floggings may also take place in public before large crowds.

Prior to a flogging, the victim is medically examined to ensure that flogging does not result in death. A doctor is reportedly required to be present at floggings to suspend proceedings should the victim be unable to withstand the full sentence administered at one time. Amnesty International has received reports of the flogging of 16-year-old boys and 60-year-old men and of women.

Twenty-three sentences of amputation of the hand for convicted thieves and robbers are known by Amnesty International to have been passed by military and Islamic courts since 1977. To date, no sentence is known to have been implemented, although one sentence had been confirmed by the Federal *Shari'a*, Islamic, Court in June 1982.

Amnesty International has expressed its concern and issued frequent appeals on receipt of detailed allegations of torture, when floggings have been ordered or when it is feared sentences of amputation may be carried out. Amnesty International has urged the authorities on several occasions to establish independent and public inquiries into allegations of the torture of prisoners, and when deaths in detention, reportedly resulting from torture, have occurred.

In its report *Pakistan: Human Rights Violations and the Rule of Law*, published in January 1982, Amnesty International publicized the cases of 10 prisoners, including three political prisoners, whose deaths in detention during the period from January 1980 to August 1981 reportedly occurred as a result of torture. The organization received further reports of the death in police custody of people arrested for ordinary criminal offences since that date. In five of the above-mentioned cases of deaths in detention, investigations or criminal proceedings have reportedly begun, although according to information available to Amnesty International in none of these cases have proceedings led to the officials named as responsible being convicted. Nor have the findings of the investigations been published in their entirety, as Amnesty International requested. In other instances, the Government of Pakistan has responded to representations made by the organization concerning the alleged use of torture by denying that it has taken place.

The only instance known to Amnesty International of the prosecution of law enforcement personnel charged with torture occurred in April 1983. Three police officers were reported to have been sentenced to death by a Special Military Court for causing the death of one prisoner and beating three others in 1979. Amnesty International knows of no occasion when a victim of torture has been awarded compensation or redress for treatment suffered.

Philippines

Amnesty International has continued to receive credible reports of systematic torture in the Philippines during the period under review, following the pattern established since the proclamation of martial law in September 1972. In recent years, with the increased involvement of the armed forces in counter-insurgency operations, often in remote parts of the country, Amnesty International has been concerned about evidence of abuses of people taken into custody by military personnel including beatings, forcing individuals to undertake humiliating acts, and other forms of ill-treatment, referred to in the Philippines as "man-handling".

Despite the lifting of martial law in 1981, members of the armed forces have retained extensive powers of arrest and detention in cases involving alleged "subversives" and other "public order violators". Although an extensive legal framework providing safeguards in cases of such arrests exists, alleged suspects are commonly abducted without warrant and detained incommunicado and in violation of other procedural safeguards. During such periods of detention detainees have commonly been subjected to torture or other forms of ill-treatment. In most cases reported to Amnesty International, the agencies responsible for arrest were armed forces intelligence branches, in particular units of the Intelligence Service of the Armed Forces of the Philippines (ISAFP), known as Military Intelligence Groups (MIGs), and Regional Security Units (RSU) of the Philippine Constabulary intelligence service, C2.

Detainees arrested or abducted by these units were commonly taken to undisclosed and unauthorized interrogation centres, known as "safehouses", where interrogation was commonly accompanied by torture involving electric shocks, sexual abuse and beatings. Detainees may be held in these conditions for periods ranging from a few days to several months. After a period of such detention, detainees may be released or transferred to an authorized place of detention. Amnesty International also knows of instances where detainees in such "safehouses" have not been seen again and are presumed or known to have died as a result of their ill-treatment. This pattern appears to be almost standard operating procedure for intelligence units.

The *Report of an Amnesty International Mission to the Republic of the Philippines, 11-28 November 1981*, published in September 1982, outlined the organization's findings that safeguards for the protection of detainees had been systematically ignored with apparent impunity; that detainees were often tortured while under interrogation; and that investigations in cases involving complaints brought by people alleging torture and ill-treatment were deficient and that, in the rare cases where the outcome of official investigation was a recommendation for prosecution, the recommendation was not pursued by the authorities. Amnesty International made a number of recommendations to the government regarding torture, including preventive measures such as the abolition of "safehouses", the abolition of waivers known as "waivers of detention" whereby detainees waive their right to be presented to a judicial authority, and stricter implementation of existing safeguards. In its reply to the report, the government dismissed Amnesty International's recommendations, asserting that existing procedures were adequate and rejecting evidence that they had been systematically violated.

Investigations of complaints of torture have usually been undertaken by the armed forces or the Ministry of National Defense, the civil judiciary rarely intervening. Amnesty International knows of no case since 1980 in which armed forces personnel have been convicted either by a civil or a military court of offences related to a complaint of torture. In March 1982, following the arrest two weeks earlier of 23 alleged Communist Party members, 17 of them submitted complaints to the Supreme Court alleging that they had been tortured or ill-treated while held in incommunicado detention. The Supreme Court, for the first time when presented with such complaints, ordered medical examinations of the complainants, the results of which were inconclusive. The latter then presented a petition to the United Nations Commission on Human Rights alleging violations of domestic and international law following their arrest. In another case two detainees, arrested in February 1982 with four others all alleged to be associated with the Communist Party of the Philippines, complained to the Supreme Court that they had been subjected to electric shocks, denied their right to legal counsel and made to sign statements under duress. The Supreme Court in July 1982 ordered a commission chaired by a government prosecutor to investigate the allegations. The findings of the commission have not been made known. Amnesty International is aware of a number of cases where reprimands have been issued, but only with respect to alleged violations of procedural safeguards and not with respect to the torture or ill-treatment complained of. The organization knows of several instances of military personnel who had persistently been accused of torture being promoted even after receiving administrative reprimands. Government officials have persistently denied that systematic torture is used in the Philippines, pointing to the extensive array of legal safeguards designed to prevent it and to the limited number of cases in which torture has been proved.

In addition to systematic torture and ill-treatment by intelligence units, Amnesty International was concerned about the mounting evidence of random violence known as "man-handling" committed by military personnel engaged in field operations mostly against peasants and tribal people living in remote rural areas. In a typical case reported in June 1982, three members of the Subanon tribe in Zamboanga del Sur province, Mindanao, were arrested by an army detachment and taken to a local command post where one of them was reportedly ordered to perform a dance, was beaten about the ears and chest, had a cigarette extinguished on his chest and had bullets placed between his fingers which were then crushed together. Amnesty International has received similar accounts from other remote areas including Abra province, the home of the Tinggian tribe, and Samar. "Man-handling" often occurs publicly, sometimes in the presence of a whole village. In some cases, "man-handling" has been a prelude to the killing of the victim. Because the areas where these incidents occur are often remote, reports received by the organization are difficult to investigate. However, the Amnesty International mission delegation which visited the Philippines in November 1981 was presented with a number of such cases. The Philippine Government has ordered investigations into reported incidents of "man-handling", shooting and killing since August 1979 primarily by convening the so-called Barbero Committee, a standing commission of inquiry, comprising the Deputy Minister of National Defense and senior military officers. However, in those cases where the committee has recommended prosecution of named military personnel, further action has been dilatory or not forthcoming at all. All the information indicates that follow-up in such cases is often obstructed by intimidation and fear of reprisals by military personnel.

Sri Lanka

In Sri Lanka torture is prohibited by Article 11 of the 1978 constitution, the penal code and the Police Ordinance. Despite these substantial legal safeguards, torture was used, at times systematically, by the army and the police—notably the Criminal Investigation Department—during the period under review. Its main purpose seems to have been to obtain information about or confessions from people suspected of having knowledge of the activities of Tamil extremist groups operating in the north of Sri Lanka, where the Tamil minority live. Some Tamil extremist groups have resorted to violent means in seeking the establishment of a separate state and several police and army officials, as well as politicians, have been killed in recent years in the north of the country. Other allegations of ill-treatment of suspects in police custody and of deaths of ordinary criminal suspects in detention have reached Amnesty International from all parts of Sri Lanka, and mainly concern Sinhalese victims.

Torture has been a longstanding concern of Amnesty International in Sri Lanka under both the present and previous administrations. Reports of torture have regularly been put before Sri Lanka's parliament by members of the opposition and evidence of torture, supported by sworn affidavits, legal testimonies and medical reports, has been presented in Sri Lanka's Court of Appeal and in the Supreme Court. International human rights organizations, including Amnesty International and the International Commission of Jurists, have drawn attention to reports of torture in Sri Lanka on a number of occasions. On 23 May 1980 Amnesty International presented a memorandum to the government which concluded that torture had been used systematically by the police and army during the months following the 11 July 1979 emergency declaration. While similar reports of such a substantial nature did not reach the organization during 1980, an Amnesty International mission, visiting Sri Lanka from 31 January to 9 February 1982, investigated allegations that Tamil detainees held under the 1979 Prevention of Terrorism Act and held in incommunicado detention had been tortured. The Amnesty International delegation examined 10 released detainees and obtained affidavits from others still in detention which confirmed that torture had been used systematically by the security forces in the north of Sri Lanka following a bank robbery in March 1981. It was used especially by the army and also by the police in various army camps and some police stations described in the Amnesty International report. Methods of torture included hanging prisoners upside down, prolonged beatings on sensitive parts of the body, insertion of needles under finger and toe nails and insertion of chilis into sensitive parts of the body. These reports of torture were consistent with and largely similar to earlier reports received by Amnesty International. In several cases, signed statements obtained under torture were taken down in a language not understood by the detainees and reportedly without having been read to them. Such statements have subsequently been used in court proceedings, and Amnesty International understands that in several cases they were used as the main evidence on which the prosecution relied in order to obtain a conviction.

Invariably, torture occurred while detainees were held incommunicado and denied all contact with lawyers and relatives.

In September 1981 the Court of Appeal upheld allegations that two detainees, held under the Prevention of Terrorism Act, had been tortured, specifically rejecting the denials of their custodians.

Amnesty International continued to receive reports of torture after its mission visited Sri Lanka, the most serious of which concerned the death in army custody on 10 April 1983, reportedly as a result of torture, of a Tamil detainee arrested under the Prevention of Terrorism Act. A magisterial inquiry was held. The post mortem report presented at the magisterial inquiry listed 25 external and 10 internal injuries, and the magistrate, at the end of inquest procedures, returned a verdict of homicide.

Amnesty International also received several reports of assaults on ordinary criminal suspects in police stations. Amnesty International knows of five such deaths having occurred during 1981 allegedly as a result of torture, but its information on these incidents is far from complete. These reports come from all over Sri Lanka and concern members of both the Sinhalese and the Tamil communities. Such cases are regularly reported in the Sri Lanka press, and are usually followed by a magisterial inquiry. They sometimes result in investigations into police conduct, some police having been remanded in custody on charges of murder. Amnesty International is not aware of any police officials having been convicted of these offences.

The Sri Lanka Government has signed and ratified the International Covenant on Civil and Political Rights, which in Article 7 prohibits torture, and on 2 September 1982 the government made a Declaration to the Secretary-General of the United Nations that it would comply with the Declaration against Torture and would implement the principles set forth therein. Despite its international commitments, and despite repeated requests by Amnesty International and other international human rights organizations to establish independent inquiries into allegations of torture by the security forces—sometimes upheld in court—and to take measures to prevent its occurrence, the government has consistently failed to investigate these well-documented reports of torture, and has denied that torture is taking place. Furthermore, Amnesty International knows of two police officers, named as involved in reports of torture and killings of Tamil detainees, who have been promoted after the incidents took place. Amnesty International is not aware of any form of compensation having been given to victims of torture, even in cases where they were told on release they were innocent of the charges brought against them.

Under Article 126 of the Sri Lanka constitution the Supreme Court has power to hear complaints of torture, but few complaints are made to the Court because of threats of repercussions and because few detainees have the means and facilities of doing so. Moreover, complaints have to be filed within one month of the infringement of human rights alleged, thus preventing the filing of complaints by detainees held in prolonged incommunicado detention. It has therefore been difficult to prove official responsibility for torture to the satisfaction of the Supreme Court, although one Supreme Court judge in a dissenting judgment in 1981 stated his view that torture took place and that the victim had a right to compensation.

Amnesty International has recommended that, in line with the international legal instruments designed to prevent torture, the government allow all detainees arrested under the Prevention of Terrorism Act and the Emergency Regulations immediate and regular access to lawyers and relatives, that it ensure that all detainees are produced before a magistrate within 24 hours of arrest, that it introduce—in the absence of any rules for detention and interrogation of detainees held under the Prevention of Terrorism Act—detailed regulations for regular medical examination and the limitation of interrogation times and ensure the presence of a senior official throughout interrogations. Amnesty International has further recommended that the one month time limit, within which complaints of torture have to be submitted to the Supreme Court, be extended and that the government establish an independent investigative machinery to investigate complaints of torture by the security forces, that the findings of such a body be published in all cases and that criminal and disciplinary proceedings be taken against any officials responsible.

Taiwan

Reports of torture and ill-treatment of prisoners in Taiwan were less frequent in the period under review than in the previous decade. Most of the 40 prisoners convicted after a human rights demonstration in Kaohsiung in December 1979 claimed in court that their confessions admitting the charges against them were obtained by violence, sleep deprivation and threats of the death sentence in some cases. They had been held incommunicado for more than two months by the Taiwan Garrison Command (TGC) and interrogated by that agency and more than 30 of them were interrogated for a further two months by civilian prosecutors. An Amnesty International mission which went to Taiwan in February 1980 met a number of people who had been interrogated following the December demonstration and released without charges. Some of those interviewed had been interrogated continuously throughout their detention, in some cases for less than 10 hours, in others for seven days and nights. The delegates were also told about torture used during interrogation on some of the other prisoners. These included beatings with a leather belt, electric shocks and the wearing of fetters and iron balls; others were reportedly forced to squat for long periods in front of electric fans. In a memorandum to the government in February 1981 Amnesty International asked that these claims be investigated; it also called for an end to incommunicado detention and other conditions that facilitate ill-treatment in custody and the introduction of procedures to investigate complaints of ill-treatment and compensate victims.

The government replied that the defendants' allegations of ill-treatment had been investigated by the court and found to be groundless. However, to Amnesty International's knowledge, the military court that tried eight of the defendants had dismissed their requests for the interrogating officers to be examined in court and accepted statements by the military prosecutor and the Bureau of Investigation that the complaints were unfounded. Amnesty International received no indication that an independent investigation of the torture allegations took place. In its response to the government Amnesty International stressed that the isolation of suspects during interrogation, while facilitating ill-treatment, also made it difficult for the prisoners to prove their complaints and for the government to disprove them.

On 1 July 1981 the government promulgated a State Compensation Law under which a plaintiff may claim compensation for damages caused by government employees in the course of their duties.

In July 1982 the Code of Criminal Procedure was amended to allow suspects in custody to retain a defence lawyer immediately after arrest. It is believed that the amendment was hastened by the case of Dr Chen Wen-cheng, found dead on 3 July 1981, the day after he was questioned by the TGC about his political activities in the United States, and by the death in police custody in May 1982 of Wang Ying-hsien, a suspect in a robbery case. An American expert in forensic medicine who examined the body of Dr Chen found no evidence of "systematic torture" but the case prompted several government officials to call for a review of the TGC interrogation procedures. An official inquiry into the circumstances of Wang Ying-hsien's death led to the prosecution and conviction in November 1982 of five police officers for assault. To Amnesty International's knowledge, this was the first ever instance where government officials were convicted for ill-treatment of suspects.

Suspects on charges of sedition interrogated by the TGC do not benefit from the change in the law of criminal procedure. They are subject to the military criminal procedure law and are not allowed to see a lawyer before indictment. They can be legally detained incommunicado for a period of two months, renewable once. Amnesty International remained concerned about several prisoners serving long sentences for sedition who claimed they were convicted in the 1970s on the basis of confessions made under torture; it continued to appeal for these cases to be re-tried.

* * * *

In addition to the countries mentioned above, Amnesty International received allegations of some cases of ill-treatment from Laos,

Malaysia, Nepal and the Socialist Republic of Viet Nam during the period under review and was concerned about the use of caning as a judicial punishment in Hong Kong, Malaysia and Singapore.

In Hong Kong, caning was used as a punishment for various offences during the period under review. In two recent cases, tried in May and July 1983, caning was imposed on offenders convicted of possession of offensive weapons. According to press reports, either the defendants or their defence counsel had themselves sought the sentence of caning as an alternative to imprisonment, citing family circumstances. In another recent case, in May 1983, two prisoners already sentenced to death were ordered to receive eight strokes of the cane after being convicted of wounding another prisoner in Stanley prison. In all the cases reported, caning was to take place immediately after the court had obtained medical reports certifying the defendants fit for it.

Amnesty International has received reports alleging that some political detainees had been harshly treated in "re-education" camps in Laos, usually as a punishment for real or suspected attempts to escape. The alleged ill-treatment included the wearing of heavy chains and deprivation of food for varying lengths of time. In some cases detainees were allegedly held chained in an underground prison or in a hole dug in the ground. Such ill-treatment allegedly took place in Na Chong and Phou Leng-Phou Khoune "re-education" camps in Xieng Khouang province and camps in Savannakhet and Attopeu provinces.

Under Malaysia's Internal Security Act, the police have the power to arrest and detain for interrogation for up to 60 days any person whom they consider a "threat" to the security of Malaysia. Throughout the 60-day period, detainees are held in undisclosed police lock-ups or Special Branch holding centres and denied access to a lawyer or doctor, and usually also to their families. Severe psychological and physical pressure is reported to have been used during such "preliminary detention" to intimidate political opponents, or to obtain confessions from political detainees that they are engaged in pro-communist activity or represent in other ways a "threat" to the security of Malaysia. Amnesty International has also been concerned about reports indicating that defendants have recently been sentenced to strokes of the *rotan*, cane—usually six strokes—in addition to receiving jail terms for various offences. Several cases were reported in Malaysian newspapers for the first time in many years in May 1983.

Amnesty International has received occasional reports of people in Nepal detained for political reasons being subjected to severe beatings. The organization has also received reports of ordinary criminal suspects being brutally treated by the police, including cases where the victims have died in custody apparently as a result of ill-treatment. Ill-treatment of political detainees appears most often to be intended to discourage further political activity. Immediately following the arrest in late March 1982 of approximately 150 students who were delegates at a conference of the All Nepal National Independent Students Union, held in Kathmandu, many of them were reportedly beaten. There were reports of further beatings of the student detainees at the end of April 1982 when they started a hunger-strike in protest at their continued detention. Several were reported to have been seriously injured. Amnesty International knows of no cases where such reports involving political detainees have been investigated by the authorities.

Amnesty International has been disturbed about the use of caning as a judicial punishment in Singapore during the period under review. In 1973, caning was made mandatory for about 30 offences, in most cases together with a term of imprisonment. The law laid down the minimum number of strokes that should be imposed by the courts, with the minimum number varying according to the type of offence. The law exempts women, children and men over 50. However, children convicted of armed robbery may receive a maximum of 10 strokes. Caning is reportedly inflicted on the buttocks with a one-yard long, half-inch round rattan rod which can split the skin, remove strips of flesh and leave deep scars. The prisoners' hands and feet are strapped to a wooden A-shaped trestle; the body is bent at the waist and protective padding is tied over the spine. Strokes are inflicted at intervals of 30 seconds. The punishment takes place with a prison medical officer available.

Amnesty International has monitored the cases of hundreds of political detainees in the Socialist Republic of Viet Nam but the organization has received few allegations of torture during the period under review. Reports have been received concerning the use of shackles and solitary confinement where prisoners have allegedly broken camp regulations. In some cases the use of these shackles has been reported for periods of several weeks and even months.

On several occasions Amnesty International has brought its concern about the reported use of shackles to the attention of the Vietnamese authorities. Most allegations regarding the use of shackles involve prisoners detained in camp 1870 in Phu Khanh province. Amnesty International has also received several reports concerning prisoners held for long periods in solitary confinement at this camp. In one case Amnesty International intervened in May 1982 on behalf of a prisoner, Vu van Anh, who had reportedly been held in shackles for up to six months.

EUROPE

Albania

A number of former political prisoners in Albania alleged that during investigation they had been held in solitary confinement and beaten by police or state security officials in order to extort confessions or information from them during the period under review. They were generally not allowed to receive visits from their family during investigation proceedings nor did they have access to legal counsel.

Several former prisoners described being beaten while handcuffed or while chained to a chair fixed to the floor. Two said they were beaten unconscious and revived with water by police officials who forced them to sign declarations of guilt. One of these stated that he was held in Gjirokaster investigation prison in solitary confinement for five months in 1980. During the first two weeks of arrest he was interrogated daily, at night as well as during the day. Investigating officials beat and kicked him while he sat handcuffed and chained to a chair. When he fainted water was poured over him; after he had revived he was again beaten. In this way he was forced to sign a confession and a declaration that he would collaborate with the police as an informer.

One former prisoner alleged that he was tortured with electric shocks on various parts of his body while being held for investigation in Tirane in 1981. He named a doctor and investigating official who he claimed were responsible. This was the only allegation of its kind made by a person who claimed to have personally been ill-treated in this way. Several former political prisoners, however, stated that while serving their sentences they had met people who had told them that electric shocks had on occasion been used at a Tirane investigation centre to extort confessions.

The ill-treatment of political prisoners serving prison sentences was also of concern to Amnesty International. Former political prisoners who had served sentences in Ballsh, Spac and Burell prison camps alleged that guards frequently beat prisoners.

Italy

According to information available to Amnesty International, torture and ill-treatment of people detained in connection with politically motivated offences is not a usual administrative practice in Italy. However, during the first three months of 1982 there was an alarming increase in allegations of ill-treatment of detainees which had, both before and after this period, been sporadic. Four police officers who were the subject of some of these allegations were found guilty in July 1983 of "abusing their authority" during interrogations.

The allegations were in some cases supported by medical statements, either from independent doctors, or in medical reports prepared at the request of the magistrate in the period immediately following the reported ill-treatment. Further evidence has been provided by relatives and lawyers representing the detainees.

Judicial investigations into these allegations have been started in Padua, Verona, Viterbo, Rome and Venice. Five police officers were charged in June 1982 by the magistrates in Padua with kidnapping, coercion and inflicting injuries on members of a left-wing armed group, the Red Brigades, in January 1982. One of the detainees alleged that he was illegally removed from the police station for interrogation and all have alleged that they were beaten and threatened by the police during interrogation.

Article 13 of the Italian constitution of 1948 states that "physical or moral violence against persons placed under any form of detention shall be punished". Although the crime of torture as such does not exist in Italian law, criminal proceedings for crimes ranging from assault and battery to murder may be brought under the criminal code and code of criminal procedure. Government officials who are charged with such acts against prisoners or detainees bear the full civil and criminal liability on conviction.

In July 1983, four of the police officers on trial in Padua were found guilty of abusing their authority while interrogating a Red Brigades member by using blows, tying him to a table and forcing him to drink large quantities of water. They were sentenced to suspended prison terms of one year to 14 months. A fifth was released because, in the June election, he was elected a deputy and thus benefited from parliamentary immunity.

Throughout the period under review Italy has been the scene of violent attacks against the institutions of the state by armed groups.

These have been accompanied by a program of murder, arson, bombing and kidnapping carried out by clandestine political groups of both the extreme left and right.

In consequence, over recent years, legislation has been introduced increasing the powers of the police to combat such violence. The most recent example of legislation of this kind was Decree Law No. 625, introduced in December 1979 and converted into law in February 1980 as "Urgent Measures for the Protection of the Democratic Order and Public Security".

Under this law, the police may hold suspects for no more than 48 hours before either releasing them or transferring them to prison. Notice of and reasons for the arrest must be given to the procurator of the Republic within the same 48-hour period. Within a further 48 hours the findings of the inquiry conducted by the police must be passed to the procurator. In cases of urgency people may be questioned by the police in the absence of a lawyer but the information obtained cannot be used in their trials.

Amnesty International received information on allegations of torture or ill-treatment in approximately 30 cases during the first three months of 1982. They came mostly from alleged members of the Red Brigades who were detained after the rescue by the police of the kidnapped NATO Chief of Staff, General James Lee Dozier, on 28 January 1982. Following the General's release, further allegations of ill-treatment were made by detainees allegedly connected with other acts of violence.

The allegations refer to incidents of torture or ill-treatment which took place in the interval between arrest and transfer to prison, in police stations, police barracks and other places which could allegedly not be identified because the detainees were hooded or blindfold. The unauthorized removal of a suspect from police premises to unidentified locations is one of the main charges in the trial of the police officers in Padua.

Methods of torture reported to Amnesty International included prolonged beatings and forcing detainees to drink large quantities of salt water. Burning with cigarette ends, exposure to jets of icy water, twisting of feet and nipples, tearing of hair, squeezing of genitals and the use of electric shocks was also alleged.

It was alleged that these methods were used to induce detainees to collaborate with the police by providing information on the circumstances of criminal incidents and the names of the associates of the detainees.

The Minister of the Interior made a speech on the subject of the allegations in the Chamber of Deputies on 15 February 1982. He assured the Chamber that the fight against terrorism would be, and always had been, carried out "within the framework of republican legality and with all democratic guarantees". In a speech made on 19 March 1982 the then Prime Minister, Giovanni Spadolini, said "The government can affirm with a clear conscience that torture is a practice unknown to this State born of the Resistance."

On 16 March 1982 Amnesty International wrote to the Minister of the Interior, Virginio Rognoni, to express concern about the number and scope of the recent allegations of torture and ill-treatment and requested the Minister to undertake an immediate review under his own authority of the procedures followed by the police in those cases which had been the subject of public allegations. It also expressed the view that the number of allegations made it imperative to undertake comprehensive investigations of arrest procedures and treatment in custody and that this investigation should not be limited to the cases raised in the letter. No reply was received from the Italian Government.

Poland

Amnesty International received information that police had beaten people who had been arrested and held in custody as a result of their non-violent political activities on several occasions during 1980 and 1981. Reports of such incidents greatly increased after martial law was imposed in Poland on 12 December 1981. In the cases reported to Amnesty International the majority of victims of police beatings were members or supporters of the suspended (and later banned) trade union Solidarity.

Reports typically alleged that police used rubber truncheons to beat detainees in police stations about the head, body and legs or kicked and punched them. There were also occasions when detainees who were arrested were subjected to the so-called "health walk"— that is they were forced to run the gauntlet of truncheon blows between a double row of police.

The police forces reported to have been involved included members of the riot police, the civic militia and state security officials. There were also incidents in which guards beat convicted prisoners and detainees in internment camps. The information received by Amnesty International related almost exclusively to prisoners of conscience.

Amnesty International's information was based largely on the accounts of victims published in underground Solidarity bulletins and in reports by unofficial human rights groups. In some cases this information was supported by affidavits, the findings of a local procurator's office or other material.

An unofficial human rights group, the Helsinki Committee in Poland, listed in a report published in February 1983 on human rights violations in Poland under martial law occasions on which arrested demonstrators had been subjected to the "health walk". It cited, among others, the testimonies of individuals who said they had been beaten in this way in police stations in Pruszcz Gdansk (30 December 1981), Warsaw (10 November 1982), Elblag, Gdansk and Lublin (4 May 1982), Wroclaw, Lubin, Krakow, Katowice and Warsaw (31 August 1982).

Amnesty International received information about some 30 other cases in which individuals were alleged to have been beaten at police stations, usually while being held in custody (under Polish law a person may be held in custody without charge for up to 48 hours). In some cases little information was supplied, but in others the incidents were described in circumstantial detail. The aim of beating appears to have been variously to intimidate detainees, to obtain information or to force confessions from them.

Unofficial sources cited over 10 cases in which it was alleged that people had died as the result of the beating they received from police following arrest. Among such cases, that of the 19-year-old high school student, Grzegorz Prezemk, attracted considerable public attention. He was reportedly arrested on 12 May 1983 in Warsaw and taken to a police station in Jezuicka Street. He died in Solec hospital two days later from severe injuries to the spleen and liver. On 16 May the Warsaw Srodmiescie procurator opened an investigation into his case. By July 1983 the investigation had not been concluded.

Amnesty International also received several reports of incidents in which guards were alleged to have beaten people detained in internment camps. These were centres set up after martial law was imposed in which over 10,000 people spent time, without charge or trial, officially on the grounds that the interests of the security of the state required their confinement. (The camps were closed on 23 December 1982.) Such incidents were said to have taken place at Wierzchowo Pomorskie camp on 13 February 1982, at Ilawa camp on 25 March 1982 and at Kwidzyn camp on 14 August 1982. The Military Procurator's Office in Koszalin investigated the incident at Wierzchowo Pomorskie camp. It was established that 37 internees were beaten by guards with fists and truncheons after they had protested, by whistling and banging their foodplates, against the infliction of the punishment of solitary confinement on two internees. The Procurator's Office discontinued criminal proceedings against two lieutenants who had been supervising the guards at the time on the grounds that they had a good record and that the victims of the beatings had acted provocatively.

At Kwidzyn over 60 internees were reported to have been beaten by guards after they had voiced their protest when the prison authorities refused entry to family members who had come to visit them. Up to 20 internees were allegedly so badly injured that they required treatment in hospital. On 24 May 1983 five internees involved in this incident (four of whom had reportedly suffered concussion) were sentenced to terms of imprisonment of between one and two years on charges of having barricaded entrances to buildings at the camp and of having thrown objects at prison officials who quelled the protest. Earlier, in February 1983, the Elblag Military District Procuracy reportedly decided to close an inquiry into this incident on the grounds that there was insufficient proof that the guards named by complainants had been responsible for the beatings.

Amnesty International was also concerned about instances in which convicted prisoners were alleged to have been severely beaten by prison guards. Prisoners in Gdansk prison (including some 15 prisoners of conscience) were said to have been attacked and beaten by guards on 23 July 1982 after rumours had circulated within the prison that inmates were about to start a hunger-strike. In addition, some 20 young prisoners were reportedly forced to take very hot showers and then again beaten. Police dogs were alleged to have been set on certain prisoners. An account of this incident, based on the testimony of several prisoners, and certified by a Gdansk lawyer, was presented in August to the Polish Primate, Archbishop Glemp. Unofficial sources referred to other occasions on which convicted political prisoners were alleged to have been beaten: at Hrubieszow (on 22 and 23 September 1982), Wroclaw (11 November 1982), Potulice (11 June 1982) and Fordon (29 April 1982). In these incidents, at least 16 prisoners of conscience were allegedly beaten by guards. In April 1983 four police officers were reported to have received sentences of between two and two and a half years' for having beaten Krzysztof Szymanski, a village chairman of Rural Solidarity, on 29 April 1982 in Wegrow police station. Amnesty International on a number of occasions enquired of the Polish authorities about allegations that individual prisoners of conscience had been beaten in detention and urged that they be given necessary medical treatment. On two occasions in 1982 Amnesty International informed the Polish authorities that it wished to send delegates to Poland to discuss its concerns with them, but received no response.

Romania

Amnesty International received a number of allegations that people detained for political reasons, mostly would-be emigrants or religious dissenters, had been beaten while being held in police custody during the period under review. In particular, people arrested while attempting to leave the country without official authorization were said to have been beaten by border guards. One such case was that of Gheorghe Sirbu who was arrested in November 1980 near the border with Yugoslavia while making his third attempt to leave Romania without official permission. He was alleged to have been attacked by guard dogs and so severely beaten by frontier guards and members of the security forces that he had to be admitted to hospital. He was subsequently sentenced to 10 months' corrective labour.

There were also allegations that during investigation proceedings prisoners of conscience had been slapped, beaten or threatened with the use of force in order to extort confessions from them. During this period they were often held incommunicado or given only minimal access to family or defence counsel. For example, Klaus Wagner, a member of the Brethren Church from Sighisoara, was reportedly arrested with two others in October 1981 after the authorities had discovered and confiscated a large number of Bibles on a ship which docked at Turnu Severin. He was charged with helping to smuggle these Bibles into Romania and distributing them. During his pre-trial detention, Klaus Wagner was allegedly severely beaten by police officials and had to be confined to hospital for intensive care. It was also alleged that during investigation proceedings neither he nor his two co-defendants had access to defence counsel.

In November 1982 Amnesty International appealed to the Romanian authorities on behalf of several members of Romania's Hungarian minority from Cluj and Oradea who were arrested after they had published a memorandum claiming that the minority was the object of an official policy of assimilation. They were alleged to have been ill-treated following their arrest and to have been threatened with charges of treason. Among these people was Karoly Toth, who was arrested at his home in Oradea on 7 November 1982. Amnesty International received allegations that during the following four days police officials who conducted his interrogation kicked him, knocked his head against a wall and beat him with a rubber truncheon on his head, neck and back. On 11 November he was released. However, marks of the beating he had received were allegedly still visible two weeks afterwards.

Several accounts of prison conditions by former prisoners of conscience spoke of guards beating convicted prisoners with rubber truncheons for minor infringements of prison rules.

Spain

There was persistent use of torture or ill-treatment of detainees in Spain during the period under review. Evidence is provided by sworn statements from former detainees, certificates from official medical sources and independent doctors, detainees' families, the church, lawyers and human rights groups. In February 1981 a detainee in Madrid died after nine days in custody, showing clear signs of torture, and in March 1983 two police officers were convicted of torturing a detainee in Bilbao.

Torture and inhuman or degrading treatment or punishment are prohibited by the Spanish constitution and punished by the penal code.

The Code of Criminal Procedure contains a long list of safeguards for detainees, but the constitution permits the suspension of certain "safeguard rights" in connection with the investigation into the activities of "armed groups and terrorist elements". However, the crucial right of the detainee to legal assistance while in custody cannot be suspended although it can be regulated by law.

The current anti-terrorist law, Organic Law 11/80 of 1 December 1980, covers a range of active, violent offences against the person or the state and offences of publicly excusing or collaborating in these acts. People detained under this law are held incommunicado, denied access to a lawyer and have no right to independent medical treatment or to inform their families, for a period of 72 hours. In order to complete their investigations, the police may request permission from the *Audiencia Nacional*, National Court, for an extension of seven days up to a total of 10 days. Such permission is easy to obtain.

In Amnesty International's view these features of this law facilitate torture or ill-treatment because incommunicado detention removes the safeguard of access to a lawyer or others during the crucial phase of the police investigation. Nearly all cases of torture or ill-treatment known to Amnesty International have taken place during this period. Judges and prosecutors may visit police stations, providing by their presence a limited protection for detainees. In practice, this rarely happens.

Between the introduction of the law in December 1980 and

March 1983 official statistics record 3,205 incommunicado detentions under this law. An extension of seven days was granted in 1,470 cases. The number of arrests both before and after this period are reportedly not significantly different. Amnesty International believes the official figure for detentions to be a considerable understatement since it does not include short-term detainees who are misleadingly informed by the police at the time of their arrest that they are being held under the anti-terrorist law, but who are then released without the court being informed. The majority of detainees reflected in the official statistics are alleged members of the different factions of *Euskadi Ta Askatasuna* (ETA), Basque Homeland and Liberty. Nearly 10 per cent of all detentions were of alleged members of right-wing armed groups and over a thousand were from other miscellaneous movements. The majority of arrests have been in the Basque country and Madrid, where armed groups have most often attacked police and security forces, public installations and banks and kidnapped for ransom.

The police stations of Indauchu (Bilbao), via Layetana (Barcelona), the *Guardia Civil*, Civil Guard, post of la Salve (Bilbao) and the *Dirección General de Seguridad* (DGS), Security Headquarters, in Madrid, are the places mentioned most frequently in the allegations. The use of torture is uncommon in prisons, as opposed to police stations or Civil Guard posts, and Amnesty International has no record of the involvement of the army in such offences. The Civil Guard and the *Cuerpo Superior*, Higher Corps, of the police are the units most frequently used.

Medical personnel attached to police stations have allegedly treated some injured detainees who are in custody but have either refused or not bothered to record their findings in writing or report them to the court.

Since 1980 Amnesty International has been informed of between 25 and 30 substantive allegations a year of torture or ill-treatment of detainees under the anti-terrorist laws. Nearly all of these allegations have been the subject of judicial complaints against the police or Civil Guard. In some cases, the complaints are supported by medical evidence which records a pattern of injuries consistent with the allegations of torture. In addition, four Amnesty International missions have interviewed first-hand witnesses such as fellow detainees, lawyers and relatives whose testimony confirms these allegations. Other cases have been investigated and denounced by the *Asociación pro Derechos Humanos*, Association for Human Rights, the press, doctors, the Colleges of Law and the Human Rights Commissions of the autonomous parliaments of the Basque country and Catalonia. Amnesty International considers that the result of these investigations shows a pattern of persistent use of torture or ill-treatment.

Sporadic instances have been reported in the Spanish press of torture or ill-treatment being inflicted on detainees under the normal criminal legislation which permits 72 hours' detention before a person is presented to a judge or released. Amnesty International has no figures for these types of case.

The main object of torture or ill-treatment appears to be to obtain confessions, even though the detainee will often disown them in court. The document will then be set aside and a new statement recording the allegations of coercion will be taken.

In September 1980 Amnesty International published a *Report of an Amnesty International Mission to Spain* which described cases of torture in Spain. The government made no comment although it was sent a copy of the text before publication. The authorities in Spain usually reply to urgent appeals from Amnesty International by referring enquiries to the courts responsible for conducting the investigations. No separate and wider public investigation has been conducted by the government.

The courts have failed to react to judicial complaints even when they are supported by medical evidence. Exceptionally, in March 1983 two police officers were sentenced in Bilbao to 10 months' imprisonment and 10 years' suspension of civil rights for torturing a detainee whose case is described by Amnesty International's 1980 report. Amnesty International knows of no other convictions. No allegations against the Civil Guard have been passed by the military judges who are empowered to decide at the investigation stage.

The new socialist government formed in December 1982 has said it will retain the anti-terrorist laws. However, a draft reform bill on detainees' rights to legal assistance was published in March 1983. A bill providing *habeas corpus* was promised for March 1983 but has not been published within the period under review.

Under the terms of the draft bill on legal assistance incommunicado detainees would not be permitted either unrestricted access to legal assistance or the right to designate a lawyer. This would be done *de officio*. The law specifies that the lawyer may only be present as a silent witness when the detainee gives a statement to the police. The terms of the draft law appear to allow the police to take statements for their own purposes when a lawyer is not present, before allowing the detainee access to legal assistance. Under this draft detainees would still be effectively deprived of legal assistance during the crucial preliminary police investigation.

Amnesty International has continued to receive allegations of torture and ill-treatment since the new government took office in

December 1982. The Minister of the Interior stated in March 1983 that, while torture had not been used during the three months of his term of office and would not be tolerated, ill-treatment had occurred. The continued use of torture and ill-treatment was confirmed by an Amnesty International mission in May and June 1983.

Turkey

Torture of political detainees was already a major concern of Amnesty International prior to the military coup of September 1980. An increasing number of torture allegations had led to an Amnesty International research mission to Turkey in May 1980, when Amnesty International concluded that torture was widespread and systematic and that most people detained by police and martial law authorities were subjected to torture, which in some cases was alleged to have ended in death. The increased number of torture allegations and reports of deaths in custody received after the September 1980 coup is undoubtedly related to the increased number of people detained and the lengthening of the detention period since the coup by amendments to Martial Law No. 1402.

Although most of the allegations of torture received by Amnesty International concern political detainees, it does occasionally receive reports of ordinary criminal suspects being tortured in order to induce confessions and information received over a long period of time strongly suggests that the torture of ordinary criminal suspects is routine practice in Turkish police stations. Most of these reports describe beatings, in particular *falaka*, the beating of the soles of the feet. However, all the detailed information concerning torture in the possession of Amnesty International relates to political prisoners, the majority of whom are subjected to some form of ill-treatment during the detention period. Some well-known detainees —notably those detained in connection with the Turkish Peace Association and former members of parliament held immediately after the coup—have apparently not been tortured, but they constitute a small minority of cases known to Amnesty International.

In most cases torture was allegedly inflicted by the police and takes place in police stations, but Amnesty International has received detailed allegations that torture has been inflicted in military establishments in Diyarbakir and in Diyarbakir Military Prison. Reports of ill-treatment of prisoners in Mamak Military Prison near Ankara and Metris Military Prison in Istanbul have also been received. Following the death in custody of the detainee Ilhan Erdost on 7 November 1980, the Commander of Mamak Military

Prison, Colonel Raci Tetik, made this statement to the Ankara
Martial Law Prosecutor:

> "I had given orders that after the preliminaries were
> completed all prisoners with the exception of the aged,
> women and children, the lame and the diseased, should be
> struck with a truncheon once or twice each below the waist
> in their rude places [buttocks] and on the palms of their
> hands and they should be warned not to come to prison
> again. I am not going to deny my order. My aim is to
> ensure discipline."

Methods of torture included electric shocks, *falaka*, burning with
cigarettes, hanging from the ceiling by hands or feet for prolonged
periods and beating and assaults on all parts of the body, including
the sexual organs.

The most severe torture usually took place during the detention
period when the detainee is held incommunicado. The main
purpose appeared to be the extraction of information and confessions,
although intimidation was also an important element. The routine
beatings which took place in military prisons, where people were sent
after being charged or convicted, seem to have been for the sole purpose of maintaining discipline. Amnesty International knows, however, of some instances of prisoners having been taken again for
interrogation and subjected to torture again, even after several
years in prison.

Evidence of torture in Turkey includes the testimony of prisoners
and former prisoners, in some cases supported by medical reports,
evidence presented in court and sworn affidavits made by fellow
prisoners and relatives. Since the September 1980 coup Amnesty
International has repeatedly asked the authorities to investigate
allegations of torture, in particular when it is alleged that a death
has resulted. Amnesty International has submitted to the authorities
the names of nearly 100 people alleged to have died in custody since
September 1980. In reply Amnesty International has received information from the authorities concerning 74 of these cases. In 25
cases trials or investigations were said to be in progress. Other
replies indicated deaths as a result of suicide, accident or illness or
referred to lack of information or any record of detention. In eight
cases the person concerned was still alive. Where no replies have
been received Amnesty International does not know whether any
investigations took place.

On 16 March 1982 the Minister of State, Ilhan Oztrak, acknowledged publicly that 15 people had died as a result of torture since 12
September 1980. However, a report issued by the Chief of the

General Staff's Office on 29 October 1982 stated that investigations into 204 deaths alleged to have been caused by torture had determined that in only four cases were the deaths caused by torture. Twenty-five deaths were said to be from natural causes, 15 had been suicides, five people were killed while trying to escape and 25 had been killed during clashes. The same report said that by 4 October 1982 the martial law authorities had opened a total of 540 investigation files following claims of torture. Investigations into 316 of these cases continued; in 171 cases there were no grounds for prosecution; trials concerning 37 cases were still continuing and trials concerning 16 cases had been concluded. Thirty-four people were acquitted and 15 were given various sentences. Of those being tried 17 people were in custody and 76 were not.

It is doubtful if all allegations of torture reported to the authorities are subjected to investigation. In the Turkish press alone there have been reports of hundreds of defendants in political trials retracting statements which they allege were made as a result of torture. F.H. Koers, a Dutch lawyer who attended hearings in three mass trials in Turkey in January 1983, on behalf of the Netherlands Trade Union Federation (FNV), the Netherlands Council of Churches and *Yeralti Maden IS*, the Turkish Mine-workers' Union, reported that in each trial defendants stated that the statements being used as evidence had been obtained by torture. At the opening session of the trial known as the "Fatsa trial" on 12 January, one of the defendants refused to cooperate in establishing his identity until the Court first heard his complaints concerning treatment in detention and during interrogations. The spokesperson for the court said that complaints should be filed at "the appropriate place" and that they were not in order at that time. The defendant replied that up to that time the many complaints made by the detainees had yielded no results. Many of the original 53 defendants in the DISK, Confederation of Progressive Trade Unions, trial made statements alleging ill-treatment during detention, but as far as Amnesty International knows, no investigation into their allegations has taken place.

While welcoming the prohibition of torture contained in Article 16 of the new Turkish constitution introduced in November 1982, Amnesty International has urged the martial law authorities to issue clear public instructions to all members of the security forces prohibiting the use of torture in all circumstances, and to allow prisoners access to families and lawyers throughout the detention period. An Amnesty International delegation which visited Turkey in April 1981 to discuss the organization's concerns with the authorities raised with both military and civilian authorities the issue of alleged torture in police stations and prisons. Since that time Amnesty International has frequently appealed to the authorities to investigate allegations of torture and has issued public statements of its concern.

Union of Soviet Socialist Republics

Prisoners have been subjected to ill-treatment in Soviet corrective labour institutions and in prison while awaiting trial during the period under review. Many prisoners of conscience compulsorily confined to psychiatric hospitals have been forcibly administered disorienting and pain-causing drugs and some are reported to have been beaten.

Conditions in Soviet corrective labour institutions are marked by hard physical labour, inadequate diet and medical neglect. Within this context Amnesty International believes that in some cases Soviet officials have deliberately countermanded the recommendations of doctors in order to punish individual prisoners of conscience who have protested against their conditions and received publicity abroad. Amnesty International has information on six such cases in which severe physical suffering has resulted. Two of these prisoners —one in Lvov and the other in Perm region—were medically certified as invalids before they began their terms of imprisonment, but were stripped of this status and its privileges by a decision of the director of their corrective labour colony. They were required to do hard physical labour and were set the output norms of an able-bodied person.

Since 1980 at least 36 prisoners of conscience—among them three women—are alleged to have received beatings from ordinary criminal prisoners at the instigation of, or in the presence of, officials of the Ministry of Internal Affairs—or, in some identifiable cases, with the participation of officials. Victims are said to have sustained injuries ranging from bruising and cuts to fractures, deafness, and, in one reported case, confirmed by the Procuracy office of Perm region, damage to the skull and brain. Eleven of these allegations concern prisoners awaiting trial, who were put in cells with convicted criminals between interrogations. Amnesty International knows of no case in which the Procuracy has conducted a thorough investigation of such allegations, or in which anyone has been held responsible and punished.

Allegations of ill-treatment have been made by prisoners in petitions at their trials; by prisoners and relatives in complaints to Soviet officials and international bodies; and by Soviet citizens unofficially engaged in monitoring violations of human rights in their own country. According to the Fundamentals of Corrective Labour Legislation of the USSR, which form the basis of the Corrective Labour Codes operating in each Union Republic, prisoners are entitled to send uncensored complaints about their treatment to the Procuracy. However, Amnesty International knows of cases in which the complaints of prisoners have been confiscated by officials of the corrective labour institution concerned.

Many prisoners of conscience indefinitely confined to psychiatric hospitals are reported to have been given forcible treatment with disorienting and pain-causing drugs by doctors—in particular haloperidol, chlorpromazine and trifluoperazine. In some cases these drugs have been given in excessive quantities without the necessary correctives and in disregard of contra-indications. Other forms of punishment have included insulin-shock therapy and various forms of fixation and immobilization.

In one known case a prisoner's health deteriorated so dramatically that in 1982 doctors offered to grant him invalid status. He is Vladimir Khailo, a Baptist, who was confined to Dnepropetrovsk special psychiatric hospital in 1980.

Some people confined indefinitely to psychiatric hospitals are reported to have been beaten, sometimes severely. Reports of this type come most often from special psychiatric hospitals, which are administered by the Ministry of Internal Affairs, and where convicted criminals serve as ward orderlies. It is widely reported that prisoners of conscience have been put under pressure by psychiatrists to renounce their beliefs and former activities as a pre-condition for their release.

Amnesty International believes that the official Soviet procedures for compulsory confinement facilitate psychiatric abuse. They make it easy for people of dissenting views to be confined arbitrarily and hard for such people to defend themselves through legal means. Formally, individuals may only be put in psychiatric hospitals against their will if they are shown to be both mentally ill and an "evident danger" to themselves or others. In practice, however, these conditions have not been met in many political cases.

Although the Procuracy is legally charged with supervising psychiatric hospitals there is no guaranteed procedure for inmates to submit complaints about their treatment. They may write letters only at the discretion of doctors and then usually only to relatives. Their letters are censored. Numerous people confined to psychiatric hospitals are known to have been punished for describing their conditions in diaries, letters, or messages smuggled outside. Inmates of special psychiatric hospitals are especially vulnerable to arbitrary treatment and powerless to protest. They are kept closely confined in conditions of secrecy, and are often too far away from their relatives to receive regular visits.

Reports of ill-treatment have come from every republic of the USSR. Former prisoners of conscience and other inmates have been released from confinement and have circulated unofficial accounts of their treatment. Relatives of others still confined have appealed to international bodies for help in securing their release. In recent years former victims who have emigrated from the USSR have given detailed accounts of their treatment and other cases of abuse known to them. Some have undergone psychiatric examination abroad and have been diagnosed as showing no symptoms justifying compulsory confinement then or previously.

Individuals who have reported on the treatment they received in psychiatric confinement are known to have been arrested and imprisoned, or, in some cases, re-confined to psychiatric hospitals against their will. One important source of evidence has been an unofficial "Working Commission to Investigate the Use of Psychiatry for Political Purposes", set up in Moscow in 1977. The commission collected information from friends and relatives of victims and travelled to the provinces to attend court hearings and visit hospital staff and patients. It was helped by a lawyer, Sofia Kalistratova, and two psychiatrists, Dr Alexander Voloshanovich and Dr Anatoly Koryagin. By 1981 all the active members of the Working Commission, including Dr Anatoly Koryagin, had been arrested and sentenced to up to 12 years' imprisonment and exile on charges of "circulating anti-Soviet slander" or "anti-Soviet agitation and propaganda".

Yugoslavia

Most allegations of ill-treatment of prisoners received by Amnesty International related to the autonomous province of Kosovo and to the period following the outbreak of nationalist demonstrations by ethnic Albanians in the province during March and April 1981. Widespread arrests followed the demonstrations, and by September 1982, according to official sources, 527 people had been criminally prosecuted and sentenced for political offences. Press access to these trials was generally restricted to correspondents of the official Yugoslav newsagency, *Tanjug*, which provided only limited information about the charges and sentences. In April 1982, however, an article in the Yugoslav press noted that allegations of ill-treatment in pre-trial detention had been made in a number of political trials of ethnic Albanians. Amnesty International also received allegations that many defendants were ill-treated following arrest with the aim of extracting information or confessions from them.

In December 1982 Amnesty International wrote to the Federal Secretary of Justice referring to the fact that it had received allegations of ill-treatment of ethnic Albanians charged with political offences and raising three specific cases. Amnesty International urged that a judicial inquiry be undertaken into the alleged ill-treatment of Hydajet Hyseni, Halil Alidema and Ukshin Hoti. Hydajet Hyseni was alleged to have been severely ill-treated following his arrest in December 1981. He did not appear at the trial of 18 co-defendants in Pristina in July 1982 because, the court was informed, he was in a depressive state. In August he was said to be in the psychiatric section of Belgrade prison hospital. On 18 November he was sentenced to 15 years' imprisonment. Halil Alidema and Ukshin Hoti, who were also alleged to have been physically ill-treated during pre-trial detention, were sentenced to 11 and nine years' imprisonment respectively in July 1982. There was no response to Amnesty International's letter and to the organization's knowledge no inquiry was carried out.

Amnesty International also received on several occasions allegations from other parts of Yugoslavia that individuals arrested as the result of their non-violent exercise of their human rights had been threatened by police with the use of force or with reprisals against their families. Other forms of psychological or physical pressure were also cited; for example, one prisoner of conscience alleged that following arrest he was deprived of food for five days.

Under Yugoslav law the extortion of confessions is a punishable offence. Amnesty International did not learn of any cases in which police had been prosecuted for this. However, several trials were reported in the press in which police had been convicted of beating to death people they had arrested. In one such case, in September 1982, a court in Skopje sentenced three militia men to between 13 and 14 years' imprisonment.

Amnesty International was also concerned about allegations it received of the ill-treatment of convicted prisoners, both ordinary criminals and political prisoners. The most serious of these allegations was made by a group of Albanian political prisoners from Kosovo. In a complaint addressed to the Secretariat of Justice of Croatia they described the ill-treatment they had allegedly suffered during transport from Pristina district prison to Gospic prison in Croatia and while detained in Gospic. They alleged, among other things, that on arrival at Gospic prison on 15 November 1981 they were forced to undress and then assaulted by guards who beat them about the face and body. Two prisoners were allegedly beaten on the genitals by guards who taunted them that they would never engender children. The account referred to injuries sustained by named prisoners and stated that the corridor where the incident occurred was stained with blood. A group of some 20 more prisoners from Kosovo who arrived at Gospic on 26 December 1981 were said to have received similar ill-treatment. Two prisoners who complained to the Director of the prison about ill-treatment were alleged to have been beaten unconscious in reprisal on 12 December 1981.

Accounts by former prisoners indicated that elsewhere in Yugoslavia the beating of individual prisoners was commonplace in certain prisons. In September 1982 a Belgrade criminologist addressed an open letter to the Serbian Secretary of Justice concerning the treatment of prisoners in Belgrade District Prison, based on his personal observation while serving a month's sentence there for a non-violent political offence. He wrote that prisoners were often beaten and were threatened literally every day with beating. He noted that guards were apparently persuaded that beating was a legally sanctioned disciplinary measure despite the fact that corporal punishment was abolished in Serbia in 1873.

Similar assertions were made by former prisoners of conscience about prisons in other republics, most notably Stara Gradiska in Croatia and Zenica in Bosnia-Hercegovina.

* * * *

In addition to the countries mentioned above, Amnesty International has received allegations of some cases of ill-treatment from Bulgaria, Czechoslovakia and Greece.

From Bulgaria, Amnesty International has received a number of allegations that political prisoners have been subjected to severe psychological and sometimes physical pressures during investigation proceedings. A number of former prisoners of conscience complained that guards had beaten prisoners for minor breaches of discipline.

Amnesty International has received reports of prisoners of conscience and people under interrogation being beaten in Czechoslovakia during the period under review.

Reports have been received concerning the alleged ill-treatment of both political and ordinary criminal prisoners in police stations and prisons in various parts of Greece. The allegations referred variously to beatings, *falaka* (beatings of the soles of the feet) and electric shocks. Amnesty International raised these allegations in letters to successive Ministers of Justice in 1981, 1982 and 1983, but received only one response. In June 1982 Minister of Justice Efstathios Alexandris informed Amnesty International, in relation to a case of alleged torture in Patras prison in February 1982, that "after conclusion of the preliminary investigation, the criminal file assembled on the four police employees said to be responsible has been sent to the Third Prosecutor of Patras with instructions to conduct the main investigation of the above police employees . . .". Amnesty International has not been informed of any further developments concerning this case.

THE MIDDLE EAST AND NORTH AFRICA

Bahrain

During the period under review, Amnesty International received reports that political detainees in Bahrain were tortured or ill-treated while in the custody of the Bahraini security forces. These allegations, which came largely from opposition sources abroad or from prisoners' relatives and friends, concerned members of illegal trade union organizations and Muslim fundamentalists who were arrested for security reasons.

Of particular concern to Amnesty International were the reports of four deaths in custody following alleged torture in 1980 and 1981. Twenty-four-year-old Muhammad Hassan Abdullah Madan who was arrested on 14 February 1981 reportedly died in prison the same day. His body was never returned to his family and it is reported that fellow prisoners who helped with his burial saw his corpse covered with burns and the marks of beatings. Jamil Ali, aged about 25, reportedly died around 10 May 1980 in Salmaniyya hospital in the capital, Manama, after being arrested approximately two weeks earlier for taking part in a demonstration in protest at the execution in Iraq of a religious leader. His family, who were able to take photographs of the body and to bury it, claim it had been burned and beaten and that bones in the left hand and in both legs had been fractured. The other two alleged victims were Abdul Karim Al Habishi, who died on 10 July 1980, and Sheikh Jamal Ali Asfour, who died on 19 August 1981.

Political suspects were often subjected to prolonged periods of incommunicado detention without access to families and lawyers, and it is to this period that allegations of ill-treatment referred. Seventy-three people charged with plotting to overthrow the government alleged during their trial in March 1982 that they had been tortured during interrogation. They had been arrested in November or December 1981 and held incommunicado for up to two months until they were first brought before an examining magistrate in

January or February 1982. After their sentencing in May 1982, they are reported to have been held in continuous incommunicado detention and to have been subjected to further ill-treatment, and their families and lawyers have not been able to visit them or communicate with them in any way.

The Bahraini authorities have been unwilling to allow independent investigation into allegations of ill-treatment. In the March 1982 trial mentioned above, and in an earlier political trial in 1981, both held *in camera*, defendants alleged in court that they had been ill-treated during interrogation. Defence lawyers in both cases called for an independent medical examination of their clients, but in both cases doctors employed by the Ministry of Interior were appointed. Their reports mentioned no evidence of ill-treatment. Amnesty International called on the Bahraini authorities to carry out an independent investigation into reports of torture and ill-treatment on a number of occasions, but the organization has never received a reply from the authorities and as far as is known no such independent investigation has ever been carried out.

Egypt

Reports of torture or ill-treatment in Egypt were rarely received by Amnesty International until October 1981, following the assassination of President Sadat, when thousands of people were arrested. Between October 1981 and March 1982 Amnesty International received numerous and consistent reports of torture and ill-treatment, mostly relating to alleged members of militant Islamic groups, notably *Al Jihad*, but also including several left-wing detainees.

According to reports received by Amnesty International torture and ill-treatment were inflicted by members of the *Mabahis Amn ad-Dawla*, State Security Investigation Service, in its own buildings or in prisons such as the Citadel, Tora Reception Prison, and Al Marg Prison, in order to obtain confessions from the detainee and information about other individuals.

State of emergency detention procedures in force between October 1981 and June 1982 facilitated the infliction of torture and ill-treatment by permitting prolonged incommunicado detention. Most allegations referred to beating with sticks, lengths of rubber hosepipe or whips; suspension by the hands or feet for prolonged periods and burns inflicted with lighted cigarettes were also alleged. Some detainees claimed to have been threatened with murder or sexual assault directed both at themselves and female members of their families.

Some of these people were among the 302 accused in the *Jihad* case who, during their trial which began in December 1982, complained in court of their torture and ill-treatment, and some reportedly identified those responsible inside the court room. The Supreme State Security Court examining their case ordered that they undergo medical examination by forensic doctors in early 1983. Amnesty International has had access to some official forensic medical reports which conclude that the clinical evidence is consistent with the detainees' allegations of torture and ill-treatment. To Amnesty International's knowledge, however, no public inquiry has been initiated into these allegations.

The Egyptian constitution contains comprehensive safeguards against torture or ill-treatment (Article 42) and provides for compensation of victims and the initiation of related criminal proceedings with no statutory limitation period (Article 57). In addition, under Article 126 of the penal code, torture is punishable by between three and 10 years' imprisonment.

In June 1982 Amnesty International addressed a memorandum (which formed the basis of the publication, *Egypt: Violations of Human Rights* in February 1983) to the Egyptian Government which contained extracts from 10 medical reports of detainees claiming to have been tortured and recommended that the President of Egypt issue, and make widely and forcefully known, a statement that the government condemns and will not permit prisoners to be subjected to torture or ill-treatment in Egypt. The organization further recommended that the Egyptian Government establish impartial machinery to investigate thoroughly all allegations of torture or ill-treatment of detainees in accordance with Article 9 of the Declaration against Torture. Such a measure would be a positive step in giving force to the Egyptian Government's declared intention of 24 June 1981 to comply with the Declaration and to apply its provisions "by legislative and other effective measures". It was also recommended that the Egyptian Government make efforts, in accordance with Article 126 of the penal code and Article 10 of the Declaration against Torture, to bring to justice those responsible for the infliction of torture and that adequate compensation be awarded to the victims in accordance with Article 11 of the declaration.

During a mission to Egypt in May 1983 Amnesty International delegates had talks with government and other officials and discussed ways in which to prevent torture and ill-treatment from occurring by introducing legislative and other safeguards. Amnesty International sought information in particular about the methods employed in investigating prisoners' complaints of torture or ill-treatment and inspecting prisons, and amendments in legislation governing arrest and detention procedures, including certain provisions allowing prolonged incommunicado detention which were abolished in June 1982.

Iran

According to information received by Amnesty International during the period under review, torture, which did not appear to take place systematically immediately following the revolution of February 1979, has become a routine practice in at least some Iranian prisons. It is alleged to have been inflicted by *Pasadaran*, Revolutionary Guards, who carry out arrests and also serve as guards within the prisons. Torture is also alleged to have taken place immediately following arrest and during interrogation in *Pasdaran* Headquarters and *Komitehs*, the equivalent of local police stations, all over Iran.

Two kinds of ill-treatment of prisoners took place which were of concern to Amnesty International: the officially sanctioned punishment of prisoners by whipping and the torture of prisoners held in incommunicado detention, which occurs during interrogation in order to extract confessions and is not acknowledged by the authorities. There does not always appear to be a clear distinction between whipping in order to extract information or a confession and whipping as a judicial punishment. This is compounded by the arbitrary nature of judicial proceedings, which take place within the prisons. A few instances of the amputation of fingers or hands and of stoning to death as judicial punishments have been reported in the press outside Iran.

Whipping as a judicial punishment was inflicted on both ordinary criminal and political prisoners. Amnesty International's information about torture for the purpose of extracting information or confessions, or for intimidation, concerns only those perceived as being opponents of the government, who included people engaged in violent opposition, but also many detained because of their non-violent political or religious beliefs or their ethnic origin, or simply because of their relationship with people who have been active politically.

Many former prisoners interviewed by Amnesty International have testified about torture. Other reports have come from former prisoners and prisoners' relatives in Iran. In some cases the testimony of former prisoners who have escaped from Iran has been supported by medical examinations carried out by Amnesty International doctors.

The most common methods of torture described to Amnesty International are whipping on all parts of the body with cables while the prisoner is suspended by the wrists or strapped to a bed and the beating of the soles of the feet. Other methods reported include burning with cigarettes, burning with an iron, electric shocks, hosing with water and mock executions.

Some allegations of torture described the torture of relatives in order to induce people to give themselves up or to intimidate the family as a whole. In other cases tortured prisoners were shown to their families so that the families would persuade the prisoners to confess to avoid further torture. In many cases Amnesty International is told that people have died under torture and that their deaths have subsequently been announced as executions.

Torture "for the purpose of extracting confessions or gaining information" is prohibited by Article 38 of the Iranian constitution. In a reply dated 3 July 1979 to a United Nations Questionnaire on Torture and Other Cruel, Inhuman or Degrading Treatment or Punishment the Iranian Government stated that torture and cruel treatment were prohibited under Iranian law and that any violation was punishable under Articles 131, 132 and 136 of the penal code.

In December 1980 Ayatollah Ruhollah Khomeini, Iran's revolutionary leader, ordered an inquiry into reports of torture in prisons. The findings of the Torture Probe Commission, announced on 17 May 1981, were that: "In general it could be said that torture is not an instrument of policy in the prisons, but certain exceptional cases of torture were observed in some of the prisons." The commission's report refers to some prisoners' complaints about *Tazir*, the corporal punishment prescribed by Islamic Canon Law, but indicates that this is not considered to be torture by the commission itself. The report states that in those cases where claims of torture were found to be reasonable those who had inflicted the torture would be "dealt with by the competent legal authorities". However, Amnesty International is not informed of any case of someone being charged with and tried for ill-treatment of a prisoner in Iran.

Since this inquiry took place the number of people arrested for political reasons has increased. The reports received by Amnesty International indicate not only that most people arrested were submitted to some form of ill-treatment, but that the ill-treatment has increased in severity.

In December 1981 Amnesty International urged the Iranian authorities to hold "a new investigation into allegations of torture" and to issue "a public, unequivocal condemnation and prohibition of torture from the highest level''. Subsequently, Amnesty International reiterated its concern about allegations of torture and asked the Iranian Government to receive a delegation from Amnesty International to discuss this and other human rights violations in Iran. No response was received from the government.

In December 1982 Amnesty International issued a report received from Iran which described in detail the ill-treatment of prisoners in five Iranian prisons: Evin, Qasr and Komiteh in Tehran; a former dairy farm, Salehabad, between Tehran and Qom; and Vakilabad near Mashad. The report was based on testimony taken from released prisoners and prisoners' relatives, belonging to various political groups and including people who had not themselves been politically involved.

Iraq

Amnesty International has received frequent reports of the torture of political suspects and members of illegal parties, including the Iraqi Communist Party (ICP), the Kurdish Democratic Party (KDP), the Patriotic Union of Kurdistan and *Al Da'wa Al Islamiya*, the Islamic Call, while they were held in the custody of the Iraqi security forces. Some reports have indicated that people have died under torture.

The reports received by Amnesty International indicate that torture most often occurred immediately after arrest and during interrogation in pre-trial detention when detainees were allegedly held incommunicado, despite the fact that torture is prohibited by Article 22(a) of the Iraqi constitution and Article 127 of the Code of Criminal Procedures. Articles 332 and 333 of the penal code further provide that a government employee or civil servant who subjects any accused person to torture for the purpose of obtaining a confession or information relating to a crime is liable to a maximum of one year's imprisonment or a maximum fine of 100 dinars or both.

In almost all cases the purpose of torture was reportedly to extract confessions and information on the views of the victims and other individuals; in some cases torture was inflicted to force the detainee to renounce his or her illegal political affiliation. The interrogation methods of the security forces have often resulted in permanent physical or mental damage to the victims, and are reported to have included crude physical assaults with fists, boots, truncheons and whips; *falaqa*, sustained beating of the soles of the feet; systematic electric shocks on various parts of the body; mock executions and sexual abuse.

In April 1981 Amnesty International published medical findings of torture in *Iraq: Evidence of Torture*. The findings were based on interviews with and medical examinations of 15 Iraqi exiles who said that while in the custody of the security forces in Iraq between September 1976 and August 1979 they were questioned under torture about their own and others' views and in some cases pressed to join the *Ba'ath* Party. Some victims said they were hung by their hand-cuffed wrists from hooks; the examining doctors found circular scars consistent with those made by handcuffs. Some reported being burned with cigarettes and special tools; the doctors found 35 scars on one victim. *Falaqa* was frequently reported and a number of those interviewed said they were sexually molested and threatened with rape. Some described being subjected to mock executions. The medical examinations, carried out from seven to 37 months after the torture, also found evidence of long-term effects: in addition to the physical scars, some victims still suffered from impaired memory, loss of concentration and energy, nervous and sexual problems, depression, fear, insomnia and nightmares.

In every case the team of Amnesty International doctors who examined them found that the symptoms and signs observed during the medical examination were consistent with the torture methods described by the victims. Moreover, the victims' accounts were mutually consistent, even though they had been arrested independently and at different times and places.

Amnesty International has consistently drawn the Iraqi Government's attention to these allegations of torture. In 1983 the organization approached the government about the cases of at least 20 people who were reported to have died under torture while in custody between 1979 and 1981, and urged the authorities to make impartial inquiries into these cases and to make the methods and findings of such inquiries public. Amnesty International had previously approached the government in connection with some of these cases, submitting the names and particulars of detainees who had reportedly died under torture, as well as providing material indicating the nature of the ill-treatment inflicted and naming those agencies responsible.

The Iraqi authorities seldom replied to such appeals during the period under review. In cases where they have, they dismissed the allegations as untrue. Responding to Amnesty International's publication *Iraq: Evidence of Torture 1981*, the Government of Iraq described the report as "without foundation" and stressed that torture was banned by Iraq's constitution and other legislation. The government did not, however, deal in any detail with the cases described in the report; nor did it respond to the report's recommendations. After the publication of the report Amnesty International called on the Iraqi Government to receive an Amnesty International mission to discuss the conclusions and recommendations in the report and aspects of legal and administrative practice. The government agreed to receive an Amnesty International delegation at the beginning of 1983.

Following the Amnesty International mission to Iraq in January 1983 the organization submitted a memorandum to the Iraqi Government in May 1983 in which it stated that widespread torture still occurred in Iraq, that arrest and detention procedures for political suspects, as laid down in the Iraqi Code of Criminal Procedure, were not followed and that the legal prohibition on torture in Iraq's constitution was disregarded in practice. Amnesty International recommended that the President of the Republic issue a personal statement prohibiting torture and ill-treatment under all circumstances and introduce safeguards against torture.

In its reply to Amnesty International's memorandum published in *Report and Recommendations of an Amnesty International Mission to the Government of the Republic of Iraq 22-28 January 1983 (including the Government's Response and Amnesty International Comments)*, the Iraqi Government said the main aim of the torture allegations "is to discredit the people of Iraq and its Revolutionary Government", and that Amnesty International's recommendations set forth in the memorandum "focus on legal procedures and ethical principles already applied in Iraq and suggest nothing fresh".

Israel and the Occupied Territories

In September 1980 Amnesty International recommended in its *Report and Recommendations of an Amnesty International Mission to the Government of the State of Israel, 3-7 June 1979* that "a public and impartial committee of inquiry should be established to investigate the allegations of ill-treatment in their totality and the administrative and legal procedures and practices relevant to the arrest, confinement, interrogation and trial of security suspects". The Israeli authorities replied to these recommendations by saying that they "conduct an ongoing review of the treatment of security detainees, and there is thus no need for the committee of inquiry you recommend".

Amnesty International has continued to receive reports of ill-treatment during the period under review in the form of testimonies from former detainees held in the Occupied Territories, statements from lawyers and eye-witness accounts. The frequency and consistency of these reports indicate that some Palestinians from the Occupied Territories arrested for security reasons and interrogated by the *Shin Beth*, intelligence services, in a number of different detention centres have been hooded, handcuffed and forced to stand without moving for many hours at a time for several days, and have been exposed while naked to cold showers or cold air ventilators for long periods of time. Detainees have also been deprived of food, sleep, and toilet and medical facilities, and have been subjected to abuse, insults and threats against themselves and the female members of their families.

Amnesty International has also received a number of detailed reports of individual prisoners being beaten, sometimes severely, during interrogation in the Occupied Territories. One such case is that of Nassim Abd Al Jalil Audi Ahmad Daoud, from Yabroud, who was arrested on 30 January 1982 and interrogated in a detention centre about his activities as a member of *Al Fatah* organization. He alleged that, while hooded, handcuffed and sometimes stripped naked, he was, over a period of two weeks, beaten all over the body, including the genitals, with clubs and fists. His head was also repeatedly hit and banged against the wall causing injury and necessitating medical treatment.

There have been many reports of Palestinians in the Occupied Territories being ill-treated as a form of harassment and intimidation by the Israeli Defence Forces (IDF), either immediately upon arrest or in places of short-term detention. These allegations referred to military premises in Hebron and Ramallah and Al Fara'a detention centre near Nablus.

A security suspect in the Occupied Territories can be held for up to 18 days without access to a lawyer and before being brought before a court (in accordance with Security Provision Order 378). The International Committee of the Red Cross (ICRC) is, by arrangement with the Israeli authorities, notified of arrests within 12 days and permitted to visit security suspects within 12 to 14 days. However, an "escape clause" allows for the exemption of an individual from the 12-day rule for imperative reasons of security, but Amnesty International does not know how often this is invoked. In Israel proper a security suspect can be held incommunicado for up to 15 days, in accordance with the Criminal Procedures Law of 1982 (Article 29(f)). In addition, the confession often constitutes the main body of the evidence against the accused in the military courts and so offers an incentive to investigating personnel to ill-treat arrested suspects.

The Israeli authorities have often told Amnesty International that specific allegations of ill-treatment are investigated. In Israel proper, following criticism of the procedure whereby complaints of ill-treatment by police officers of ordinary criminal suspects were investigated by the police and brought before its disciplinary court, changes were agreed to in June 1983. These changes were based on recommendations proposed by the Eitan-Sirota Commission and included the establishment of a national unit to carry out internal investigations, the addition of a civilian member to the police disciplinary court, and provision for the public to complain directly by letter to the Attorney General or the Interior Minister.

In the Occupied Territories the detaining authority is the IDF, and they have their own internal procedures for investigating complaints brought by security suspects of ill-treatment by IDF regulars, Border Police and the Military Police. Between November 1982 and February 1983 five members of the IDF were prosecuted after three IDF reserve officers filed complaints about the excessive use of force by the army during demonstrations in the West Bank in the spring of 1982. They were charged with beating up Palestinian teenagers in their custody under orders from two local commanders, which the court declared were illegal. They were sentenced by a military court to between two and six months' imprisonment. In August 1982 two women soldiers were sentenced to one and three months' imprisonment for assault, after a complaint lodged by a British citizen who had been detained.

However, lawyers claim that few complaints lodged by individual Palestinians are thoroughly investigated since many people are discouraged from filing complaints because they fear repercussions such as charges being brought against them if they do. Furthermore, few complaints lead to prosecutions because the incommunicado nature of the detention and interrogation procedures makes it very difficult to produce sufficient evidence to make a case. Some complaints do not receive a reply, such as the one filed in August 1982 by the lawyer of Nassim Abd Al Jalil Audi Ahmad Daoud concerning his ill-treatment, referred to above.

After the Israeli invasion of Lebanon in early June 1982, Amnesty International received eye-witness accounts alleging that Palestinians, Lebanese and people of other nationalities, captured by the IDF and held in temporary detention centres in Sidon, were, at least until the third or fourth week in June 1982, ill-treated as a form of intimidation, and in some cases in order to elicit information. These accounts reported indiscriminate and often severe beating and exposure all day to the sun, treatment which was reported to have led to serious injury, illness and in seven or eight cases to death. Further allegations of ill-treatment in Lebanon have continued in 1983.

Palestinian and Lebanese prisoners captured by the IDF in Lebanon were not accorded prisoner of war status nor given rights under Israeli law. They were subjected to longer periods of incommunicado detention than is legally permissible in the Occupied Territories. It was five weeks before the ICRC was permitted to visit Al Ansar camp where the majority of detainees were held. Most prisoners, before being transferred to Al Ansar, and if not released, were held incommunicado without access to the ICRC for a month or more during interrogation. This took place in detention centres in Israeli military bases in southern Lebanon or, at least during 1982, in prisons in Israel proper. In addition, none of the detainees were allowed to see a lawyer, even though on 11 May 1983 the authorities decided that certain Israeli lawyers would be allowed to meet Al Ansar detainees.

Amnesty International urged the Israeli authorities on a number of occasions to investigate the allegations of ill-treatment in their totality and to publish the findings. Amnesty International has received unconfirmed reports that some investigations into allegations of ill-treatment in Lebanon have been carried out, but the organization has no further details.

Libya

Reports of torture and ill-treatment in Libya were rarely received by Amnesty International until after the February 1980 official call for the "physical liquidation of enemies of the 1969 revolution living abroad, and of counter-revolutionary elements within Libya". In the months following the declaration Amnesty International received reports that hundreds of people were arrested in Libya and that at least three people who were former members of the Ba'ath Party died in custody, reportedly under torture. A request for an autopsy in the case of 'Amer Deghayes, a lawyer who died in custody in late February 1980, three days after he had been summoned for questioning by the police, was refused by the authorities who claimed that he had committed suicide. In March and April 1980 Amnesty International observers attended parts of the trial of 18 prisoners of conscience during which defence lawyers complained that many of the 18 defendants had been subjected to beatings on their arrest, and that they had been held incommunicado in solitary confinement for a period of three months.

Towards the end of 1980 first-hand testimonies about torture and ill-treatment reached Amnesty International. Torture was inflicted mainly to obtain confessions and information about "the enemies of the revolution" and their activities. Detainees were allegedly tortured immediately after arrest during interrogation in various centres belonging to the Revolutionary Committees and the intelligence services in Tripoli and Benghazi. The basement of the Military Intelligence Headquarters in Tripoli, in what was formerly the Ministry of Planning building, is mentioned in most reports as the main torture centre. Detainees were allegedly held incommunicado for unlimited periods and their families were not informed of their whereabouts. The torture techniques reported include: beating; kicking; whipping with cables while chained to the wall; *falaqa*, beating on the soles of the feet; electric shocks, in particular on the head and genitals; placing a beetle under an inverted cup on the stomach of the torture victim; verbal humiliation; threats of execution; and threats of sexual abuse.

On 30 April 1980 Amnesty International addressed a memorandum to Colonel Mu'ammar Gaddafi in which it expressed concern about allegations of torture and called on the Libyan authorities to take remedial measures.

During 1982 and the early months of 1983 allegations of ill-treatment and torture were frequent and consistent. They indicate that torture of political suspects by the intelligence services and Revolutionary Committees during interrogation is routine and systematic.

In August 1982 Amnesty International received the names of three students who were said to have died under torture. Saleh Al Kounayti from Misratah, Ahmed Ismael Maklouf and Naji Bahouia from Benghazi, arrested in April 1982 following student demonstrations at Benghazi University, had allegedly died while in the custody of the security services. Their bodies were returned to their families in sealed coffins at the end of July. In a letter to Colonel Mu'ammar Gaddafi on 6 October 1982 Amnesty International requested that an immediate inquiry be made into these allegations. To Amnesty International's knowledge, no such inquiry has been undertaken.

It was reported that two Libyan citizens residing in the Federal Republic of Germany were tortured by members of the Revolutionary Committee at the residence of the Secretary-General of the Libyan People's Bureau in Bonn. On 13 November 1982 Elhadi Elghariani and Ahmed Shaladi were allegedly held inside the Secretary-General's residence and were released 24 hours later, after they had submitted written and recorded confessions about their political activities. Their confessions were said to have been extracted under torture, including beating, kicking, threats of execution and verbal humiliation. Amnesty International had access to the findings of the medical examination, by an independent doctor, of one of the victims. They show that the clinical evidence is consistent with the detainees' allegations of torture and ill-treatment. The culprits, two Libyans residing in Bonn, Dr Mustapha Zaidi and Abdullah Yahia were prosecuted and brought to trial on charges of torturing fellow Libyans. However, the trial was called off after the West German authorities decided to exchange the accused for eight West German nationals detained in Libya. On 15 May 1983 the two accused were released and returned to Libya.

Morocco

Amnesty International was concerned that certain aspects of Moroccan legal provisions and practice, particularly those related to *garde à vue*, incommunicado detention by the police, created the preconditions for torture and ill-treatment. Frequent and consistent allegations given to the organization suggested that torture and ill-treatment of opposition political activists, trade unionists, students, writers and other political prisoners and prisoners of conscience has taken place during the period under review. The organization is also concerned about the fate of a number of "disappeared" prisoners.

On arrest, political detainees are held in the exclusive custody of the police under the *garde à vue* provisions, with no access to lawyers or their families. The period of *garde à vue* is normally limited to 48 hours with a 24-hour extension possible. However, in cases involving *sûreté intérieure ou extérieure de l'Etat*, offences against the internal or external security of the state, all these periods may be quadrupled and as many extensions as necessary may be secured.

Throughout the 1970s it was common for political detainees to remain under *garde à vue* for many months and in some cases for up to several years; in the period under review such extended periods have become less common, although in some recent cases *garde à vue* appears to have lasted several months.

It is to the *garde à vue* period that most allegations of torture refer. These allegations cite, among forms of torture meted out to detainees during interrogation, beatings, electric shocks, cigarette burns, suspension in unnatural positions for long periods from iron bars often accompanied by *falaqa*, beating on the soles of the feet. In addition, political detainees under *garde à vue* have been kept blindfold and handcuffed for extended periods, with no exercise permitted. Prisoners also state that medical care during the *garde à vue* period is of the most rudimentary sort.

Amnesty International has also taken up the cases of approximately 60 individuals who were reportedly taken into custody by the Moroccan forces in connection with the war in the Western Sahara and who have since "disappeared"; and is concerned about the fate of approximately 100 military prisoners still held because of their involvement, in 1971 and 1972, in attempts to assassinate King Hassan II. Although the Moroccan authorities have refused to reveal their whereabouts, many of these military prisoners are believed to have been held in a secret detention centre near Tazmamert and Amnesty International has received reports that at least 15 of these prisoners have died and that deaths have continued to occur. These deaths are believed to be a result of the appalling conditions in which they are held—windowless, filthy and unventilated cells, extremes of temperature, solitary confinement, arbitrary punishments and beatings, inadequate food—and the complete lack of any medical care. Amnesty International fears that a similar fate awaits the remaining military prisoners and may await other "disappeared" people as well, whose numbers may reach several hundred.

During an Amnesty International mission to Morocco in 1981, officials were unable to allay any of these concerns, which were described in May 1982 in Amnesty International's *Report of an Amnesty International Mission to the Kingdom of Morocco*. Despite the fact that several Moroccan officials stated that a new code of criminal procedure that might substantially improve *garde à vue* procedures was under consideration at the time of the 1981 mission and would shortly be submitted to Parliament, as far as the organization is aware, this had not yet occurred. To Amnesty International's knowledge the Moroccan judicial and executive authorities have taken no significant steps to reduce the likelihood of torture or ill-treatment, to act on complaints that such abuses have occurred or to respond in substance to appeals concerning these and related human rights violations.

In February and March 1981 several activists of the *Union socialiste des forces populaires* (USFP), Socialist Union of Popular Forces, arrested in Tiznit in January 1981 showed the court marks on their bodies which they said were evidence of ill-treatment by the police. The court refused their request for a medical examination to justify their claims. When Taieb Sessy, President of the Bar Association of Agadir, member of the administrative committee of the *Association marocaine des droits de l'homme* (AMDH), Moroccan Association for Human Rights, and member of the administrative committee of the USFP, claimed that he had been badly beaten after being taken into custody on 11 July 1981, no official investigation was made.

In October 1981, members of the UN Human Rights Committee considered the Moroccan Government's report on the implementation of its obligations under the International Covenant on Civil and Political Rights. They asked, among other things, whether there were any grounds for believing that people had "disappeared" and in how many cases public officials had been prosecuted for brutality or ill-treatment. Morocco's representative answered many of the other questions but avoided answering these. In May 1983 the lawyer Abderrahman Ben Ameur, member of the administrative committee of the AMDH, appeared injured at his trial and claimed that his injury had been inflicted by the police after his arrest, but the court refused his request for medical examinations to be carried out to establish his claim. Finally, the Moroccan Government has not answered the many questions raised by Amnesty International, as well as by other international human rights organizations, regarding the current status, whereabouts and fate of the approximately 100 military prisoners cited above, nor regarding the many other "disappeared" people, who may number in the hundreds.

Saudi Arabia

Amnesty International received a number of complaints of torture or ill-treatment of detainees in Saudi Arabia during the period under review. These allegations have come in the form of first-hand accounts by present or former detainees as well as through relatives and defence counsels.

Most of the complaints have come from people detained for ordinary criminal offences and they suggest that ill-treatment of detainees occurs most often during the period after arrest while the victim is being held in custody awaiting trial or release. Some allege that because, in the absence of witnesses, the law requires a confession to convict for certain offences, this has in the past increased the risk of ill-treatment of detainees during interrogation in pretrial detention.

In several cases people were detained for many months incommunicado and/or in solitary confinement. For example, two Thai carpenters, Pilarn Pucharoen and Boonsri Prakarnnung, who were arrested in April 1980 on suspicion of complicity in the murder of a Yemeni shopkeeper, were reportedly held in solitary confinement for over two years. Boonsri Prakarnnung alleged that after his arrest he was not allowed to see daylight until 2 June 1982. Both have also alleged that since there were no witnesses to the crime, they had been tortured by whipping and electric shocks in order to extract confessions from them.

In one case which has been brought to Amnesty International's attention the Saudi authorities are reported to have carried out an investigation into allegations of torture and disciplined those responsible. Keith Carmichael, a British subject, was held incommunicado in Aleysha detention centre from 2 November 1981 until 31 January 1982. During this time requests by the British Consulate to visit him were reportedly denied. When he was eventually allowed access Keith Carmichael complained that he had been threatened with sexual assault by a prison guard and that on the night of 17 November 1981 his feet were padlocked to the back of a chair and the soles of his feet were beaten with a cane. As a result his feet and ankles became swollen and he was hospitalized for over two weeks.

Although the Saudi authorities had not responded to an Amnesty International request for an investigation into these allegations, the organization has learned from other sources that an inquiry was conducted, with Keith Carmichael identifying some of those responsible for his ill-treatment. At least one prison guard is reported to have been imprisoned. The findings of the inquiry have not been made public.

Amnesty International also understands that cruel, inhuman or degrading treatment was inflicted in the form of floggings or the amputation of limbs. *Shari'a*, Islamic Law, provides for amputation of the hand as punishment for repeated theft where there are no mitigating circumstances. Since the beginning of 1980 Amnesty International has learned of five cases where this punishment was carried out (one in 1980; one in 1981; and three in 1982). In the case of Salah Fariah Shukair, a national of the Yemen Arab Republic, reports indicate that following the severing of his right hand with a knife in a public square in the town of Najran on 7 August 1982, he was immediately transferred to a hospital for treatment.

Floggings were also inflicted as a form of judicial punishment, mainly for alcohol offences, during the period under review. In some cases a sentence of flogging was carried out instead of a term of imprisonment, the victim being given the choice. In other cases it was inflicted in addition to imprisonment, the sentence being carried out shortly before release. Sentences which have come to Amnesty International's attention in the past few years have ranged from 30 to 300 lashes carried out over a period of several days or months.

According to Saudi officials, this form of punishment is designed to humiliate and rehabilitate rather than cause pain. The official administering the blows holds a copy of the Quran under his cane arm, using only his lower arm to wield the cane, and the strokes on the clothed back and buttocks are reportedly not allowed to draw blood.

However, Amnesty International has also learned of cases where offenders have been flogged on their bare backs causing weals and bruising.

All the cases of floggings reported to Amnesty International during the period under review have been those of foreign nationals. During this period Amnesty International received no information that Saudi nationals had been flogged, although the organization is unable to state that such floggings did not occur.

Syria

Amnesty International has continued to receive allegations of torture or ill-treatment of prisoners in Syria during the period under review, as in previous years. Most of the allegations indicate that torture or ill-treatment usually occurs during the period immediately following arrest while the victim is held in the custody of the arresting authority. In most cases the victim was detained by a branch of the security forces, was held incommunicado in one of their detention centres and was interrogated to obtain a confession or information regarding other individuals.

Most reports of torture or ill-treatment have come from former detainees, prisoners' relatives, and lawyers, and include many first-hand accounts. The extent, consistency and detail of these allegations, which have been received persistently over the years, some of them being supported by medical evidence, suggest that torture is used systematically during interrogation both in order to extract confessions and as a form of punishment.

Amnesty International believes that the fundamental rights of people in custody in Syria, particularly those held in preventive detention under the State of Emergency law of 1962, are routinely infringed by the Syrian security forces. Detainees are usually not informed, at the time of arrest, of the reasons for the arrest and are denied legal assistance and the right to a prompt medical examination after arrest. Moreover, under the procedures followed during the state of emergency in Syria, there appears to be no clear limit to the length of time the security forces may hold a person incommunicado—it could be for a few days or several months or years.

Allegations of torture have been received by Amnesty International concerning people of widely differing ages, representing many professions and coming from every province in Syria. They include individuals held on account of their alleged membership of or support for a variety of organizations or parties legal or banned, as well as relatives held as hostages until the suspects are taken into custody.

The types of allegation received have included reports of beatings or whipping on all parts of the body; suspending the victim, sometimes upside down, for lengthy periods; showering or pouring boiling or cold water over the victim alternately or at different times; plucking hairs or extracting finger-nails; applying electricity to all parts of the body, particularly the genitals; extinguishing cigarettes on sensitive parts of the body; forcing the victim to sit on bottle necks or inserting sticks or heated metal skewers into the rectum.

Instruments reportedly used to torture victims have varied from simple belts, sticks or whips to more sophisticated devices such as *al-'Abd al-Aswad*, the Black Slave: strapping the seated victim onto an apparatus which when switched on inserts a heated metal skewer into the anus, or the *Bisat al-Rih*, Flying Carpet: strapping the victim to a piece of wood shaped like a human silhouette and beating or applying electricity all over the body.

Since 1980 Amnesty International members have made a number of urgent appeals on behalf of detainees who have been held incommunicado in Syria and where the organization feared that they had been ill-treated. In several cases in 1982, including those of Riad al-Turk (First Secretary of the Communist Party Political Bureau), Fateh Jamus (a mechanical engineer and member of the banned Party for Communist Action) and Maître Muwaffaq al-Din al-Kozbari (President of the Prisoners' Care Association and First Secretary of the Syrian League for the Defence of Human Rights), they had also been transferred to hospital for urgent medical treatment. The Syrian authorities did not respond to any of these appeals.

Torture and ill-treatment are prohibited under the Syrian constitution and Article 391 of the Syrian penal code provides that any person who subjects another to any form of violence not permissible under law for the purpose of obtaining a confession or information relating to an offence is liable to imprisonment for between three months and three years. If the violent acts result in illness or injury to the victim, the law prescribes a minimum penalty of one year's imprisonment for the person responsible.

In April 1983 Amnesty International submitted a memorandum

to the Syrian Government assessing human rights violations by the Syrian security forces. The organization cited several extracts from the torture testimonies of former detainees, and included the record of a medical examination of a former detainee which took place in London in September 1980. (The victim was detained and released in September 1979.) Amnesty International drew the government's attention to the "General Comments" made by the United Nations Human Rights Committee on 27 July 1982, according to which it is not sufficient for State Parties merely to prohibit torture by law, and recommended that the Syrian Government examine current legislation and practice designed to prevent abuses by the security forces and allegations of torture or ill-treatment. Amnesty International further recommended that the government should bring those responsible for the infliction of torture to trial, and that it should make adequate compensation to the victims in accordance with Article 11 of the Declaration against Torture.

Tunisia

Numerous and consistent allegations of torture and ill-treatment or punishment of political detainees in Tunisia have reached Amnesty International over a number of years and have continued during the period under review. Following arrest political detainees are taken into police custody for interrogation before they appear before an examining judge. This period, known as *garde à vue*, has no defined maximum limit and in the case of one group of detainees who were arrested in October 1982 exceeded 40 days. During *garde à vue* detainees are held incommunicado. Relatives often experience difficulty in tracing them, and determining their exact whereabouts, and may meet with denials from the police that the person is in detention at all. It is during this period of *garde à vue* that torture and ill-treatment reportedly occur.

The methods of torture most consistently reported during the period under review include beatings on sensitive parts of the body, particularly the soles of the feet, with sticks, iron bars and lengths of rubber hosepipe, often after the detainee has been stripped naked. Detainees are also subjected to the "swing", whereby they are suspended in an inverted position, their ankles and wrists bound together, from an iron bar inserted behind the knees. Other forms of torture and ill-treatment include burns inflicted with cigarettes and enforced standing for prolonged periods.

Political detainees, including prisoners of conscience, have consistently claimed during their trials that their confessions were obtained as a result of torture, and have called for independent medical examinations in order to substantiate their claims. Such requests are not known to have been acted upon. Amnesty International knows of cases where detainees have lodged complaints against individuals whom they claimed were responsible for the infliction of torture, but is not aware of any disciplinary measures having been imposed on the perpetrators, or of compensation having been paid to the victim.

Pressure from within the country has been brought to bear on the Tunisian authorities by members of the legal profession, various political parties or movements and *la Ligue tunisienne pour la défense des droits de l'homme*, Tunisian League for the Protection of Human Rights, to set up an independent inquiry into allegations of torture and ill-treatment. Similar demands have been made to incorporate further safeguards against torture into existing legislation governing arrest and detention procedures, including a short and defined term for the *garde à vue* period.

Amnesty International has repeatedly called on the Tunisian Government to demonstrate its commitment to Article 7 of the International Covenant on Civil and Political Rights, which Tunisia ratified on 18 March 1969, by initiating a thorough investigation of all allegations of torture and ill-treatment. Amnesty International has urged that the investigation be undertaken by individuals who enjoy the respect and confidence of all those involved, and that the findings be made public. To Amnesty International's knowledge, no such inquiry has been undertaken.

In addition, Amnesty International has drawn attention to Article 103 of the Tunisian penal code which provides for five years' imprisonment for those who have used or ordered the use of violence towards, or ill-treatment of a defendant, witness or expert, for the purpose of obtaining confessions or statements. The same article provides that threats to inflict ill-treatment are punishable by a maximum penalty of six months' imprisonment. During the period under review Amnesty International knows of no cases in Tunisia where law enforcement officials were sentenced under this provision, or of victims of torture or ill-treatment receiving compensation.

* * * *

In addition to the countries mentioned above, Amnesty International has received allegations about some cases of torture or ill-treatment from Algeria, Jordan, Kuwait, Lebanon, Oman and the United Arab Emirates.

Amnesty International received sporadic reports of ill-treatment and bad prison conditions from Algeria during the period under review. Some of these reports referred to ill-treatment of individuals detained in the Kabyle region following protests in March and April 1980, and to four prisoners sentenced by a military tribunal at Blida in 1980 and serving their terms in the prison of Tazoult-Lambese. The organization has been unable to verify these reports.

Amnesty International was also unable to investigate several reports of ill-treatment received from Jordan during the period under review.

Amnesty International received allegations that prisoners have been tortured in order to extract confessions and that arbitrary ill-treatment of prisoners by prison guards may have taken place in Kuwait during the period under review, but has been unable to verify these reports.

Amnesty International was concerned that many of the detainees held since late 1982 by the Lebanese army and security forces had not been permitted visits by their lawyers, relatives or outside observers. The organization received reports that some detainees had been tortured and that several may have died as a result of their ill-treatment, and although it was unable to confirm these reports it has urged President Amin Gemayel to investigate them and to ensure that all detainees be allowed their full legal rights.

Amnesty International received several reports that political prisoners have been tortured in order to extract confessions in Oman, but was unable to substantiate them.

Amnesty International received allegations that prisoners had been subjected to ill-treatment in the United Arab Emirates in order to extract confessions and that arbitrary ill-treatment of prisoners by prison guards may also have taken place during the period under review, but the organization was unable to substantiate these reports. Amnesty International has also received reports that certain offences such as murder, rape and adultery can be punished by flogging, but was unable to ascertain the extent to which such sentences have been carried out. Adultery can also be punished by stoning to death, but the organization was unable to confirm whether such sentences have been carried out during the period under review.

The prevention of torture

Amnesty International believes that any government that wishes to stop torture has the means to do so. It is a question of political will. In adopting the Universal Declaration of Human Rights, the Declaration against Torture and other statements of international law and human rights, governments have accepted the illegality of torture and agreed to abolish it (see Chapter 4).

Two international instruments currently being elaborated would provide additional protection: the draft Convention Against Torture and Other Cruel, Inhuman or Degrading Treatment or Punishment and the draft Body of Principles for the Protection of all Persons Under any Form of Detention or Imprisonment. The former would establish universal jurisdiction in respect of alleged torturers and give legally binding force to the standards included in the Declaration against Torture; the latter includes additional safeguards such as the right of arrested people to notify their families. They should be adopted as soon as possible, including the strongest possible measures of protection against torture.

Also currently under discussion, both regionally and in connection with the draft Convention and the draft body of Principles, are proposals for national and international systems of independent visits of inspection to places of detention, which would help to provide additional protection against torture.

Without waiting for these new international instruments to be adopted, however, governments should review the safeguards against torture available in their own countries in the light of the provisions of the Declaration against Torture. Among other measures to be taken, they should make the text of the Code of Conduct for Law Enforcement Officials available to all law enforcement officials in their own language and ensure that those officials are fully trained in the prohibition of torture as a criminal act.

Amnesty International has compiled a list of some of the principal measures which governments should take to prevent torture, reflecting the recommendations made in Chapter 6. The following 12-Point

Program for the Prevention of Torture has been compiled from existing international standards and from the recommendations which Amnesty International itself has made over the years to governments of countries where torture is inflicted. The organization believes that the program and the standards on which it is based should be publicized widely. The various points in the program can be used as a test of a government's willingness to prevent torture.

Governments must act to fulfil their responsibility for the prevention of torture but efforts can also be made by non-governmental groups in fighting torture by disseminating practical information to victims and potential victims on prisoners' rights, procedures to be followed in lodging complaints of torture, or on what medical, financial or legal aid is available.

Bar associations and individual lawyers and judges can press for the adoption of legal safeguards against torture; members of parliament can send appeals through international channels and seek to prevent torture through investigative missions and special reports or hearings; journalists can expose torture by locating torture centres, identifying individual torturers and obtaining testimonies and photographic evidence. Once reports of torture are published, the news media should follow up the story to see whether the government conducts an impartial and effective investigation of the allegations and brings those responsible to justice. Among other individuals and groups which can help to prevent torture are religious leaders, who can denounce torture as incompatible with religious teachings and encourage action against it; trade unionists, who can mobilize support for their colleagues and others who have been tortured at home or abroad; women's organizations, which can take action concerning the special degradation faced by women at the hands of male torturers; and teachers' organizations, which can ensure that the issue of torture is raised within schools and universities in the context of human rights education. Medical organizations can investigate allegations of the participation of members of their profession in the infliction of torture and can impose appropriate disciplinary sanctions where involvement is proved. Organizations of military, police and prison officials can press for training programs which instil a personal conviction that torture must not be inflicted.

Elsewhere, individuals should raise their voices to appeal for an end to the illegal and shameful practices described in this report, either working on their own or through the various NGOs engaged in programs of education and action, of which Amnesty International is one.

Amnesty International

12-Point Program for the Prevention of Torture

Torture is a fundamental violation of human rights, condemned by the General Assembly of the United Nations as an offence to human dignity and prohibited under national and international law.

Yet torture persists, daily and across the globe. In Amnesty International's experience, legislative prohibition is not enough. Immediate steps are needed to confront torture and other cruel, inhuman or degrading treatment or punishment wherever they occur and to eradicate them totally.

Amnesty International calls on all governments to implement the following 12-Point Program for the Prevention of Torture. It invites concerned individuals and organizations to join in promoting the program. Amnesty International believes that the implementation of these measures is a positive indication of a government's commitment to abolish torture and to work for its abolition worldwide.

1. Official condemnation of torture

The highest authorities of every country should demonstrate their total opposition to torture. They should make clear to all law-enforcement personnel that torture will not be tolerated under any circumstances.

2. Limits on incommunicado detention

Torture often takes place while the victims are held incommunicado—unable to contact people outside who could help them or find out what is happening to them. Governments should adopt safeguards to ensure that incommunicado detention does not become an opportunity for torture. It is vital that all prisoners be brought before a judicial authority promptly after being taken into custody and that relatives, lawyers and doctors have prompt and regular access to them.

3. No secret detention

In some countries torture takes place in secret centres, often after the victims are made to "disappear". Governments should ensure that prisoners are held in publicly recognized places, and that accurate information about their whereabouts is made available to relatives and lawyers.

4. Safeguards during interrogation and custody

Governments should keep procedures for detention and interrogation under regular review. All prisoners should be promptly told of their rights, including the right to lodge complaints about their treatment. There should be regular independent visits of inspection to places of detention. An important safeguard against torture would be the separation of authorities responsible for detention from those in charge of interrogation.

5. Independent investigation of reports of torture

Governments should ensure that all complaints and reports of torture are impartially and effectively investigated. The methods and findings of such investigations should be made public. Complainants and witnesses should be protected from intimidation.

6. No use of statements extracted under torture

Governments should ensure that confessions or other evidence obtained through torture may never be invoked in legal proceedings.

7. Prohibition of torture in law

Governments should ensure that acts of torture are punishable offences under the criminal law. In accordance with international law, the prohibition of torture must not be suspended under any circumstances, including states of war or other public emergency.

8. Prosecution of alleged torturers

Those responsible for torture should be brought to justice. This principle should apply wherever they happen to be, wherever the crime was committed and whatever the nationality of the perpetrators or victims. There should be no "safe haven" for torturers.

9. Training procedures

It should be made clear during the training of all officials involved in the custody, interrogation or treatment of prisoners that torture is a criminal act. They should be instructed that they are obliged to refuse to obey any order to torture.

10. Compensation and rehabilitation

Victims of torture and their dependants should be entitled to obtain financial compensation. Victims should be provided with appropriate medical care or rehabilitation.

11. International response

Governments should use all available channels to intercede with governments accused of torture. Inter-governmental mechanisms should be established and used to investigate reports of torture urgently and to take effective action against it. Governments should ensure that military, security or police transfers or training do not facilitate the practice of torture.

12. Ratification of international instruments

All governments should ratify international instruments containing safeguards and remedies against torture, including the International Covenant on Civil and Political Rights and its Optional Protocol which provides for individual complaints.

The 12-Point Program was adopted by Amnesty International in October 1983 as part of the organization's Campaign for the Abolition of Torture.

Appendices

Standard Minimum Rules for the Treatment of Prisoners

Adopted by the First United Nations Congress on the Prevention of Crime and the Treatment of Offenders on 30 August 1955 and approved by the United Nations Economic and Social Council on 31 July 1957
Articles 31, 32 and 33.

31. Corporal punishment, punishment by placing in a dark cell, and all cruel, inhuman or degrading punishments shall be completely prohibited as punishments for disciplinary offences.

32. (1) Punishment by close confinement or reduction of diet shall never be inflicted unless the medical officer has examined the prisoner and certified in writing that he is fit to sustain it.

(2) The same shall apply to any other punishment that may be prejudicial to the physical or mental health of a prisoner. In no case may such punishment be contrary to or depart from the principle stated in rule 31.

(3) The medical officer shall visit daily prisoners undergoing such punishments and shall advise the director if he considers the termination or alteration of the punishment necessary on grounds of physical or mental health.

33. Instruments of restraint, such as handcuffs, chains, irons and straitjackets, shall never be applied as a punishment. Furthermore, chains or irons shall not be used as restraints. Other instruments of restraint shall not be used except in the following circumstances:

(a) As a precaution against escape during a transfer, provided that they shall be removed when the prisoner appears before a judicial or administrative authority;

(b) On medical grounds by direction of the medical officer;

(c) By order of the director, if other methods of control fail, in order to prevent a prisoner from injuring himself or others or from damaging property; in such instances the director shall at once consult the medical officer and report to the higher administrative authority.

APPENDIX II

The United Nations Declaration on the Protection of All Persons from Torture and Other Cruel, Inhuman or Degrading Treatment or Punishment

("Declaration against Torture")

The United Nations General Assembly adopted on 9 December 1975 a Declaration condemning any act of torture or other cruel, inhuman or degrading treatment as "an offence to human dignity". Under its terms, no state may permit or tolerate torture or other inhuman or degrading treatment, and each state is requested to take effective measures to prevent such treatment from being used within its jurisdiction.

The declaration was first adopted and referred to the General Assembly by the Fifth United Nations Congress on the Prevention of Crime and Treatment of Offenders, held in Geneva in September 1975. In adopting the declaration without a vote, the assembly noted that the Universal Declaration of Human Rights and the International Covenant on Civil and Political Rights provide that no one may be subjected to torture or to cruel, inhuman or degrading treatment or punishment.

The assembly has recommended that the Declaration serve as a guideline for all states and other entities exercising effective power.

The text of the declaration follows.

* * * *

Article 1

1.   For the purpose of this Declaration, torture means any act by which severe pain or suffering, whether physical or mental, is intentionally inflicted by or at the instigation of a public official on a person for such purposes as obtaining from him or a third person information or confession, punishing him for an act he has committed or is suspected of having committed, or intimidating him or other persons. It does not include pain or suffering arising only from, inherent in or incidental to, lawful sanctions to the extent consistent with the Standard Minimum Rules for the Treatment of Prisoners.

2.   Torture constitutes an aggravated and deliberate form of cruel, inhuman or degrading treatment or punishment.

Article 2

Any act of torture or other cruel, inhuman or degrading treatment or punishment is an offence to human dignity and shall be condemned as a denial of the purposes of the Charter of the United Nations and as a violation of the human rights and fundamental freedoms proclaimed in the Universal Declaration of Human Rights.

Article 3

No State may permit or tolerate torture or other cruel, inhuman or degrading treatment or punishment. Exceptional circumstances such as a state of war or a threat of war, internal political instability or any other public emergency may not be invoked as a justification of torture or other cruel, inhuman or degrading treatment or punishment.

Article 4

Each State shall, in accordance with the provisions of this Declaration, take effective measures to prevent torture and other cruel, inhuman or degrading treatment or punishment from being practised within its jurisdiction.

Article 5

The training of law enforcement personnel and of other public officials who may be responsible for persons deprived of their liberty shall ensure that full account is taken of the prohibition against torture and other cruel, inhuman or degrading treatment or punishment. This prohibition shall also, where appropriate, be included in such general rules or instructions as are issued in regard to the duties and functions of anyone who may be involved in the custody or treatment of such persons.

Article 6

Each State shall keep under systematic review interrogation methods and practices as well as arrangements for the custody and treatment of persons deprived of their liberty in its territory, with a view to preventing any cases of torture or other cruel, inhuman or degrading treatment or punishment.

Article 7

Each State shall ensure that all acts of torture as defined in article 1 are offences under its criminal law. The same shall apply in regard to acts which constitute participation in, complicity in, incitement to or an attempt to commit torture.

Article 8

Any person who alleges that he has been subjected to torture or other cruel, inhuman or degrading treatment or punishment by or at the instigation of a public official shall have the right to complain to, and to have his case impartially examined by, the competent authorities of the State concerned.

Article 9

Wherever there is reasonable ground to believe that an act of torture as defined in article 1 has been committed, the competent authorities of the State concerned shall promptly proceed to an impartial investigation even if there has been no formal complaint.

Article 10

If an investigation under article 8 or article 9 establishes that an act of torture as defined in article 1 appears to have been committed, criminal proceedings shall be instituted against the alleged offender or offenders in accordance with national law. If an allegation of other forms of cruel, inhuman or degrading treatment or punishment is considered to be well founded, the alleged offender or offenders shall be subject to criminal, disciplinary or other appropriate proceedings.

Article 11

Where it is proved that an act of torture or other cruel, inhuman or degrading treatment or punishment has been committed by or at the instigation of a public official, the victim shall be afforded redress and compensation in accordance with national law.

Article 12

Any statement which is established to have been made as a result of torture or other cruel, inhuman or degrading treatment may not be invoked as evidence against the person concerned or against any other person in any proceedings.

APPENDIX III

Code of Conduct for Law Enforcement Officials

Adopted by the United Nations General Assembly on 17 December 1979
Article 5 with Commentary

Article 5

No law enforcement official may inflict, instigate or tolerate any act of torture or other cruel, inhuman or degrading treatment or punishment, nor may any law enforcement official invoke superior orders or exceptional circumstances such as a state of war or a threat of war, a threat to national security, internal political instability or any other public emergency as a justification of torture or other cruel, inhuman or degrading treatment or punishment.

Commentary:

(a) This prohibition derives from the Declaration on the Protection of All Persons from Being Subjected to Torture and Other Cruel, Inhuman or Degrading Treatment or Punishment, adopted by the General Assembly, according to which:

> "[Such an act is] an offense to human dignity and shall be
> condemned as a denial of the purposes of the Charter of the United

Nations and as a violation of the human rights and fundamental freedoms proclaimed in the Universal Declaration of Human Rights [and other international human rights instruments]."

(b)   The Declaration defines torture as follows:

". . . torture means any act by which severe pain or suffering, whether physical or mental, is intentionally inflicted by or at the instigation of a public official on a person for such purposes as obtaining from him or a third person information or confession, punishing him for an act he has committed or is suspected of having committed, or intimidating him or other persons. It does not include pain or suffering arising only from, inherent in or incidental to, lawful sanctions to the extent consistent with the Standard Minimum Rules for the Treatment of Prisoners."

(c)   The term "cruel, inhuman or degrading treatment or punishment" has not been defined by the General Assembly but should be interpreted so as to extend the widest possible protection against abuses, whether physical or mental.

APPENDIX IV

General Comments on article 7 of the International Covenant on Civil and Political Rights

Adopted under article 40, paragraph 4 of the International Covenant on Civil and Political Rights by the Human Rights Committee at its 378th meeting (16th session) on 27 July 1982

General Comment 7 (16) (article 7)

1.   In examining the reports of States parties, members of the Committee have often asked for further information under article 7 which prohibits, in the first place, torture or cruel, inhuman or degrading treatment or punishment. The Committee recalls that even in situations of public emergency such as are envisaged by article 4 (1) this provision is non-derogable under article 4 (2). Its purpose is to protect the integrity and dignity of the individual. The Committee notes that it is not sufficient for the implementation of this article to prohibit such treatment or punishment or to make it a crime. Most States have penal provisions which are applicable to cases of torture or similar practices. Because such cases nevertheless occur, it follows from article 7, read together with article 2 of the Covenant, that States must ensure an effective protection through some machinery of control. Complaints about ill-treatment must be investigated effectively by competent authorities. Those found guilty must be held responsible, and the alleged victims

must themselves have effective remedies at their disposal, including the right to obtain compensation. Among the safeguards which may make control effective are provisions against detention incommunicado, granting, without prejudice to the investigation, persons such as doctors, lawyers and family members access to the detainees; provisions requiring that detainees should be held in places that are publicly recognized and that their names and places of detention should be entered in a central register available to persons concerned, such as relatives; provisions making confessions or other evidence obtained through torture or other treatment contrary to article 7 inadmissible in court; and measures of training and instruction of law enforcement officials not to apply such treatment.

2.   As appears from the terms of this article, the scope of protection required goes far beyond torture as normally understood. It may not be necessary to draw sharp distinctions between the various prohibited forms of treatment or punishment. These distinctions depend on the kind, purpose and severity of the particular treatment. In the view of the Committee the prohibition must extend to corporal punishment, including excessive chastisement as an educational or disciplinary measure. Even such a measure as solitary confinement may, according to the circumstances, and especially when the person is kept incommunicado, be contrary to this article. Moreover, the article clearly protects not only persons arrested or imprisoned, but also pupils and patients in educational and medical institutions. Finally, it is also the duty of public authorities to ensure protection by the law against such treatment even when committed by persons acting outside or without any official authority. For all persons deprived of their liberty, the prohibition of treatment contrary to article 7 is supplemented by the positive requirement of article 10 (1) of the Covenant that they shall be treated with humanity and with respect for the inherent dignity of the human person.

3.   In particular, the prohibition extends to medical or scientific experimentation without the free consent of the person concerned (article 7, second sentence). The Committee notes that the reports of States parties have generally given little or no information on this point. It takes the view that at least in countries where science and medicine are highly developed, and even for peoples and areas outside their borders if affected by their experiments, more attention should be given to the possible need and means to ensure the observance of this provision. Special protection in regard to such experiments is necessary in the case of persons not capable of giving their consent.

APPENDIX V

Principles of Medical Ethics

Adopted by the United Nations General Assembly on 18 December 1982

Principles of Medical Ethics relevant to the Role of Health Personnel, particularly Physicians, in the Protection of Prisoners and Detainees against Torture and Other Cruel, Inhuman or Degrading Treatment or Punishment

The General Assembly,

Recalling its resolution 31/85 of 13 December 1976 in which it invited the World Health Organization to prepare a draft code of medical ethics relevant to the protection of persons subjected to any form of detention or imprisonment against torture and other cruel, inhuman or degrading treatment or punishment,

Expressing once again its appreciation to the Executive Board of the World Health Organization, which at its sixty-third session, in January 1979, decided to endorse the principles set forth in a report entitled "Development of codes of medical ethics" containing, in an annex, a draft body of principles prepared by the Council for International Organizations of Medical Sciences and entitled "Principles of medical ethics relevant to the role of health personnel in the protection of persons against torture and other cruel, inhuman or degrading treatment or punishment",

Bearing in mind Economic and Social Council resolution 1981/27 of 6 May 1981, in which the Council recommended that the General Assembly should take measures to finalize the draft Principles of Medical Ethics at its thirty-sixth session,

Recalling its resolution 36/61 of 25 November 1981 in which it decided to consider the draft Principles of Medical Ethics at its thirty-seventh session with a view to adopting them,

Alarmed that not infrequently members of the medical profession or other health personnel are engaged in activities which are difficult to reconcile with medical ethics,

Recognizing that throughout the world significant medical activities are being performed increasingly by health personnel not licensed or trained as physicians, such as physician-assistants, paramedics, physical therapists and nurse practitioners,

Recalling with appreciation the Declaration of Tokyo of the World Medical Association, containing the Guidelines for Medical Doctors concerning

Torture and other Cruel, Inhuman or Degrading Treatment or Punishment in relation to Detention and Imprisonment, adopted by the twenty-ninth World Medical Association, held at Tokyo in October 1975,

Noting that in accordance with the Declaration of Tokyo measures should be taken by States and by professional associations and other bodies, as appropriate, against any attempt to subject health personnel or members of their families to threats or reprisals resulting from a refusal by such personnel to condone the use of torture or other forms of cruel, inhuman or degrading treatment,

Reaffirming the Declaration on the Protection of all Persons from Being Subjected to Torture and Other Cruel, Inhuman or Degrading Treatment or Punishment, unanimously adopted by the General Assembly in its resolution 3452 (XXX) of 9 December 1975, in which it declared any act of torture or other cruel, inhuman or degrading treatment or punishment an offence to human dignity, a denial of the purposes of the Charter of the United Nations and a violation of the Universal Declaration of Human Rights,[1]

Recalling that, in accordance with article 7 of the Declaration adopted in resolution 3452 (XXX), each State shall ensure that the commission of all acts of torture, as defined in article 1 of that Declaration, or participation in, complicity in, incitement to or attempt to commit torture are offences under its criminal law,

Convinced that under no circumstances should a person be punished for carrying out medical activities compatible with medical ethics regardless of the person benefiting therefrom, or be compelled to perform acts or to carry out work in contravention of medical ethics, but that, at the same time, contravention of medical ethics for which health personnel, particularly physicians, can be held responsible should entail accountability,

Desirous of setting further standards in this field which ought to be implemented by health personnel, particularly physicians, and by Government officials,

1. *Adopts* the Principles of Medical Ethics relevant to the role of health personnel, particularly physicians, in the protection of prisoners and detainees against torture and other cruel, inhuman or degrading treatment or punishment set forth in the annex to the present resolution;

2. *Calls upon* all Governments to give the Principles of Medical Ethics, together with the present resolution, the widest possible distribution, in particular among medical and paramedical associations and institutions of detention or imprisonment in an official language of the State;

3. *Invites* all relevant inter-governmental organizations, in particular the World Health Organization, and non-governmental organizations concerned to bring the Principles of Medical Ethics to the attention of the widest possible group of individuals, especially those active in the medical and paramedical field.

[1] Resolution 217 A (III)

Annex

Principle 1

Health personnel, particularly physicians, charged with the medical care of prisoners and detainees have a duty to provide them with the protection of their physical and mental health and treatment of disease of the same quality and standard as is afforded to those who are not imprisoned or detained.

Principle 2

It is a gross contravention of medical ethics, as well as an offence under applicable international instruments, for health personnel, particularly physicians, to engage, actively or passively, in acts which constitute participation in, complicity in, incitement to or attempts to commit torture or other cruel, inhuman or degrading treatment or punishment.[2]

Principle 3

It is a contravention of medical ethics for health personnel, particularly physicians, to be involved in any professional relationship with prisoners or detainees the purpose of which is not solely to evaluate, protect or improve their physical and mental health.

Principle 4

It is a contravention of medical ethics for health personnel, particularly physicians:

(a) To apply their knowledge and skills in order to assist in the interrogation of prisoners and detainees in a manner that may adversely affect the physical or mental health or condition of such prisoners or detainees and which is not in accordance with the relevant international instruments;[3]

(b) To certify, or to participate in the certification of, the fitness of

---

2 See the Declaration on the Protection of All Persons from Being Subjected to Torture and Other Cruel, Inhuman or Degrading Treatment or Punishment (General Assembly resolution 3452 (XXX), annex), article 1 of which states:

"1. For the purpose of this Declaration, torture means any act by which severe pain or suffering, whether physical or mental, is intentionally inflicted by or at the instigation of a public official on a person for such purposes as obtaining from him or a third person information or confession, punishing him for an act he has committed or is suspected of having committed, or intimidating him or other persons. It does not include pain or suffering arising only from, inherent in or incidental to, lawful sanctions to the extent consistent with the Standard Minimum Rules for the Treatment of Prisoners.

"2. Torture constitutes an aggravated and deliberate form of cruel, inhuman or degrading treatment or punishment."

Article 7 of the Declaration states:

"Each State shall ensure that all acts of torture as defined in article 1 are offences under its criminal law. The same shall apply in regard to acts which constitute participation in, complicity in, incitement to or an attempt to commit torture."

3 Particularly the Universal Declaration of Human Rights (General Assembly resolution 217 A (III), the International Covenants on Human Rights (General Assembly resolution 2200 A (XXI), annex), the Declaration on the Protection of All Persons prisoners or detainees for any form of treatment or punishment that may adversely affect their physical or mental health and which is not in accordance with the relevant international instruments, or to participate in any way in the infliction of any such treatment or punishment which is not in accordance with the relevant international instruments.

Principle 5

It is a contravention of medical ethics for health personnel, particularly physicians, to participate in any procedure for restraining a prisoner or detainee unless such a procedure is determined in accordance with purely medical criteria as being necessary for the protection of the physical or mental health or the safety of the prisoner or detainee himself, of his fellow prisoners or detainees, or of his guardians, and presents no hazard to his physical or mental health.

Principle 6

There may be no derogation from the foregoing principles on any ground whatsoever, including public emergency.

APPENDIX VI

United Nations: Unilateral Declarations against Torture and Other Cruel, Inhuman or Degrading Treatment or Punishment

In resolution 32/64 of 8 December 1977, the United Nations General Assembly called on all member states to reinforce their support for the UN Declaration against Torture by making unilateral declarations against torture and other cruel, inhuman or degrading treatment or punishment along the lines of a model text appended to the resolution. This model text comprised a statement of the government's intention to comply with the Declaration against Torture and to implement the provisions of the Declaration through legislation and other effective measures. Resolution 32/64 further urged member states to give maximum publicity to their unilateral declarations.

---

from Being Subjected to Torture and Other Cruel, Inhuman or Degrading Treatment or Punishment (General Assembly resolution 3452 (XXX), annex) and the Standard Minimum Rules for the Treatment of Prisoners (*First United Nations Congress on the Prevention of Crime and the Treatment of Offenders: report by the Secretariat* (United Nations publication, Sales No. 1956. IV. 4.), annex 1.A).

The following is a list of the countries which had made unilateral declarations against torture as of mid-1983.

* * * *

	Signature/non-binding Declaration (day/month/year)
Africa	
Mauritius	03/10/79
Rwanda	12/11/82
Senegal	07/09/79
The Americas	
Bahamas	14/09/81
Barbados	16/02/79
Canada	18/12/82
Chile	03/10/80
Mexico	27/06/80
Nicaragua	24/06/80
Panama	16/07/80
Saint Vincent and the Grenadines	26/03/82
Asia	
Australia	16/10/81
India	23/06/79
Japan	28/12/78
Philippines	26/10/79
Sri Lanka	02/09/82
Europe	
Belgium	08/12/77
Denmark	19/09/78
Finland	19/09/78
France	30/09/82
Iceland	19/09/78
Italy	10/04/78
Luxembourg	09/01/78
Netherlands	05/12/78
Norway	15/09/78
Portugal	13/09/78
Spain	01/12/78
Sweden	19/09/78
Yugoslavia	22/10/79
Middle East and North Africa	
Egypt	24/06/81
Iran	08/02/78
Iraq	03/09/79
Qatar	25/05/79
Yemen, Democratic	25/06/79

APPENDIX VII

United Nations Voluntary Fund for the Victims of Torture

In 1981 the United Nations General Assembly decided that, in addition to adopting instruments to eliminate torture, assistance should be given to torture victims. General Assembly resolution 36/151 of 16 December 1981 therefore established the United Nations Voluntary Fund for Victims of Torture.

This fund is designed to distribute voluntary contributions for assistance as humanitarian, legal, and financial aid to individuals whose human rights have been severely violated as a result of torture and to the relatives of such victims. Donations are collected from United Nations member states and distributed through established channels of humanitarian aid.

Contributions and pledges received from governments as of 20 October 1983 were as follows:

Governments	Pledges (US$)	(day/month/year)	Contribution (US$)
Cyprus	200	(20/09/83)	500.00
Denmark			114,600.00
Finland			81,729.00
France			19,480.52
Germany (Federal Republic of)	57,600	(14/07/83)	
Greece			5,000.00
Luxembourg	1,858.74	(30/09/83)	2,019.84
Netherlands			45,000.00
Norway			100,000.00
Sweden			150,000.00

AMNESTY INTERNATIONAL is a worldwide movement which is independent of any government, political grouping, ideology, economic interest or religious creed. It plays a specific role within the overall spectrum of human rights work. The activities of the organization focus strictly on prisoners:

— It seeks the *release* of men and women detained anywhere for their beliefs, colour, sex, ethnic origin, language or religion, provided they have not used or advocated violence. These are termed *"prisoners of conscience"*.

— It advocates *fair and early trials* for *all political prisoners* and works on behalf of such persons detained without charge or without trial.

— It opposes the *death penalty* and *torture* or other cruel, inhuman or degrading treatment or punishment of *all prisoners* without reservation.

AMNESTY INTERNATIONAL acts on the basis of the United Nations Universal Declaration of Human Rights and other international instruments. Through practical work for prisoners within its mandate, Amnesty International participates in the wider promotion and protection of human rights in the civil, political, economic, social and cultural spheres.

AMNESTY INTERNATIONAL has more than 500,000 members, subscribers and supporters in over 150 countries and territories, with over 3,000 local groups in more than 50 countries in Africa, Asia, Europe, the Americas and the Middle East. Each group works on behalf of at least two prisoners of conscience in countries other than its own. These countries are balanced geographically and politically to ensure impartiality. Information about prisoners and human rights violations emanates from Amnesty International's Research Department in London. No section, group or member is expected to provide information on their own country, and no section, group or member has any responsibility for action taken or statements issued by the international organization concerning their own country.

AMNESTY INTERNATIONAL has formal relations with the United Nations (ECOSOC), UNESCO, the Council of Europe, the Organization of American States and the Organization of African Unity.

AMNESTY INTERNATIONAL is financed by subscriptions and donations of its worldwide membership. To safeguard the independence of the organization, all contributions are strictly controlled by guidelines laid down by the International Council and income and expenditure are made public in an annual financial report.